Chinese Women Writers
on the Environment

Chinese Women Writers on the Environment

A Multi-Ethnic Anthology of Fiction and Nonfiction

Edited by
Dong Isbister, Xiumei Pu *and*
Stephen D. Rachman

McFarland & Company, Inc., Publishers
Jefferson, North Carolina

ISBN (print) 978-1-4766-6698-3
ISBN (ebook) 978-1-4766-4013-6

LIBRARY OF CONGRESS AND BRITISH LIBRARY
CATALOGUING DATA ARE AVAILABLE

Library of Congress Control Number 2020031700

Front cover artwork: *South of Colorful Clouds* by Burao Yiling
(Burao Yiling is a Va artist living in Yunnan Province, China)

Printed in the United States of America

McFarland & Company, Inc., Publishers
Box 611, Jefferson, North Carolina 28640
www.mcfarlandpub.com

Table of Contents

Acknowledgments

This anthology emerged from a conference in River Falls, Wisconsin, in October 2014 and the National Women's Studies Association Annual Conference in Puerto Rico in November 2014. It has been made possible with support from various groups of people and institutions in China and the United States.

Collectively, we express our gratitude to Rhonda Herman, Amy Donley, and Layla Milholen at McFarland for encouraging us to submit a book proposal after the NWSA conference (2014) and providing support at every step of the project. We give special thanks to Layla for closely working with us in the long process of developing and completing the anthology and showing her patience and passion. We also thank the Association for the Study of Literature and Environment for awarding us a translation grant (2016) that recognized the importance of the anthology and supported us in the editing process. Our thanks also go to the authors who trusted us to best represent their voices and answered our questions whenever needed; and the translators who did their best to help make those voices heard in English.

Dong Isbister would like to extend her gratitude and appreciation to Stephanie Branson whose question after Isbister's presentation in River Falls planted the seed for the five-year-long project; Qiu Shanshan, a prolific and renowned Chinese writer, for her guidance to contacting the selected authors to obtain permissions to translate their works in the development stage of the project; and Lin Yang from the Copyright Administrative Management Department of China Writers Association for reaching out to the authors and collect signed permissions and contact information and continually replying to inquiries and answering questions afterwards. Isbister is also grateful to Dr. Mark Bender who, with years of translating and research experience in Chinese ethnic minority literature, met with her in his office at the Ohio State University and communicated with her via email to generously offer much-needed advice, recommend translators, and share information that helped her consider the direction the anthology took in the development stage and beyond.

Isbister has also been touched by all the support and encouragement from her friends, students, and colleagues who took the time to help in different stages of the project. Dr. Li Xiangzhen at Wuhan University recommended two pieces for the anthology and had many conversations with Isbister, sharing his knowledge of ethnic cultural practices in China; Xiaomei Du, Qiuju Ge, Leilei Huang, Chi Jiang, Yixing Sun, Desong Yuan, and Lei Zhang located materials in Chinese or purchased books in Chinese whenever Isbister contacted them for assistance; Marsha Weaver closely read "Eternal Spirits" and provided insightful feedback; Evan Larson and Danica Larson went above and beyond to proofread "Dalema's Sacred Tree" and share invaluable comments; Lynnette Dornak, Tonya Harris, Frank King, Marianne Maili, Lea Popielinski, Chris Underwood, James Valiga, and Rich Waugh would make time for Isbister when she revised her own translation or edited the other translated pieces in the anthology. Thank you all for your support, encouragement, and belief in the contribution of the anthology!

Special thanks go to University of Wisconsin–Platteville, where Isbister is currently teaching. The College of Liberal Arts and Education awarded Dean's Travel Funds to assist the development of the project. The Provost's Office and Office of Research & Sponsored Programs awarded the project two Scholarly Activity Improvement Funds (2016–2017; 2018–2019) to assist the completion of the project.

Finally, Isbister would like to express her deepest gratitude to her family members, particularly her parents, Li Zhifang and Li Fulong, who supported her with love and belief in the long process. The numerous conversations they had with Isbister about the anthology were inspiring.

Xiumei Pu would like to thank Christy Clay and Brent Olson from the Environmental Studies Department at Westminster College for offering their support and being mindful of her teaching schedule along the way, and her research assistants Eliza Van Dyk and Jack Jacob for reading a draft of her translation "Mokuqin the Cow" and providing valuable feedback.

Stephen D. Rachman expresses his appreciation of the College of Arts and Letters and the Department of English at Michigan State University for their generous support in the development and completion of the anthology.

Finally, the editors would simply like to acknowledge that their names are arranged alphabetically by last name and that they contributed equally to the project.

Introduction

Ecomemories: The Tasks of the Translators

Translation makes global literature and global literary study possible. This edited collection of twenty-two pieces of ecologically-oriented writing by contemporary female authors from thirteen different Chinese ethnic minorities were translated from the original Chinese into English (with two exceptions) by a host of translators under the direction of the three editors. The anthology is an expression of a hope that through translation into English we might expand the horizons of global literary study, ethnic literary study, environmental study, and the study of women writers.

The voices found in this volume represent a range of ethnic groups that constitute smaller slices of the Chinese demographic puzzle: Daur, Evenki, Hui, Kazakh, Manchu, Mongol, She, Tujia, Uyghur, Va, Xibo, Yi, and Zhuang. China officially recognizes 56 distinct ethnic groups, of which the majority Han population makes up its 1.38 billion people. The officially recognized ethnic minorities number approximately 117 million people, and the numbers represented by the groups featured in this collection would be approximately 74 million.

Geographically, the peoples represented by the various authors in this volume conform to the general population distribution of Chinese ethnic minorities which are widely distributed in the Western and border areas of modern China. These areas generally have smaller population densities (compared to ethnic Han regions), but overall, they do not fall into any neat geographical patterns. They range from the northeastern to the northwestern provinces, and they also extend to central and southern regions of China. Some of these ethnic populations are concentrated in relatively small, relatively traditional regions, such as the Tujia of the Wuling Mountains, others such as the Hui, Manchu, Mongol, and Uyghur—while regionally identified—are much more widely dispersed. Others still, such as the Evenki, have been *de facto* relocated and their migrations directly correlate to their contemporary history.

1

Ethnic minority is the official term that China uses to designate these demographic entities, but from a literary point of view the term indigenous, with some qualifications, might equally apply. The voices here do indeed express, in manifold ways, connections between people and the local habitations and environments, frequently in terms and ways that are not wholly separable. Furthermore, as one frequently encounters in global indigenous literature, the literary voices collected here often describe the changing roles that women have played in these groups, as bearers of traditions, children, and burdens. The displacements of peoples from lands and traditions have arguably structured this common collective experience. The stories, essays, and poems collected here express in manifold ways the consequences of modernity on indigeneity—what it means to be from a particular place in a time of rapid change. The deep and time-tested connections among peoples and the lands they inhabit, the foods they eat, the animals they keep and hunt, and the myriad particulars of local knowledge, are all expressed in these pieces. Taken separately or as a whole, these pieces amount to a kind of ecomemory palace. Through the agency of human recollection, they offer a collective description of China that is deeply particular in its attachments to rivers and mountains, fields and forests, plants and animals in spaces and times that are epochal in scale.

Much has been written about the economic development of China since the 1970s, and this collection seeks to give a global voice to another kind of development: the rich and unprecedented flourishing of several generations of women writers in China. As a whole, these authors articulate subjects that reach deep into history and time yet also speak to the present—the changing demographics and social conditions that this economic and social development has set into motion. Some stories, such as "Daliangpo: Egg, Water, and Milk" by the Uyghur author, Patigül, describe a largely Muslim community in western China, possessing a richly intimate inter-ethnic community in which Hui, Uyghur, and Kazakh families live and mix like, as the title expresses it, egg, water, and milk. Other stories detail the migrations of animals and humans brought on by economic change. The impact of these kinds of relocations or displacements on the structures of traditional villages are described through the perspective of a small reindeer in a piece by the Evenki author, Dekeli, or a family along the far northern Chinese Huorili River in the story by the Daur author Yilan. The voices of resistance to change mix with those that merely recognize its inevitability, sometimes both at the same time. These themes can be heard in the Kazakh "Nomad Songs" of Ayinuer Maowuliti in which trendy salads sit uneasily beside traditional foods and the geriatric lumber saboteurs in "Dalema's Sacred Tree" by the Daur author Sana, who try to stave off rapid deforestation. In other stories, the voices of young people coming of age mix with those of old people coming to terms with age. Many authors express the profound difficulties of keeping the voices of one's ancestors alive in these times of urbanization and deforestation. Many of these voices find their own power in the cultural fight to give voice to the mountains, rivers, animals, and flowers that are losing their names and purposes. The mist-shrouded Ava Mountain, the dancing Gen River, the Kazakh eagles with more names than the Inuit have for snow, the lives of some Xibo house cats, the snow lotuses blossoming at altitude in icy crevices, and the multi-ethnic egg-shaped village of Daliangpo—these are all powerful images that run through this collection. These images and many more express the world in terms that make the ethnic and ecological indivisible. Some of these changes are dramatic upheavals registered in the broadest of terms, others are as subtle as a change in attitude toward the commonest and humblest of staple crops, buckwheat. Through these narratives, large swaths of cultural history are written in personal, filial, communal, regional, and national terms.

Educational journeys that reflect broad trends in China for women are also expressed here. The development of many of the authors in this collection are the direct or indirect result of the re-opening of the universities in the late 1970s, having taken place through the writing programs in Beijing and other centers of learning. Some authors in this anthology refer directly to this experience, such as Burao Yilu in "Four Generations of Va Women," but the biographical notes reveal a general pattern of literary education and training that has fostered this burgeoning of women's voices. A large number of the authors in this collection have participated in the Advanced Writers Seminars at Lu Xun Literary Institute in Beijing, another cluster of them hold degrees in ethnic or folkloric study from national universities. In these ways, the Chinese educational system since the 1970s has fostered the growth of literary, ethnic and ecological consciousness.

The stories are arranged alphabetically by author, and we will leave it to readers to select the themes and topics that resonate the most, but in our role as contributing translators and coeditors of this anthology, we have selected the term ecomemory as one theme that runs through all of them. Ecomemory expresses the tension between the environmental (the entire material cultural surround at any scale, either built or natural) and memory (artistic acts of simulated recollection that enhance, supplement, or critique empirical findings.) As a cross-section of environmental writings from contemporary Chinese authors, these works represent a turn toward the personal, political, social, and ecological in ways that argue for a conceptual fusion of external, shared systems of ecology and the private and subjective realm of memory. The writings move between traditional elements of memoir and ecological representation, attempting to speak simultaneously to problems of environment, environmental destruction and to connect these issues to particular histories of the ethnic peoples, the lands that these peoples have inhabited, and the landscapes that embody and emblematize these histories and relationships. As such, these writings strive to serve simultaneously personal and environmental purposes. In many ways, this anthology explores the convergence of environmental destruction and ethnographic migration or displacement and the ways in which a new literature has attempted to respond and reimagine these contemporary developments.

* * *

This book's genesis began in 2014 at a conference in Wisconsin entitled, "Gendered Planet: Ethics, Ecology, and Equity." At the conference, Dong Isbister delivered a presentation on Sana's story, "Dalema's Sacred Tree." After her presentation, she was asked by a member of the audience when she was going to translate the story. Isbister, who had long experience with translation, having translated Nathaniel Hawthorne's *The Scarlet Letter* into Chinese and having worked as a medical translator/interpreter and translation instructor for many years, was wary. She knew the pitfalls of translation, be it from English to Chinese or vice-versa.

Xiumei Pu, who participated in the conference as part of a plenary session, was also in the audience at Isbister's presentation and they began discussing the importance of these literary voices from China and the need for English-language versions of these works if they were going to be introduced into classrooms in U.S. universities or English-speaking classrooms, and more generally, become part of global literary study. After some brainstorming Isbister and Pu drafted a call, soliciting translators who were interested in contemporary ethnic minority women's environmental literature in China and from that small beginning, the anthology was born. When they had assembled the Chinese authors that best represented this diversity and thematic range of topics and also recruited a team of translators with backgrounds in Chinese, the idea of this collection clearly came into view.

Early into the project, Isbister and Pu were wrestling with a translation of one of the pieces in the collection, the Zhuang author Cen Xianqing's meditation on the rock paintings of Huashan Mountain, "Eternal Spirits." They had worked and reworked many drafts of it, but to little satisfaction. Isbister contacted Stephen D. Rachman, a professor of English who she had worked with at Michigan State University, to help solve some of the translation issues. From that point forward a collaboration was born, and the three editors have worked steadily, largely over Skype, with translators as each piece was revised and honed into the versions found in this anthology.

It is fitting that the challenges of translation brought this team together. Rendering Chinese into English while retaining the voice of the original always presents a number of difficulties. In Chinese, word order can be very different than that found in English, and tenses are typically implied rather than clearly indicated. All of the original pieces in this collection were written by women writers and many of them deal explicitly with gender and identity (sometimes the gendered identity of animals)—and yet the original Chinese texts frequently do not indicate gender. Given this situation, we were often torn between the demands of context and that of literal accuracy. How should we render a reference to a beloved animal? The context might indicate "she" or "he," but the Chinese character used was undoubtedly "it." This was one type of editorial dilemma we continually faced, and without going into too much detail it stands in for a host of others.

The meanings of Chinese characters can change significantly when added to other characters and the significance of any one character can often expand in English to long complex phrases, making strict translation difficult or impossible. Finding an English phrase that may be adequate in one sense may just as easily lose shades of meaning, and with them, the implied associations and traditions that the Chinese reader would regularly perceive. Because of its context-driven nature, Chinese often allows for a greater repetition of words and phrases without hindering flow or musicality, where this might wear on the English-language reader who is taught to be wary of overuse of repeated words and phrases.

These fundamental issues were compounded by the scale at which we were working. Some twenty-odd Chinese authors writing prose and poetry, fiction, memoir, and reportage are assembled here. A similar variety of translators were also assembled. Both the original authors and the translators brought their own styles, sensibilities, and idiomatic preferences to bear, and it was certainly daunting to achieve stylistic consistency and accuracy while retaining the diversity of voice and vision that is at the core of such an anthology.

Indeed, the linguistic and ethnic diversity of the source texts often presented challenges in choices for diction, phrasing and register for these translations. In almost all cases, the translators worked from Chinese originals (the Kazakh texts translated by Guldana Salimjan are the exception), and these texts are frequently flavored with terms derived from the various ethnic languages of the authors. In some cases, the linguistic nuances simply could not be fully conveyed. For instance, the Chinese title of Hui author Ma Jinlian's story, 孔雀菜, has been translated as "Bitter Greens." While the English title is, in our opinion, both accurate and deeply appropriate, the original Chinese characters refer to a play on words and mispronunciation of the name of this plant central to the story's theme. The author could have chosen other Chinese characters to represent this same mispronunciation, but the ones used contain a kind of hidden beauty—the image of a peacock (孔雀)—suggesting an even greater complexity of feeling. In such cases, we must simply agree in the interest of clarity and readability that poetry is sometimes what is lost in translation.

However, in many instances in which the ethnic inflection of the use of words imported into Chinese from the Daur, Evenki, Kazakh or other languages from which it was derived, we felt it was crucial to preserve those inflections in translations, wherever possible. For example, in the translated excerpt from "Huorili River, Huorili Mountain," by the Daur writer Yilan, a Chinese reader might readily perceive that *tunzi* is a northern term that can mean village in one context and creel in another, so in those cases we have retained the word in italicized pinyan and offered the English meaning of the term parenthetically. In another example, in the story entitled, "Kangnalikan the Little Reindeer," by the Evenki author Dekeli, the name of the reindeer, Kangnalikan (Black Boy), had been transliterated by Dekeli into Chinese as 考淖日刊 and rendered in pinyin by the translators as Kaonaorikan. The tonalities in this representation of the Evenki word distorted it in such a way that a Mandarin speaker might easily be tripped up in pronouncing it while reading it out loud in the translated text. It had effectively lost its ethnic musicality and so we have returned, after consultation with Dekeli, to the Evenki name and transliterated that into English directly. In this way, we strove to retain a crucial marker of linguistic ethnicity.

In a similar way, Salimjan's translation of "A Houseful of Birds" by the Kazakh author Nuryla Qiziqan, retains the term *aq-yiq* for the eagles of the Altay Mountains, rather than translating it into English as "white shoulders." The translator's reasoning stems from the fact the Kazakh language has more than forty terms for eagles that connect to a bird's markings and habitat. Rather than simply using a common English term, we wanted to preserve the Kazakh taxonomy for eagles that is untranslatable. This amounts to an eco-linguistic marker of ethnicity, and, as such, constitutes a keyword that we wish to preserve for readers of these translations. In this way, we always strived for readability in these translations. We did not wish to sacrifice those ethnic and ecological elements which give these works their distinctive flavor and points of view. Consult the Notes on Style for more details on the ways we have tried to indicate these elements to the reader.

Notes on Style

In a book of this kind, it is inevitable that variant forms of place names and terms germane to various ethnicities and languages will appear. When these occur in these translations, we have endeavored to represent them with as much accuracy and consistency as possible. Here are a few basic guidelines that we have followed.

1. Where Chinese words are rendered, they are presented in the italicized pinyin system followed by an English-language clarification in parentheses. For example, we render the term *xiaorenshu* (illustrated storybooks).

2. Occasionally, where the text relies on pronunciation in a crucial way, we have rendered the italicized pinyan with the appropriate diacritic indicating the tone. For example, in "Herbs Living in the Body" the medical terms are rendered this way: *wàng* (observation), *wén* (auscultation and olfaction), *wèn* (inquiry), and *qiè* (pulse feeling and palpation).

3. In the cases of place names that have long been established with Wade-Giles spellings, those have been retained. For example, Tsinghua University is mentioned in "Four Generations of Va Women" and is rendered as such.

4. Where names of geographical features are named, we represent them by (one of) the accepted English language names for these places. For example, the river which runs along the Chinese-Russian Border is rendered as the Argun River, that being the name most familiar to English speakers.

5. In some stories we have retained Chinese units of measure and currency. For example, in "Shujuan the Black Bear," a Chinese measure of weight *jin*, roughly equal to 1.1 pounds, is used. Upon first usage, we have supplied a footnote offering an English equivalent.

1

From Nomad Songs

AYINUER MAOWULITI

Destiny

The blood from my umbilical cord
Did not fall on the grasslands.
And so I am destined to this life of drifting and distress.
The totem of my tribe,
Forgotten in the dust of history.
A descendant of nomads,
Wandering through the seasons;
The nomad path stretches into the distance.

The Corner

The moss grows quietly in the shade,
Foregoing the generosity of the sun.
The ants are hard at work
Persisting in their very own dream.
The wind chances by,
The seasons follow one another.
A dog naps in the shade.
In this corner,
There are no footsteps.
A world so at peace.

Revelry

At a Kazakh bistro in Ürümqi
We eat a trendy foreign salad,

Translated by Ann Waltner, Rivi Handler-Spitz, Ben van Overmeire, Rachel Kronick, Han Jiangxue, Li Kan, Jiang Yuanxin, Gao Ruchen, Eric R. Becklin, Lars Christensen

And drink fine wine from Ili.
Traditional foods
Sit a bit uneasily on the linen-decked table.
Kazakh singers from abroad sing songs
In their mother tongue.
Wafting in the breeze
An air of mixed blood.
We dance to our heart's content.
The grasslands and the snowy peaks,
We cast them far behind us.

2

Patterns of the Sun

Bamo Qubumo

Meanings of the patterns:

1. The sun and sun rays
2. Dodecagon: twelve animals calendar
3. Decagon: ten-month solar calendar
4. Octagon: eight directions
5. Quadragon: east, south, west, north

Lead singer: Walking barefoot under the blazing sun
Do you remember Zhige'alu[1]
For seven days, he called out to the suns
    Day and night were jumbled together
Nary a leaf on the beech trees
One could only hear the melancholy descending
    Flailing little ice-cold hands
        Brush up against clear and murky forces
Chorus: The dance of the twelve beasts, a sacrifice
Lay out the twelve ritual fields
Drumbeat faintly heard
The twelve divining sticks are set out as a forest
Ritual bells chime sending forth the long cries of all souls
Clean sacrifice like white silk
We are like small waves converging on the mountain

---

1. In the Yi mythology there were seven suns. Zhige'alu shot down six of them and was acclaimed and worshiped as a hero.

Translated by Ann Waltner, Rivi Handler-Spitz, Ben van Overmeire, Rachel Kronick, Han Jiangxue, Li Kan, Jiang Yuanxin, Gao Ruchen, Eric R. Becklin, Lars Christensen

The twelve banners of the Nuosu people
Tracing the shape of the sun with blood:
We are all descendants of the Black Tiger
Lead singer: Cosmic chaos still prevails cosmic chaos still prevails
Black Tiger transforms into ten thousand things
Left eye becomes the sun
Right eye becomes the moon
Whiskers transform into sunlight
White teeth transform into stars
Backbone transforms into the high plains
Chorus: The high plains undulate like a baha serpent[2]
Charging forward through the misty swirling Heishui River
The sun shines on the wilderness like a clear mirror
Our tears gush out like a waterfall
Our deep faith in the dark of the night
Turns every single perilla seed into a splendid star
Shining on our endless generations
Lead singer: Walking barefoot on thorns
You must remember your own ancestors
The perils they went through and the hardships they endured

---

2. The baha is a snake-like creature, companion of Zhige'alu.

3

Four Generations of Va Women

Burao Yilu

I had a dream. I dreamt that my daughter and I soared through the sky, the black hair streaming from our heads had morphed into pairs of golden wings. The sun shone on the horizon. Streaming sunbeams formed a ladder of light to the sky-world. We flew toward the ladder. Beneath us many mountain people sang by a flowing creek.

A delicate light red flower, lifting its head from beneath a rock, bloomed on a slope. The melodic ring of bells from a passing horse caravan shattered the silence. A "cave man" threw a sprig of wild red berries to me. I was frightened. I held my daughter in my arms and ran to the millet field. The entire mountain ridge was moving, changing its shape.... Several wild gnu were charging toward us.

Then I seemed to be in my village, in the mist-shrouded Ava Mountain. The grass hut where my grandmother and mother used to live swayed on its stilts in the wind. My mother's laughter and my own laughter echoed in the village. My dreams and my daughter's dreams hovered over the mountain tops....

Grandmother, Woman of the Mountain

My grandmother was the daughter of the Va chief. As the child of a Va chief, my grandmother should have had the privilege of going to school, but she did not because she was a girl. True to her native roots as a Va girl she never left the mountain and was illiterate.

In the past, the Va people had a shortage of table salt, calico, and rice wine. Grandfather had to go down to the local town market. After he came back, he contracted a miasmic disease, a fairly common disease among the

---

Translated by Alexandra Draggeim

---

people living in remote mountains. Not long after that, Yongde Menghong Va Village invited him to a conference of elders. A few days later, a "chicken feather messenger" delivered the news that grandfather was dying. My maternal uncle from Nanla rode on horseback, day and night, to Yongde to be with his father, but soon after he arrived, our grandfather passed away, leaving his jaundiced body to the mountains forever.

Grandfather didn't go quietly. Even as he drew his last breath, he was still grumbling about the poverty of the Va people. After he left us, my widowed grandmother never remarried. She raised their children alone and struggled to make a living deep in the mountains. She often worked on the barren mountain slopes, farming millet, digging sweet potatoes and taro. She would return in the evening, drenched in sweat, hunched over like a small mountain. Grandmother's time and energy were consumed with making ends meet that she had no time and energy for her children, and so my mother was neglected like an unwanted child. Like the gnarls on the banyan tree, she weighed down grandmother's shoulders.

It was said that Mother had a strange disease as a child. She couldn't eat a bite or drink a sip of water and would just cry. Grandmother scoured the mountains in search of an herb to expel the evil spirit. At the age of four or five, mother still couldn't climb a single stone step. Whenever her condition worsened, her face would appear gaunt, her eyes dim. Without doctors and medicine, Mother was hovering between life and death, and seeing this Grandmother held her in her arms and cried for a long while. She eventually wrapped my mother up in a piece of traditional black cloth and placed her near the fire to keep her warm. She thought to herself: if my daughter's condition doesn't improve in the morning, I will take her into the mountains, dig a hole in the red dirt, and bury her in it. Upon waking up the next morning, Grandmother unraveled the cloth, only to find that Mother was bawling. Magic! She had come back to life!

Grandmother immediately sent for her brother to divine our future and a chicken was killed. My great uncle put some Va medicine in a wooden bowl, which he then filled with water. Standing in the center of the grass hut like a shaman, he stirred the water with two fingers and mumbled incantations. Then he said: "All of this is because the widowed woman has offended the spirits, and she cannot stay." He wanted my grandmother to take her children and leave. She would have to make a living elsewhere.

Some time later, Grandmother borrowed some money and opened an inn on the main street in town. It served as a convenient stopping place for those transporting goods to and from the mountains to feed and water their horses. Grandmother cooked delicious Va-style rice with chicken. The red rice wine she brewed was sweet and fragrant, but the grilled wild game was even more enticing....

My oldest uncle's sign was the snake. Grandmother had requested a Va Moba (a sacrificial priest) to foretell his future, and the Moba said that my uncle was born under a lucky star, that he was going to attend college and eventually become a high-ranking government official. My uncle received a good education, but he was never able to become a government official. The Moba looked up our genealogy and suggested that our family line had too many snakes in it, and so his luck had run out. My uncle, who was very poor, had to scratch out a living with his children as a "slash-and-burn" farmer in the mountains.

When they were young, my second and third uncles served in the army. For seven or eight years they excelled and were promoted to platoon leader, battalion leader, and other such positions. They were commended several times for their leadership. Unfortunately, my hometown was hit by a flood, and my uncles, who had been expected to rise even higher in the ranks, decided independently of each other to return to Ava Mountain, into Grandmother's embrace.

My fourth uncle was young, ambitious, and optimistic. He found a good job away from home. As he was preparing to take the national entrance exam to a top-tier college, grandmother was hit by a horse cart that had come out of nowhere and suffered a severe bone fracture. Grandmother asked second uncle to write a letter to fourth uncle, saying: "My youngest son is not here, and it feels as if one of the legs of the bench in our house were missing. If you don't come home soon, you are not a good son and I can't die in peace." Upon receiving this letter, fourth uncle set out immediately in the middle of the night, first by train, then by bus, then by horse carriage, and, finally, on the back of a donkey. Grandmother left this world several days later. She was laid to rest in the red earth of the leeward side of the mountain ridge. At some point, her tomb had become overgrown with microbial weeds (people said that, before the founding of the People's Republic of China, Japan had air-dropped eupatorium seeds in this area). In the end, Grandmother did not leave an estate to her children and grandchildren, nor did she bring good luck to her youngest son. Having run out of other options, fourth uncle decided to work as a mailman, hauling a heavy mail bag, traveling on foot through mountains and woods, valleys and forests, climbing over steep mountain ridges. By delivering packages, telegrams, and letters, he fulfilled grandmother's wishes by doing good deeds and serving others.

Grandmother lived in the Ava Mountain area until the day she died. What she always said to her own children can be said with equal truth to her grandchildren and great grandchildren: "Life is really about living simply and just getting by. Too much money is a burden. It only brings about misfortune and trouble. People tend to become lazy as they get rich, and disaster naturally follows. Hard work is the essence of what it means to be Va."

After China launched its economic reforms, my great uncle returned to the Ava Mountain area from Taiwan. During his brief stay, he made sure to pay a visit to Grandmother's grave and erect a black marble gravestone for her. Before saying goodbye to the family and taking his leave, he returned to her grave and placed on it an azalea bouquet he had picked in the mountains. Then he kowtowed a few times to express regret for saying the words that had hurt Grandmother, hoping that she would rest in peace after a life of toil and strife.

Mother, the Runaway Bride on the Mountain Ridge

Mother was born and grew up in the mountains. Like a peach tree growing in Ava Mountain's rich soil, she blossomed into a woman, pretty, elegant, and strong. But Mother was unaware of the wilderness that flowed in her blood, or the mountain face that she wore through life. The Va people's hardscrabble life, enduring and overcoming every hardship, had carved her features.

When Mother was young, bandits often made forays across the Yunnan border. She chafed at being housebound and isolated, but she had to wait until she was ten to enter first grade at the village elementary school. Most of the teachers were capable Han Chinese from beyond the mountains. One senior teacher was very strict with the girls who started their education late. Students didn't understand why he was so strict. If students were inattentive and he happened to be in a bad mood, he would punish them with a beating. Mother had her palm slapped dozens of times with a bamboo stick. Filled with dread, she would submit her right hand for punishment.... After returning home in the late afternoon, she would have to finish her homework as soon as possible in excruciating pain, before climbing the hills to collect a basketful of grass for the cows. Otherwise, the cows would wail throughout the night.

After graduating from elementary school (fourth grade), Mother could not continue her schooling. To support her family and help grandmother's sons, she had to tie her younger brother to her back and carry him around.... Yet, even as life was tying her down, she found a way to free herself by taking up weaving and embroidery. In the mountains, whether one had food and clothing was a matter of survival. Mother was a kind person. Just to make her younger brothers and sisters happy, she would sometimes use the money made from weaving brocades to buy them *ganbaba* (buckwheat cake) or candy. The Va people have been making colorful brocades for centuries, and every Ava Mountain girl bears the responsibility of keeping up the tradition.

From the day a Va girl is born, she gives almost her entire life to the

mountains and to the uncles on her mother's side of the family; the maternal family serves as a "checkpoint" to her future. Like a mountain camellia,
Mother blossomed, and it was time for her to marry. On an auspicious day
in the Va calendar, wine and local foods were served to welcome the groom's
wedding convoy. But Mother ran away, up the lily-covered mountain pass,
and, having rejected our traditions, fell in love with a man from a Wu family.
He became my father.

Va people seldom married outside of their clan or ethnic group, and
the case of my mother, the daughter of the chief of the Liu family in Nanla,
was virtually unheard of. Fearful for her daughter's happiness, Grandmother
stood on the rocky promontory and said, "Just look at that man named Wu.
He is so skinny that he won't be able to carry the lightest basket of grain on
his back; he won't be able to carry a single bamboo tube of water on his back;
and he speaks with a weird accent. How can you marry such a useless man?"

Mother broke free from the marriage traditions of the Va and, in this
way, she was something of a pioneer in our clan. As she was working hard to
prepare for her new life, her wedding was a small, silent, matter-of-fact affair:
no relatives, no dowry, no processional, aside from a few childhood friends
trailing in the back, not even a room for her wedding night…. Mother was
like a silver pheasant on Ava Mountain, taking her life into her own hands,
and stitching for herself the best possible marriage out of the threads that life
had offered her.

Several years later, Mother, riding on a donkey, followed the horse cara-
vans with their jingling bells out of the mountains. Like a traveling monk on a
celestial pilgrimage, she and her children rode for more than two weeks over
the far mountains and through old forests. When she arrived at the township
of Baoshan, at last she got off her emaciated donkey and discovered that her
legs were swollen like lotus roots, and her lower back ached as if stabbed
by knives…. Over the next few days, she took several buses which snaked
along the Burma Road by mountains and rivers before entering Kunming,
the provincial capital. From there she set off to search for my father, who
had already obtained a level-six benchwork certificate there. The money for
the journey came from Mother's years of hard work weaving cloth and em-
broidering flowers. Luckily, Mother found her true love. In the eyes of the Va
people Mother was a century ahead of her time.

In 1958, my father was accused of being a "right-wing counter-
revolutionary" and taken away in a car. Mother was like a wounded elk,
destitute, and a social outcast, left to care for her children without help. A
twenty-six-year-old woman full of hope, she never imagined that her husband—her mechanical engineer husband, her highly accomplished techno-
logically innovative husband, her committed, loving husband, dedicated to
Va, wife, children, colleagues, and society—would be sent to the labor camp

on a dead lake at the foot of the Western Mountain to be re-educated. What law had he violated? People said it was serious! What was the crime? To this day, Mother does not know.

During the "movement" Mother would read a few paragraphs out of the newspaper or some lines from various official governmental papers to her co-workers, who were generally illiterate. One day, at the left-leaning Little Steel factory (now a subsidiary of Kun Steel) near the border with Yunnan, Mother was reading with great feeling when someone interrupted her, blurting out, "She is the spouse of a counter-revolutionary, she has no right to discuss politics with us." Nobody knew why this person wished to drag Mother down and put her on trial in this way. As if struck by a stick, Mother suddenly lost her "ethnic minority" temper and stormed into the factory director's office. "Even if my husband comes from a family of counter-revolutionaries," she argued. "I come from a solid, modest family, several of my brothers are military commanders. If a man has violated the law, he alone should bear the consequences. Why should his wife and children take the blame? Is this a Communist Party policy?" What she said was so clear and logical that it won the factory director over.

After Father left, Mother went to work making steel and forging steel balls in a workshop at the Little Steel factory. After that, she worked converting mountains into arable land and then farming them on a May Seventh Farm. After that, she hauled heavy steel oxygen tanks at the factory's delivery terminal; she also loaded and unloaded coal and other cargo from the railway carriages at Dushupu Railway Station. Mother earned only eight *jiao* a day to support her family. When she was unable to do heavy labor with her rheumatic legs, she offered to look after the children of two neighbor families…. For her, everyday there was always tasks to be done and every year, more work to be completed.

During the winter, separated from us by netting, Mother would work by lamplight hand-sewing new clothes and shoes for the children. The repetitive rhythm of mother's needle and thread would lull us to sleep. Once, I was frightened awake by a thunderstorm in the deep of the night, and I saw the flicker of Mother's tired shadow in the darkness…. Tomorrow always held some new task that needed doing—her first-born son was to attend a winter sports meeting; her daughter was to dance at the June 1 International Children's Day…. Mother safeguarded her children's dreams with her warm, strong hands!

During a famine year, there was a severe cold snap. One day, as Mother was walking home, she saw a stranger dying of hunger near the steel plant in the Dianxi Road (the Southern Silk Road.) The stranger was surrounded by a crowd of onlookers who were laughing and mocking…. Without a second thought, Mother took some of the food she was carrying home, a steamed bun sprinkled with a little brown sugar, and gave it to the stranger. As she was leaving, she also handed the stranger a bag of corn, making a great deal of trouble for herself. At a public denunciation, people made a point of saying that Mother was no friend of the working class but a friend of the lazy; they claimed that "brown-sugar buns" are vestiges of a capitalist lifestyle and so forth. Mother stood like a statue in the cold wind without speaking a single word. She was weighed down by her sadness, yet there was nothing to say. She had learned to remain silent and keep her thoughts to herself.

As soon as we heard the Ma family dog barking in the mountain pass across from the Long family house, we knew father had come home for the weekend. Mother would eagerly fix her gaze on the mountain, waiting for him to come into view. Like a child, she would scamper down the terraced rice fields to Shahewan to meet Father. Greeting Father was always a happy event. Water flowed easily and time passed lazily. No one had much to say, but everyone was ready to laugh. Mother was surrounded by the descendants of the Va. They had crossed an old wooden bridge overhung by a dead tree, had run along a footpath through sweet, fragrant fava bean fields, and skirted the water chestnut ponds that smelled of silt to arrive, at last, to this meeting place with Father—a eucalyptus grove in the mountains.

...

Three years ago, Mother turned sixty in the fall. Throughout her burdensome life, from that day to this, her children had never heard a single word of complaint cross her lips. Using the money I received for articles published in *China Society News*, I bought a short, iron-gray wool coat for Mother. I regretted that I had been working for so many years away from home and had not been able to take care of her. Mother tried on the coat. The wrinkles on her cheeks had become more pronounced; her face had slackened, but it was still clear whether she felt joy or sorrow. Her face was overcome with melancholy, one could see a lifetime of hardship there. Mother was still so kind, so beautiful!

My Itinerant Life as a Writer

I spent my childhood in the old forests on Ava Mountain, in western Yunnan province. At my command, golden raspberry and kapok tree blossoms obediently fell off. I don't know if it was because of the changing seasons; I always felt that I had the power to transform rivers and mountains or make grass and trees sway. But when the setting sun lit up the red hills of the mountains, a *Da* (Va elder male) returned with silver pheasant, muntjac, and other game tied to the shotgun or crossbow slung over his shoulder. I followed his tracks in search for the beginning and end of life.

I have a good-looking friend with a disability that makes her less agile, but she has a distinctive personality and her own way of thinking about things. On rainy days, we couldn't go out to pick the white michelia covering the mountains. Instead, we went to play over at her house, which was small and made of wood. I was intrigued when I saw that she had a notebook tightly wrapped in thick brown kraft. My curiosity got the better of me, and I peeked inside: in her diary, she wrote about how we climbed Maobi Mountain to pick tiny pink wildflowers, tiny like the rice-grain-sized birds that like to eat them, and white sephora flowers; at Whetstone River we played with "Water Mother" (a water-strider).... She also wrote about how I was a mischievous schoolgirl. At playtime, I stealthily undid the teacher's head scarf, unveiling her cropped head and in the process revealing to the entire class, the teacher's secret. Reading the diary was my first inspiration for writing, and then I wrote, "That Little River in My Hometown." It immediately became a model for other students to imitate.

In midsummer, I was living in a six-square-meter apartment adjacent to the local village elementary school, and I could hear the students' voices as they recited texts or happily babbled to one another on their way home. One day, a vaguely familiar face appeared in my doorway, saying that he was a teacher from the school. He said he had written a new poem, "In Praise of Red Plum Blossoms," and asked if I would share with him my opinion of it. Without holding back or mincing my words, I replied, "There are a bit too many slogans in your poem, it's not vivid enough...." and so forth, amusing and amazing him with my astuteness. Actually, I was a complete amateur in writing, a mere observer who hadn't so much as written half a line of poetry, yet somehow I dared to drag him down to the wide sea of creative writing and get his feet wet.

It was that year that Kun Steel decided to increase production, hiring people as if they were buying grain on a quota system (the children of steelworkers were hired and assigned positions in the factory based on a ratio of men to women.) So, I started work at the Kun Steel subsidiary plant, Qiaogang, where my father had been condemned, and I ended up working there for a decade. For ten years, I wore a thick, heavy worker's uniform and tight, wind-proof suede and leather shoes. Day in and day out, I rushed to the massive factory and my dusty workshop. I was tied down at the ripe age of eighteen, a cold fog had enveloped me and clipped my imaginative wings, preventing any flights of fancy. In the evening, I would jot down some *dayoushi* (doggerel) and temporarily leave behind or ignore the social world and all its relations in a mountain valley. In order to get my hands on the classics of world literature, I had to borrow books and promise to return them to the lender in three days or sometimes just twenty-four hours. I only managed to pick several titles at random to speed-read, which has left me with an anemic knowledge of literature that persists to this day.

One day, someone from the Provincial Writers' Association came running to my house with a face streaming with sweat. I was told that Jiang Shui, the chief editor of *Dongchuan Art*, needs a first-time female author's piece for publication and I was asked if I had anything at hand that could be used. This is when I decided to piece together my shattered thirty-two-year-old soul, in early middle age wielding my pen methodically, finally finding my niche. I started to draft my piece. My writing process was extraordinarily tortured, filled with setbacks and false starts. I started with the baseline "The Beginning of Fall," changed it to the lyrical "Scent of Golden Osthmanthus," then to the feature-article-sounding title, "Ode to Autumn," finally settling on the prosey, "Early Autumn." I went from that to this and this to that, trying to find the exact right words. When I finally got all my ideas together in a form that I was somewhat happy with, I delivered my manuscript to those sunshine-filled offices. It was then I learned that the editor, Jiang Shui, had died a few days earlier. I was shocked and I tasted the autumnal bitterness of my dead essay, my firstborn brainchild. I was set adrift for a long, long time....

Today, others see me as a skinny, dark-skinned woman from an ethnic minority group who is not satisfied with the status quo, who carries a bright green and red Va satchel and "wanders about." ... For many years I have been wandering, roving, collecting material, and devoting myself to my writing. I like spontaneity when it comes to writing and maybe I am even a bit presumptuous.... I hope that we, the Va people, will not merely harvest isolation and desolation, but rather harvest confidence and courage.

Fifteen years ago, wholly by chance I pushed open the door to the Yunnan writers' circle and I became one of two female writers out of more than three million Va people. With the kind of courage possessed by young people who don't know much about the world, or as we say, with the spirit of "a bear cub who is unafraid of the wolves," I ventured out into the world. Adventure runs in my blood; I have inherited from my ancestors a fearlessness of heaven and the earth, and the courage to bargain with ghosts and spirits.

In the fall of 1994, I grudgingly left the red soil of Yunnan which had nurtured me for thirty-nine years and traveled to further my studies at the Literature Department in the Graduate School of the Chinese Academy of Social Sciences in Beijing. On the muddy, rain-soaked roads to the train station, Mother pushed my hand away.... She had lost her ability to speak following a stroke, so she used her facial expressions and gestures to urge me to continue onward. Mother had never left Yunnan, and Beijing was a place she had longed to visit her entire life. Perhaps she was living vicariously through me. As the train's steel wheels spun into motion, I could see Mother's red swollen eyes welling up with tears.... My mother's tears ran down her face. Yet, as we were about to say farewell, her dark eyes, round as longans, looked at me full of concern, full of melancholy, full of hope!

The graduate school was situated to the north of the Lido Hotel. In one of the school's snow-covered buildings, literary experts commented on my essays, "Himalayan Butterfly Bush" and "You Are a Bright Ray of Sun." At the New Year's performances, my classmates pushed me towards the stage, and so I sang the Va song "Ava Girl Pounding Rice," a Yunnan folk song, "The Trickling Stream," and the Taiwanese song, "The Olive Tree." After my classmate who happens to be a poet heard these songs, he suddenly "let his tears gush out like water from a spring," as we say. When I sang "Mother in the Candle-light" with the lyrics, "no longer can you stand tall and straight," smoke filling my throat, tears rolled down the front of my white down coat.... I felt like I had gone back home, back to my childhood; Mother wore an apricot-colored dress and stood by the bamboo, teaching her daughter to sing Va folk songs such as "New House Dance" and "Little Bird Flying High"! Some of my classmates were surprised and started probing me about where I had received "voice training," but I couldn't explain at all what kind of force was urging me on.... It was Mother, far away, ailing from lifelong hard labor, who had become partially paralyzed and lost control of the nerves to her voice box, who would never sing again!

Suddenly, I stood up. I swept my long black Va hair out of my face and wiped away my tears. I would sing for my mother!

My Daughter's Divine Dreams of Painting

My daughter is a naturally hyperactive child, like an Ava Mountain monkey. I had thought of a way to keep her still: from the age of three, I made her learn to hold a brush and to study Chinese water and ink animal paintings. But painting did not actually keep her any quieter than before, for the moment that inspiration seized her nothing could hold her back. She painted our bedsheets, tablecloths, and clothes in a riot of color. She would plaster the walls with her artistic menagerie, turning our home into a zoo. That was her imaginary world.

Before my daughter Keke (her nickname) could read, she would write characters that resembled Chinese characters but weren't quite right. There would be strokes to the left, strokes to the right, all intersecting in the middle, and she would read out her scribbles, "Dear grandmother, poor mom, dear aVa Mountain, poor wildflowers.... Mom, I am going out to the Yuantong-shan Zoo to learn to paint animals. If you're hungry when you get home, cook a few steamed buns...."

My daughter loved painting from an early age, and whenever it was about to rain, she would stare out of the window: white clouds look like the sea and the black rain clouds look like mountains. At the age of three she discovered this secret. "Keke, can you paint this?" After a little while, she tod-dled up to me with her little sketchbook to show me her work. Why did the white clouds look like two moons? I asked her a little crossly, "Can there be two moons in the sky?" My daughter drew her tiny face close to mine: "Mom, don't you know, if there are two moons in the sky, it will be *so* bright, wouldn't that be wonderful?" Who would have thought that she began to seek the light at such a young age?

Keke said: "Since I was born hyper, I like to shout and run around, and so people here said that I got ADD. My mother has shed many tears because of me. When I was in kindergarten, the boys would bully the girls, and I would stand up for the girls, but the teacher gave me the nickname, 'ji-pu-sai-nv-*lang*, Gypsy girl.' I thought it was spelled like the word '*lang*, wolf' from the phrase 'big bad wolf,' so it made me cry. But my personality is a bit wild. Whenever I see someone bullying a smaller person I can't bear it, and I want to help my weaker friends however I can. I took things into my own hands and hit one of the boys before running like a rabbit into the girls' restroom to hide. I knew that the boys couldn't go into that restroom and hit me. I hid there until the teacher realized I had disappeared and pulled me out. I think that people should be kind and respect one another."

It was common for my daughter to be in high spirits. Screeching like a cat and jumping like a monkey, she used her brush to make vivid animal paintings, each in a different pose: these "little guys," so fully human, heeded her every command....

The drawers at home were full of my daughter's drawings: sketches of exotic animals at the zoo, nature scenes painted outdoors, sketches of row-ers' arms during televised boat races, and copies of comics. When I noticed that she was being "a bit lazy" while copying comic strips by Cai Zhizhong, a Taiwanese cartoonist, I called out to her, "Keke, where is the person on the wise turtle's shell?" Without missing a beat, she replied, "Oh, that's a bad guy. If I draw him, he will hurt others." "When you're copying, you have to copy everyone, no matter if they're good or bad. What if you want to make a painting of your own and then realize you don't know how to paint bad people?" She cleverly redirected our conversation: "Also, there was no space in my drawing, so I might as well leave him out. Anyway, I like animals best." "So you don't want to learn to draw anything else, is that right?" I began to grow angry, but my daughter's anger was greater than mine: "What's the point of learning to draw bad guys like that? As soon as I see bad guys, I tremble!" Any adult looking into her big black eyes wouldn't have known whether to laugh or cry.

On my thirtieth birthday, my daughter did not go out to play. In-stead, she worked very hard to paint me a large, colorful canvas depicting room-by-room and floor-by-floor of an unusual building that combined an ancient castle with Western-style architecture. In her fairy-tale castle, depicted in a very fantastic manner, an ancient poet sits by a window, writing. Without warning, my daughter held up the painting for me to see, announcing, "Happy Birthday, Mom! I made you this gift. I hope that, just like the ancient poet in the painting, you will be able to write some decent works!" For a moment, I was very moved. This complex building and colorful painting was truly a profound birthday gift. It expressed the meaning of the Va people and illuminated our lives.

The elementary school teacher once assigned the students an essay on the following topic: "A Self-Portrait." My daughter immediately decided to discuss every aspect of her body; in her vivid style of thinking, she exemplified both the simplicity and honesty of the Va people: "I am a small Va girl, I have big bright black eyes like two black gemstones, a tall nose like a mountain range, a mouth like a grape for reciting poetry, a small face like a red apple—whenever Mother sees it, she wants to touch it. My head is neither big nor small, just right atop my neck; since I was born with a dark complexion, my classmates have taunted me, calling me 'little Africa!' 'little Africa!'"

One day after school, as soon as she walked into the courtyard of Building 56 on Beimen Street, my daughter let out a cry. When I saw her cheeks, still tear-stained, I became concerned, but without waiting for me to speak, she immediately said, "Mom, today I got into a fight with Dajiang, a boy from your art class." "Why?" "Because he doesn't treat small animals well; he crushed all legs of a gecko, but the gecko didn't die, it was just barely hanging on to its life. This is when some classmates ran over and called out, 'Look, everyone! A free, live-action fighting show!'" My daughter lowered her head. Just moments later, she raised her head, exclaiming, "Yes! These animals are just too weak. Let's go home! After what he did, I'm gonna go pick a fight with him (Dajiang) tomorrow!"

My daughter was a little kid who has always been on the lookout for adventure. On June 1, International Children's Day, she invited the children in our courtyard to go to the public well to wash their cleats. As they were cleaning the shoes, my daughter asked Xiaojie, "What do you think, how many mothers do you think a person has?"

"I don't know, probably just one, if you have more than one, then they're probably stepmothers."

"I think that everyone has two mothers," my daughter loudly insisted.

Xiaojie suddenly placed her small hand over my daughter's mouth: "Quiet, quiet, what if your mother hears?"

"I'm not scared, why should she be so worried about her feelings! Let me tell you, one mother is the one who gave birth to you, and the other is your country!"

On July 7, 1990, the Beijing Cultural Palace of Nationalities hosted the opening of the exhibit "Young Va Painter Zhang Ke," presided over by Shen Peng, Vice Chairman of the Chinese Calligraphers' Association. At the ceremony, an American professor from the Foreign Languages Department at Tsinghua University offered the following message for my daughter in English: "This child from a Chinese ethnic minority is no ordinary child. May her paintings continue to give to the people of this world!" After seeing the exhibit, a student from the Central Academy of Fine Arts shook my daughter's small hand saying, "Keke, thank you for your paintings, a child's heart is so pure! I lost my inspiration to seek this kind of purity years ago, but your artwork has helped me find it again." Middle school students from Beijing crowded around Keke's drawing table and drew a small portrait of a Va girl with the caption, "Dearest Keke, may you always remain as cute as the kittens in your paintings."

On the evening of the opening ceremony, my daughter fell asleep just like a quiet kitten…. She lay on the steps outside the exhibition hall, wearing a black and red Va dress, her sweat-covered face glistening in the lights, looking especially brilliant!

Keke was actually dreaming, dreaming that she had gone back to the Ava Mountain that had been in her thoughts for so long. The mountain was covered with a carpet of fragrant wildflowers. The wild fruit on the mountain was ripe, bright and almost translucent. The *Aya* (elderly Va women) working on the mountain picked a few fruits to relieve her thirst and hunger. My daughter asked for some fruit, but the Aya replied that the fruit was sour and tart. My daughter began to grow impatient and cried out, "I want it, I want to eat the fruit…." In her dream, her face, full of surprise, was stained with tears!

This is what people heard my daughter say as she awoke from her dream: "I hope that my paintings, like a tiny bird, may fly somewhere beautiful!"

4

Eternal Spirits

Cen Xianqing

It's a spring day. At last, I stand in front of the rock paintings of the Huashan Mountain, ancestral home of the Zhuang people.

Are these my ancestors in the paintings?

On the cliff are the rock paintings of thousands of spirits, clustering around an invisible world with a red secret. These figures have no facial features, making it hard to tell if they are filled with joy or torn by grief or if they are excited or dispirited. Are they dancing or bowing, with horse stance and outstretched arms? Does the shining, round shape symbolize a war drum or the Sun God who rules the world? Are the small animals, half-running and half-hopping, warriors' horses or ritual sacrifices?

The mountain gives no answer.

There might have been fierce battles by armored cavalry, serious threats from natural disasters and plagues, great joy for an ample harvest or a peaceful period of stability and prosperity. From this point of view, the throngs and herds could have been brave soldiers marching into battle, with loud drums and heroic cries; they could have been shamans preparing the altar for offerings in a cloud of smoke, or ploughmen and weaving women in the tranquility of the pastoral countryside.... Who knows if this is meant to be an accurate portrayal of daily life or a vision of the promised land of these Zhuang ancestors?

Unfathomable. Unknown. Revealed on the cliff is a vivid wall of passionate people and living creatures, inviting archeologists to determine its age, scholars to draw their inspiration, and the Zhuang to burn incense and honor the spirits. The cliff stands silently and mysteriously.

Only the river seems to know the secret hidden for thousands of years.

Translated by Guangrong Wan, Dong Isbister, Xiumei Pu, Stephen D. Rachman

But the river gives no answer. It flows silently, winding gently, forming a clear blue world beneath the cliffs.

Standing here and now, I find myself lost in an ancient dream permeated with a mysterious mist—aloof and dense—unveiling the mountain, the river, the trees and the people....

Looking up, I see the cliff towering over me imposingly, ready to unloose with its frightening steepness the vicissitudes of time, numerous people, countless creatures, and a great mystery.

Looking down, I see the river flowing calmly, like silk or satin. The water reflects the cloudless southern sky against which the bamboo and mountain gently sway.

A *yang* mountain, a *yin* river, a harmonious world!

I raise my hand to touch the paintings; the art and the rock mesh flawlessly together. How many years have passed since the images of my ancestors were painted here? Summer departs and fall arrives; winter retreats and spring follows; trees flourish and wither; the river rises and falls. Everything keeps changing in the quiet of time; only the images of our ancestors remain the same. The paintings, red as ever, are always watching over the silent river.

I head for the river bank where the mountain and the river join in harmony. Perhaps it is this harmony of *yin* and *yang* that inspires me to decipher the secret of the rock paintings. I head for the river bank, where *yin* is in communion with *yang*. Perhaps, it is only there that I would unravel the secret of the rock paintings.

I am surprised to discover numerous patterns, partly hidden and partly visible, on the bluestones of the riverbank all the way to the cliff paintings. I scrutinize them carefully and realize they are the fossils of small creatures, such as shells, conches, shrimps, and crabs. They are embedded in the rocks serenely with their lives enfolded into the cliff's eternal being.

Are they revealing the secret of the mountain and the river?

Oh, my Zhuang ancestors have devoted their lives to inscribing the history and souls of the Zhuang people into the cliff. Indestructibly strong, they have held onto the root for thousands upon thousands of years, facing a pool of water and leaning against countless folds of the mountain. Time, wind or rain, the red color unrelentingly battling erosive water and scraping rocks, presenting a wall of lively and dynamic lives. It is these souls that keep the ethnic group surviving and flourishing against years of hardships and difficulties. They create lives and culture with tenacity and strength and betray neither the mountain by the river nor the river around the mountain.

These are the Zhuang, as strong as the mountain and as gentle as the river.

I surmise that I finally understand the rock paintings.

The setting sun shines on the water, and the gleaming ripples reflect the cliff. A light mist rises and floats silently from behind the trees on the mountain, and the figures on the cliff begin to move to and fro. In a queer trance, I see the red people and creatures come alive, their war drum beating, their war horses neighing and their dance music ringing in my ears. The tender, small waves caress and propel me to the imposing mountain....

Come back to me, spirits of the Zhuang!

5

Herbs Living in the Body

CHEN DANLING

My woman's soul is inextricably connected with a special rosebush. Really, the whole of my all-too-brief childhood could be covered by a single rose petal.

When it happened, I was sitting upright on a wooden bench in the classroom. At that moment, any sound or look could have startled me. I was afraid to move and afraid to scream. My shyness and apprehension were repressed and hidden, but revealed shamefully by the dark red, sticky stain on the bench and my pants. Scared and worried, I realized that no one would come to the rescue. I could only stiffly sit there and wait for the bell to ring, for my classmates to leave, until I could no longer hold back my tears.

The beginning of adolescence opened up a river in my body. The river pounded against my diminishing calm; it washed away the peace of my childhood, little by little. Mud and sands sink below the surface of the river, depositing a thick and heavy layer of shame, enough to bury a person.

Physical pain also came along. "Growing up, that is the way it is." Mother's words carried a feeling of inescapable fate as I lay beneath my blanket buried in despair. It seemed to me that "growing up" was always a sacred phrase with an indescribable power to elevate and expand life.

But in this magnetic field, the only thing I could do was say goodbye, shed my skin, silently endure the pain, and set out on a journey.

Sounds, colors, scents—how vibrant life and words are. They offered a farewell to my childhood, didn't they? They made me aware of my powerlessness and pain, as if I were the butt of a cruel joke.

Because this rite of passage was the first, it was suffused with hopelessness, mischief, and pain. It felt like I was all alone at a loud party, but my loneliness was invisible. It was hidden beneath the roar of the celebration. Maybe

Translated by Stacy Jane Grover

29

the roar of the celebration would die down and I might feel better or maybe my pain and loneliness would cool off and die, but I was not sure which.

Mother took me to see *Da Gong* (my grandfather's older brother) in his herbal medicine store, the only one in the village. Seeing him gave me some peace.

The store was actually a wooden house. The chestnut-colored counter was old. The lacquer was peeling around its edges and corners. Even after the rubbing of *yijin* (the front pieces of a traditional Tujia men's double-breasted jacket) over the years, the counter still shone with a soft exquisite light. Da Gong's silvery white beard and hair were shinier than his youthful black hair I remembered. A towering herbal medicine chest stood behind the counter. It was made up of numerous separated compartments and covered the entire wall. The chest had long occupied the space; the wall behind had long been hidden out of the line of sight. The chest had high prominence in the village, similar to the prominence given to white-bearded and white-haired Da Gong. In the village, anyone who did not feel well could get medicine here.

I was led to the meeting room. Mother sat between Da Gong and me. She avoided eye contact, mumbling incessantly in the midst of shaking and nodding her head.

Da Dong used the four diagnostic methods of *wàng* (observation), *wén* (auscultation and olfaction), *wèn* (inquiry), and *qiè* (pulse feeling and palpation). To me, they were mysterious and sophisticated. At that moment, my body seemed to become a deep valley. I felt a ray of pure light softly shining on me with warmth and comfort.

I saw a prescription written on rough straw paper. A fine, smooth calligraphy brush. Ten fair, slender fingers. Ink slowly soaking into paper. Fine dust floating gently in light. Everything unfolding as if in slow motion. I was infatuated with this kind of serenity and peace. The scent of the herbal medicine in the store and on Da Gong's body had an air distinctly reminiscent of ancient times. The serenity of the scent made patients feel as if they were in an open space and provided them with a kind of essential sustenance.

"Plant a rose bush in a corner of your yard. Mix flower petals with two egg yolks and fry them. It will help with cramps, menstrual flow, and pain."

On a spring evening, Father asked his second sister for a rose bush. He planted it in the corner of our yard. A smile came over his face.

It was the beginning of blossom time. Dark green leaves, about the size of fingernails, earnestly hung on to the slender branches and stems. Hidden between the branches and leaves were thorns: thin, small, and hard to detect, like a girl's temperament. If pricked by one of these thorns, one would feel a subtle pain. The flowers were more prominent. On the tips of the branches, they enjoyed breezes and sunshine, soaked in the rain and dew and moonlight. The flowers were delicate, but they bloomed stubbornly and beautifully.

Row upon row of petals spread out in different directions. Even with a closer look, one was unable to tell one layer of petals from another. Inner feelings, folded in the petals, resembled drops of blood bursting out and splashing down on a layer of dark green leaves. The way the flower presented itself could no longer be called "blooming." "Splitting open" would be more accurate. It split open until it could not split open anymore.

A beautiful, elegant, fine rose opened on a thorny branch, like a teenage girl, beautiful in every way.

From the time I was twelve, Mother had fried two egg yolks with a cup of rose petals for me to eat every month. My younger brother was unhappy about me getting this kind of privilege. Mother would simply give him a stare without speaking a word. The privilege alleviated some of the discomfort of growing up. My shyness, fear, pain, and sensitivity were cherished and saved by a self-sacrificing flower. Since then, I have had a forbearing flower living inside me. That is how the village became a place where a rose bush and I lived.

The village was not a lonely place; it was always bustling. One could walk around the village and see plantain, benzoin, Chinese bermuda grass, wormwood, woolly grass, and cnidium monnieri. They were all reincarnated spirits filled with life's essence, pure and mysterious, tranquil and luminous, silently providing neighborly care and companionship, even sacrificing their lives in the rescue. I prefer to call them grass because I like what the word conveys: humility, endurance, tenacity, ease, friendliness, and gentleness.

Still I remember how danger always lurked at night. How Mother and the snake alarmed each other. How the venom spread through her right thumb rapidly, causing pain and swelling in her body. The blood from the wound turned darker and darker. Signs of death were more obvious every second. The hospital was too far from the village. My third aunt grabbed a flashlight and rushed out returning soon after with a *qibulian*, a plant she found on the edge of the village. She chewed it to pieces, and then applied them to Mother's wound. I did not know or see how the plant absorbed and dissolved the venom. I remembered that the herb was gone, and my mother lived on.

Years later, Grandfather was on his deathbed. His feet were deformed from edema. On his swollen left foot was a depressed scar. Earlier that year, while Grandfather was harvesting cabbage, he dropped his knife on his left foot. Blood gushed out. In that remote village, no surgeons were available. The only option was to treat oneself. Grandmother rushed to the mountain for *huibaolu*, a medicinal herb to stop bleeding and relieve pain. The herbs in Grandfather's body were engaged in a life-cycle within him: giving their lives to help him go on living. Now, the *huibaolu* lived inside Grandfather's feet and would die with him. Life ends, but certain pains persist and will never fade.

After a spell of autumn rain, daisies bloomed merrily on the stone wall of the left side of the house. As the tightly bound buds opened, the flowers were exquisite, as if glowing with the colors of all the sunrises and sunsets from the ancient sky. Mother told me that flowers and plants have hearts; they are just unable to speak. These fragrant hearts beat in the village, loving the sorrows and joys of life, and loving an all too brief spring. This short life. On the stone wall, a vast expanse of daisy hearts softened the heartlessness of the stone, activated its energy, and infused it with a stream of *qi*.

The small yard in the front of the house was Father's private village: roses, hyacinth, chives, snow parsley, pumpkin, caterpillars, and ants were forever in his heart. When my daughter was one month old, Father planted an orange tree in that yard. "It will grow with my granddaughter, and she will have a long life like the tree," he said. Years later, the tree still did not bear fruits, as if it kept a promise to my daughter: to enjoy her prolonged childhood. Father never spoke one word of dislike. He looked after his village. During the weeding season, his grandchildren helped him with joy but only made things worse. Father would stop weeding and extend his thick, powerful hand to hold the small, fine hands of his grandchildren. Happiness was exchanged between the older hands and younger hands. Peals of laughter burst forth from the children and fell upon the grass.

Year after year, the grass, trees, and the green background of the village, quietly played a healing role, a cure for the worm-eaten cabbage that is the human heart. They lived patiently and honestly; they lived peacefully and compassionately. They were often silent because they majestically lived in the hearts of the villagers and filled them with persistent calmness and equanimity.

6

Kangnalikan the Little Reindeer

DEKELI

Kangnalikan, a reindeer calf, was born in August. Extremely uncommon. It is against the law of nature for it to be born in August, not to mention that its mother had not reached the normal calf-bearing age. Perhaps its life was already shadowed by misfortune at birth.

Perhaps the mother reindeer did not even know what birth was. After spasms of excruciating pain, it saw a little thing appear before its eyes. Enclosed in its afterbirth, it looked so strange. After several unsuccessful attempts, this reddish-brown, furry, wet little thing finally stood up on all fours. When it wobbled towards the young mother, it panicked. Bewildered, it avoided this little thing. Perhaps it could tell that humans or other reindeer had touched the calf. When it tried to suckle, attempting to get close, the mother dashed away in disgust. Left alone in the herd, it cried. From a distance, shocked and unresponsive, the young mother stared at it struggling.

The other reindeer calves were born in April or May. They were much older and larger than this newborn reindeer. They had grown strong enough to endure the harsh winter to come. At the northern, fifty-second parallel, the temperature could drop below -50° C. The older calves were prepared for a freezing winter, but the newborn was unlikely to survive the cold.

The mothers could distinguish the calls of their young amid the calls of all the other calves. The mothers in turn responded, running to their babes, and their young could tell their mothers' calls, as well. It was reunion time in the smokey woods.

But the young mother ignored its newborn's call and continued to busy itself searching for green moss to eat. Perhaps this inexperienced young mother had to struggle for its own survival and was not ready to take care of an even more vulnerable young life. Perhaps it would rather the babe had

Translated by Dong Isbister, Xiumei Pu, Stephen D. Rachman

died at birth so it did not have to suffer because of incompetence. Nature follows its own rules. Only the strong survive.

Mother told me that a mother reindeer tends to abandon its first-born. The baby reindeer either starves to death or survives under the care of humans. A doe won't become a real mother unless it experiences birth firsthand. There was a time when Evenki women would sing to a doe until it roused its sense of motherly love and accepted its first-born.

Ewo—my second aunt—inherited about sixty or seventy reindeer from her parents. She and her family were moving to another place where they could find abundant green moss and spring water for their reindeer calves. It was already fall, and winter was coming.

Ewo was in her nineties but could not remember her exact age. In the Evenki language, the word *ewo* means grandmother; in Evenki culture, ewo commands the most respect. We called her Ewo not merely because she was forty or fifty years older than my mother but also because she enjoyed high prestige in the family. She never married. She helped her parents raise more than ten younger siblings. She also raised the reindeer her parents had left behind.

Because of her age, at times she was confused, at others alert. She bundled up when it was hot and wore a thin layer when it was cold. She had frequent and serious bouts of bronchitis and pneumonia. Again and again, Mother told her to dress appropriately for the weather, but Ewo continued with her own way of life. Whenever Ewo fell ill, Mother would complain, "She is such a pain. She just wants to annoy me by not taking care of herself. She does it on purpose." Ewo's matriarchal power was waning. She was no different from the other elders. People looked at her pitifully. I could tell she was in denial. She did not appreciate pity and dreaded becoming too feeble to take care of herself. She agonized over losing her authority. She found solace in her reindeer. She said she would follow them and live and die as a nomad.

Ewo no longer had the energy to take care of this abandoned calf as she would have in her prime. Still, she named it Kangnalikan, meaning "black boy" in the Evenki language. She hoped it would grow up healthy, like a sun-tanned muscular young man. Ewo carried Kangnalikan inside the tent and laid it down on her bed, which was covered with fresh pine branches and a soft reindeer hide. The calf curled up in the bed, still panicking. Ewo fed it fresh reindeer milk while scolding its young mother.

Ewo left Kangnalikan with us on a Sunday afternoon in August. By that time, the incessant rains had stopped. The forest looked even more gloomy in this cold, damp season in the north. The sun came out like a long-lost friend, cheerfully shining over the land. At dusk, the air became soft and gentle.

In the first few hours, Kangnalikan timidly looked around the strange new environment. Its innocent deep blue eyes were filled with fear and vigilance. Its soft brown fur glistened in the tender sunlight. Its hooves were not made to walk on hard and slippery floors; it was close to falling in its attempts to move around. Out of fear, it gave up.

Mother fed Kangnalikan with reindeer milk she brought back from a camp. It slept quietly that night. I did not hear it making a sound. It must be exhausted with fear.

We ran out of reindeer milk the next morning. Mother sent me to buy two bags of milk powder. We heard that someone used it for abandoned calves, but that was at a camp in the forest. We decided to give it a try anyway. Still, we were not sure if Kangnalikan would survive on milk powder and grow up in a place away from the mountains.

Mother got a feeding bottle, but it didn't know how to suckle at the nipple when we placed it in its mouth. I emptied the milk into a bowl. It worked! It lowered its head into the bowl and started to gulp down the milk. It kept hitting the bottom of the bowl with its snout as if that would bring it more milk. Mother looked at it affectionately, laughing. She said Ewo might have fed it with a bowl.

Mother loves animals, perhaps because animals are more genuine and trustworthy than humans. We had two dogs before, but they disappeared one after the other, out of the blue. Mother believed they would exhaust themselves and return home one day. Whenever she stayed at home alone, she could not help missing the dogs. Lost in her memories, she couldn't hold her tears back. Miracles did not happen. The dogs never returned home. Years passed by, Mother still could not get over the loss of the two dogs, Kaqi and Kulie. To console her, I brought home a puppy. We called it *Xiaogou* (little dog). It grew up like our child, pampered with love and care. Mother said it was so sensible and smart that it was no different from a human being except it did not speak the human language. Still, she often thought of the two dogs.

A few days later, Kangnalikan became used to the new environment and the people around it. Its reindeer nature came back. It started to call for its mother again and ran around playfully. The look of fear disappeared; naughtiness filled its deep blue eyes. It took everything soft for its mother: clothes hung on the clothesline, the screen door, us, and the puppy. It hopped around aimlessly to look for its "mother." It would realize it had made a mistake when it heard our laughter. Then it'd turn around and continue searching.

Kangnalikan annoyed me sometimes. It would unexpectedly raise its head in the middle of eating, rubbing its messy mouth against me, leaving stains all over me. I ran around the yard to avoid it, but it went after me like my own shadow. At my wit's end, I had to hold the bowl in one hand and a towel in the other so I could wipe its mouth right before it reached me.

Kangnalikan acted more and more like a child, following us everywhere like a boy attached to his mother. Clip-clop, clip-clop, clip-clop. The yard constantly echoed with the sound of its hooves. Sometimes it followed me outdoors or to the river. It would walk next to me, looking around timidly like a shy boy.

At first, Xiaogou had a grudge against this newcomer and would bark at it. Whenever we were not watching, Xiaogou attempted to sneak over to take a closer look and bite it. When we tried to stop the dog, it would walk away reluctantly, with a look of resentment. Mother said the puppy was jealous of the reindeer calf. It sensed that it was no longer a pearl in the palm; the calf got everyone's full attention: food, play, sleep, every single move. The first thing everyone did when coming home was go check the calf, talk to it, feed it, and keep it entertained. No one seemed to remember the puppy existed. The puppy must be thinking to itself: "Huh! They all love you, keep the best food for you. They ignore me, scold me, and dislike me! I will have my revenge on you! Just wait and see…."

Xiaogou never took action. It had grown fond of the little reindeer. Lonely sentient beings pine for companionship. They played together in the yard during the day. At night, Xiaogou would lie down by the side of the little reindeer, assuming the responsibility of a watchdog. They got along well and relied on each other. We all said they were brothers: the puppy was the elder brother, and the little reindeer was the younger brother.

Time went by. The little reindeer was growing like a pampered child. We could see two black round bumps glistening on the top of its head. It was about to grow antlers. I couldn't wait to see it become a strong bulk carrying its beautiful antlers, running gracefully in the forest. When the fall came, its antlers would be weapons to defeat any and all rivals. It would win the love of the most beautiful doe and become the king of the herd.

The little reindeer died a month later. It was sick. It lay in the grass all day, looking weak and lethargic, lowering its head every now and then to inhale the scent of the fresh earth. Perhaps the posture made it feel that it was back in the woods. It grew thinner and thinner until it was nothing but bones. Its satiny fur lost its sheen. On its very last day, my brother and I stayed up all night; we took turns holding the IV bottle high above it. Watching it take in every single drip of the medicine, we believed it would get better the next day. Mother would usually pamper Kangnalikan but this time she stayed away. Occasionally, she sneaked a peek at the door and walked quickly away. She seemed to be afraid of looking into its imploring eyes. It fell asleep. It looked like an innocent babe having a sweet dream.

Kangnalikan woke up to bright sunshine the next day. It opened its eyes, took one last look around, then closed its eyes for good.

My brother gently picked up Kangnalikan. The little reindeer looked as if it were sleeping. Its head rested in my brother's arms like that of a weak and skinny child. Brother carried it to the yard and laid it on the ground. Xiaogou sadly walked up to the little reindeer and licked its face. In the next few days, Xiaogou seemed to know it had lost close kin. It remained quiet for days. No barking, no running around.

My family never raised any abandoned baby reindeer away from the forest again.

Our reindeer are the spirits of the pristine forest. They would never make a home in an impure world populated by humans.

Years passed; my memory of the reindeer calf faded away. Its name came up again in our conversations with Ewo during one of her visits. She told us Kangnalikan's mother had another calf a year after its birth. This time, it acted like a real mother. I wondered if it still remembered its first-born.

The only thing left behind of Kangnalikan was a photo. The exposure was poor, but we could see the image clearly enough. It was staring at the lens in great surprise, holding a corner of my mother's shirt in its mouth. Mother was laughing, trying to get it off her.

In my mind's eye, Kangnalikan was struggling for its first walk on a hard and slippery floor. The clicking sound of its hooves was still ringing in my ears.

7

Eji's Buckwheat Field

Han Jinghui

1.

Eji sat on the buckwheat field on the hillside like a buddha, bathing in the sunshine, blathering over and over, "We'll never eat *maoerduo* (noodles shaped like cat's ears) again!"

Tana sat by her grandmother's side weaving green foxtails to make a little cat, the bright green blades of grass flying through her fingers. She was ten years old this year, the daughter of Eji's youngest son.

Tana went on silently weaving the foxtails with her small hands. Eji's chatter hovered around Tana, every minute of every hour of every day, and on top of that Eji's hearing was getting worse, so it was necessary to shout over and over before she could hear you. Tana didn't want to waste energy talking to her.

"What will you do when you have a sore or you get the runs, and there's no gut-cleaning grass?"

Eji also called buckwheat gut-cleaning grass. When Tana had an abscess on her head or face, Eji would make a paste of buckwheat flour and vinegar and apply it to the infection. One day later, it would scab over. When Tana had diarrhea, a drink of toasted buckwheat would cure her right away. Oh, and for dog bites, just rub some buckwheat dough mixed with dog fur on the wound and it will quickly stop the bleeding and the pain....

Tana knew all about what buckwheat is good for. Eji said that, though buckwheat flowers were plain little things without name or rank in the vegetal world, they could cleanse the organs, reduce heat rash, calm rheumatism, and cure diarrhea. She said that she had lived so long without the need of a single pill or injection all because of her love of buckwheat.

Translated by Anne Henochowicz

Tana also learned from Eji's babble that the farmers and herders living in Lamadi didn't appreciate buckwheat's low yield. They never planted it on good, flat land, but scattered it on the hillsides and valleys that were unworthy of other crops and let it grow and die naturally. Eji said this was unfair to the buckwheat, which also thrives in good soil near water! "But people are heartless. Buckwheat is so good to people, but people neglect it." So Eji berated others. Yet she, too, planted buckwheat on the hillside.

Tana still said nothing, focusing on her foxtails. Tana followed Eji like a puppy dog, but rarely spoke to her. She listened in silence to Eji's lectures, occasionally nodding her head. Even so, she was more accepting of Eji than her parents were. She didn't get upset by Eji's babble. Her parents had two ways of handling Eji when she started to talk. One was to ignore her and avoid her; the second was to argue with her, like with the question of Tana's education. Her parents were constantly fighting with Eji about that.

The year Tana was supposed to start school, there was no schoolhouse in the village. It had been incorporated into the county seat. Tana had no choice but to take the school bus. When Eji first took Tana to catch the bus and saw her granddaughter squeezed in like a meat pie, Eji's heart hurt, struck with fear, and she started her incessant nagging. "These days we keep getting poorer. When Tana's dad was young, the village still had an elementary school with six rows of rooms. He finished elementary school there, then attended the middle school close by. Now they've closed the school and the children have to go to the county seat. How can they learn when they have to travel so far? How is it that we keep getting poorer? How come there are fewer and fewer schools?"

For the next few days, Eji wouldn't stop her nagging. At first, Tana's dad patiently explained that school was free now, much better than before, but this only caused Eji to dig in her heels. "You think it's free, but to me it seems more expensive than before. They're always asking us for money to buy uniforms, notebooks, this thing or that. How are we saving money? When you were young, they only asked that we pay for textbooks, nothing more. How is it that we're getting poorer now? Back then, the village always would hold 'gatherings' for the new year and festivals, and at Gongyefu (the name elders used for the county seat) they could see the lanterns and the Yangko dancing! Now there are no more 'gatherings'! There's nothing! Isn't that what it means to be poor?"

Tana's dad objected. "Isn't there enough excitement on TV all the time? You can watch it every day!" When he was done shouting, he stared at Eji for a moment, then turned around and left. "How come old people are so annoying? Nagging me to death."

Not long after, on a rainy day, the school bus skidded and turned over on the muddy road. Though Tana wasn't among the injured, Eji was so frightened that she wouldn't let Tana go to school. Eji insisted that they just wait, wait until they get a bigger bus and then Tana can go back to school. They waited two years but nothing had improved. In fact, things had only gotten harder for the children. For safety, the government did not permit private vans to be used as school buses. The school didn't have the money for a bigger bus, so it left it up to the parents to resolve. Many children like Tana who at the time lived far from the school, decided not to go at all.

Eji and Tana's dad fought incessantly about whether or not to attend school. Eji's opinion was that Tana would survive if she didn't go to school. Tana's dad thought that without school Tana was finished. "Our village hasn't produced a college student in more than ten years," said Eji, "and a lot of children don't go to school. Don't they have food and clothing?"

"I don't care about other people's children. Mine is going to school." He swore he would rent a room in the county seat so that Tana's mother could accompany their daughter while she went to school. But he ran around for half a month, then came back and told Eji, "We can't afford the high rent!"

In the course of all this, Tana turned ten and she still hadn't gone back to school! Because she wasn't in school, she practically shadowed Eji every day. In this way, she became Eji's constant companion.

Eji and Tana got used to "cooperating" this way: Tana could silently amuse herself all morning beside her babbling Eji, and Eji could babble all day next to her granddaughter while the little one played. But it seemed neither could leave the other. As soon as Tana was out of Eji's sight, Eji would shout with all her breath, "Where the hell are you? Tana…. Tana…." That voice may have been old, but it could still penetrate the buckwheat-covered hillside and echo in the valley.

As soon as Tana heard Eji, she would pop her head up from the sea of buckwheat blossoms while giggling and waving, "Here I am!"

But Eji couldn't hear her. So Eji's dimming eyes would scour the landscape until they settled on Tana's silhouette. Only then would Eji stop yelling for her.

If it was Tana who lost track of Eji, the girl did not have her grandmother's composure. Tana would panic like a newborn lamb looking for its mother. She would cry and shout, but Eji couldn't hear her. Tana would go on until Eji reappeared. But Eji couldn't stand to be separated from Tana. No matter how confused Eji got, she never forgot Tana. It's just that after sitting for a while, Eji had to find a ridge between sections of the field or a tree to hide behind and pee.

Ugh, the foxtails just won't listen today. It's so tricky and slippery that Tana will never be able to weave it into a kitty cat!

Eji talked to herself again. "We'll never see the buckwheat flowers again…."

As soon as Tana heard this, she raised her head. Her face filled with worry and her hands stopped their weaving. She loved those pink and white buckwheat flowers. Tana could do without Eji's *maoerduo* and hot bowls of *gegedou* (buckwheat pasta). She could forgo Eji's buckwheat jelly made from the little stone mill. She could forget those buckwheat meat pies and buckwheat noodles. But Tana could not go without seeing these flowers. Every spring and summer Tana would go with Eji to the valley. Tana would turn somersaults in the buckwheat field. She would catch locusts or run down to the stream and catch fish and tadpoles. She would pick wildflowers. In spring the buckwheat hadn't flowered yet, but the stone flowers, marigolds, foxtails, tassel flowers, apricot blossoms, Chinese larkspurs, tundra roses, and gentians were all in bloom. These carefree wildflowers seemed pressed to appear earlier and more beautiful than each other, bursting open as if they were vying for first place. But the buckwheat flowers were never in a rush. They obeyed Eji's plan. On the day Eji would decide it was time to plant the buckwheat, *Aba* (Dad) and *Ama* (Mom) would carry the buckwheat seeds on their shoulders to plant on the mountain. On the day Eji said the flowers should bloom, on that very day, the buckwheat flowers would powder the mountain white! Hey, that really was magical. Then Tana would worship Eji, who could cover a mountain in flowers with only her words. Isn't that magical?

So Tana loved those mountain wildflowers. And she loved the buckwheat flowers even more, since Eji brought them to bloom herself.

Together, Tana and Eji beheld the fields of buckwheat flowers!

The flowers wreathed the hills and fields, floating over thin red rhizomes. They dazzled in the sunlight with fairytale beauty. They were dizzying, intoxicating. Though humble, they beckoned the bees and butterflies. Crowds of butterflies fluttered and danced in the perfumed flowers. The bees whirred back and forth in the sea of blossoms, reluctant to leave. The bees, butterflies, and wind all carried the scent of the buckwheat flowers into the valley, charming every tree, stone, even the fish and the frogs in the gurgling stream with its fragrance.

The birds of the valley circled over the buckwheat flowers, one moment perching in the trees, the next diving into the expanse of blossoms. They crowded the elms and apricot trees in chattering throngs, laughing and playing. They seemed to enjoy the buckwheat field as much as Tana, and revel in its splendid flowers and delicate perfume.

2.

Eji was making "buckwheat jelly" in the kitchen. First, she mixed the ashen flour into a fine paste with her quivering hands. Then she poured it into a basin and tottered over to the yard to put it in the sun, covering it to keep the flies off.

After she had done all that, Eji sat panting under the old apricot tree.

Eji had gotten old. Things that were so easy before were now very strenuous. Eji's pursed lips and taut cheeks told Tana how much she struggled each time she squatted down or stood up. "I used to make a huge flat basket of buckwheat jelly," Eji prattled on. "Now I can only make a big bowl of it. This is the most I can lift. In the blink of an eye, I find myself over eighty. How come the days have gone by so quickly?"

In a half day in the sun, the basin of buckwheat cooled and congealed into a lump.

Eji brought the basin inside. She cut the lump into strips and added a spoonful of vinegar, a sprinkle of minced cilantro, a pinch of chili powder, and a dash of soy sauce. There it was, a bowl of glittering, translucent buckwheat jelly.

Looking at the inviting bowl of jelly, Eji started to think aloud, as if she were crazy. "In the future, when we want buckwheat flour, we won't have it."

Tana's mom was sautéing buckwheat cakes on the stove. As soon as she heard Eji, she turned her head and shot back, "If we had money, we could buy buckwheat flour anywhere."

Eji turned to her daughter-in-law and shouted, "What did you say?"

Tana's mom repeated, "If we had money, we could buy buckwheat flour anywhere."

Eji was still shouting, "What?"

Tana's mom didn't acknowledge Eji this time. "Deaf as death," she mumbled to herself. Then she bowed her head and turned back to her buckwheat cakes.

Tana shouted into Eji's ear, "Ama says that, if we had money, we could buy buckwheat flour anywhere."

This time Eji heard it. She muttered, "No other flour will taste as good as ours. Our flour…."

As Eji babbled on, Tana's mom turned away and kept quiet. She didn't want to upset her mother-in-law anymore. She knew that if she explained one sentence her mother-in-law would blurt out a hundred more. Then her ranting would start them bickering. Eji and her daughter-in-law rarely saw eye-to-eye. They were like two strands of rope that refused to be twisted together.

Tana's village was a typical eastern Mongolian multi-ethnic community at the junction of rugged hills, grassland and forest. There were Han Chinese, Mongols and a few Manchu living there. Their culture and lifestyles had blended together over the generations so that now one person wasn't so different from the next. They had adopted each other's means of livelihood, too: some Mongols now farmed in addition to their traditional herding, and some Han herded in addition to their traditional farming. But no matter the changes that went on around her, Eji stubbornly preserved Mongol customs and language. She hoped her son and his wife would do the same, but they were like all the other young people and spoke mostly Putonghua. Her son kept studying Putonghua after he graduated from high school, only speaking Mongolian with Eji. And Tana's parents always spoke in Putonghua to their daughter so that little Tana spoke better Putonghua than Mongolian. Tana only spoke a little household Mongolian with Eji. This did not please Eji at all. She believed her son and his wife had forsaken their ancestors. Shameless ingrates, always biting the hand that feeds them.

At that moment, Tana's dad rushed past Eji and Tana through the yard into the house, where Tana's mom was still bent over the stove frying buckwheat cakes. "Ha," he shouted, "the bottom rail is on the top, now!"

Tana's mom stood up straight and looked at her excited husband, stunned, while the cakes sizzled in the pan. "What is it? You're scaring me."

Tana's dad waved his hands around excitedly and went on, "The village head said not only will our buckwheat field be requisitioned, but also our house. He said that's the only way there will be enough land for the factory. Everyone in the village is going to be relocated. And the head said they'll compensate us for the buckwheat field and the square-footage of the house. And after they've built the factory, they'll take one person from every requisitioned household to work there. The head said urbanization would start right here."

The hands of Tana's mom trembled and the spatula dropped to the floor. She stood there stupefied for a while and couldn't snap out of it. Ah, were their days of tilling the soil and herding sheep over? Would they live on a monthly salary like people in the city?

"My God, is it true?" Tana's mom felt like she was dreaming, like it wasn't real.

"True, it's true. The head said it. Absolutely true!"

At night, Tana's dad and mom lay in bed planning what they would do with the money. Tana's dad said that, as soon as they got the money, they would buy a house in the county seat. If there was any left over, then it would be best to buy a car.

Tana's mom giggled, "Then I can drive Tana to school every day.... Haha.... Haha...." She felt that she'd choke on her own happiness.

The sound of their laughter carried from their room....

Tana heard her parents loud and clear in the room next door, but Eji heard nothing.

Hearing her parents' conversation made Tana very excited. While the buckwheat flowers were pretty, they were worth giving up for a family car to take Tana to school and an apartment in the city. Tana had to tell Eji the great news.

Eji was undressing, her body quivering. It took a great effort for Eji to undress. For years now, she would wrap her legs with long black strips of cloth to keep warm. Every evening she unwrapped her legs, and every morning she would wrap them again.

Eji's sunken mouth was clamped shut, the muscles of her face pulled tight with exertion. Eji really had gotten old. Unbinding her legs was like heavy labor.

Tana whispered in Eji's ear, excitedly telling her all that her parents had said. Tana didn't dare speak in Putonghua to Eji but she had to mix in a lot of Putonghua words with her Mongolian just to make herself clear. Even if she had to use a mixture, it was always better than speaking Putonghua. If she only spoke in Putonghua, she would have to fall asleep listening to Eji's unhappy chatter from bedtime until midnight.

Eji was dumbstruck. The black cloth slid from her dried-up old hands.

She was lost in thought for a while. Then Eji tore off the bindings, shook herself off the *kang* (multi-purpose platform bed), picked up her rosewood cane, and tottered over to the other room. She didn't knock. She pushed open the door and yelled at the couple lying on the *kang*: "Who said you could sell the house? I'm not selling anything!" Then she turned around and left.

Tana's dad didn't utter a sound, because he knew that, no matter how much of a fuss Eji made, it would accomplish nothing. Could she stop the whole village? It would be a cold day in Hell before that happened!

Tana's mom was afraid that Eji's bearing could make everything fall through, but Tana's dad told her not to worry. He said, "The village head said the biggest wave can't stop the fish from swimming and the tallest mountain can't keep the sun from rising. This is how things go. It can't be stopped. You just wait for that house and that car."

Another laugh burst from their room.

Eji sat all night alone in the pitch-dark yard. Feeling alone, she looked up at the old apricot tree that had accompanied her all these years. Feeling alone, she heard the sheep grazing in their pen. Feeling alone, she breathed in the scent of green grass wafting from the marshes beyond the yard. Mournfully, she listened to the frogs and cicadas in the vegetable garden.

On this one night, Eji could hear exceptionally well. The subtlest sound rang clear as a bell in her ears.

The trees in the yard, the flowers in the garden, and the black dog curled up outside the main doorway were all shrouded in darkness. The night covered Eji's heart, snuffing out any sliver of light. She felt sad and suffocated. Although there was a night breeze, it couldn't blow away the heavy fog in old Eji's heart.

Whenever Eji was angry at Tana's parents, Tana would sit quietly by Eji's side keeping her company. Tana's parents and Eji got angry about lots of things. For example, Tana's mom made her call Eji "Nainai," but "Nainai" made Tana call her "Eji." When her mom wasn't around, Tana called Eji "Eji," but sometimes Tana got confused and accidentally called her "Nainai." Eji would get angry right away and tell Tana, "You are the progeny of the Mongol people. You should speak Mongolian." But then when Tana spoke Mongolian, her Mom would get angry and say, "You have to speak Mandarin Chinese from the very beginning. Otherwise, you'll have a hard time learning it when you're grown."

Little Tana was sandwiched between her parents and Eji. Sometimes she didn't know what to do or whom to listen to. She figured out a way to avoid both Eji and her parents scolding her: if they were all present, Tana would say nothing. While she said nothing, she almost always stood by Eji's side.

But this time Tana didn't accompany Eji, as she also wanted to ride in her family's own car and live in a clean, bright apartment building like the other children in town and go to the best school. So Tana was unhappy that Eji said she wouldn't sell the house or the buckwheat field. Unhappy Tana ignored Eji sitting in the courtyard. She turned over and fell asleep.

Eji sat weeping in the dark night. She couldn't bear to leave her buckwheat field. She couldn't bear to leave the house she had lived in all these years, but she knew that, if everyone in the village was selling their land, she couldn't stop her son.

In fact, if it weren't for Eji's stubbornness, her son would have gone to work in the city years ago and taken his wife with him. They would have fled this lifetime of toiling in the land with their backs bent over the yellow earth under the hot sun. They would have fled the life of farming and herding like most of the other young people in the village. They also yearned for the city, for the clean and tidy life of the city. But Eji wouldn't let her son have this dream, and she had done everything in her power to keep them from leaving the village.

Eji sat in the yard like a buddha. A net of silver moonlight shrouded her, lighting the entire scene and all the animals in it. Even the sad chirping of the crickets seemed shrouded in moonlight. Everything, including every blade of grass and every leaf, had lost the clarity and realness of the day. Their colors were blurred and illusory, giving one the feeling of being in a dream or hallucination.

Eji heaved a long sigh. Although it was long, it was so weak, just commingled with interminable grief. This grief, too, was quickly buried by the quiet night. Not even the insects in the meadow felt it. They went on singing happily.

This was an era when something new happened every day. This was a helpless era that Eji could not block or prevent.

In the wee hours a cool breeze blew intermittently, and the apricot tree began to tremble and rustle. It was still the three hot periods of summer beyond the Great Wall, but night was much cooler than day. Again and again, Eji wiped the tears from her face as the cold wind blew through her spine....

Perhaps she had caught a cold that night. From then on Eji continuously coughed. Sometimes she had a fever too. Every day her coughs echoed in her little room. In the middle of the night, the strange sounds emitted by Eji's throat sounded like a bellows and frightened Tana, who tossed and turned and could not sleep.

Tana's dad and mom tried to persuade Eji to go to the hospital, but Eji refused. All her son could do was buy her some cold medicine and cough suppressant, put them by her bedside, and urge her to take them. Eji, who had never touched medicine in her life, would not let a single pill pass her lips.

Every day Eji sat coughing in the buckwheat field, watching the bees fly around, watching the butterflies turn somersaults over the buckwheat flowers, watching how the buckwheat flowers fell and revealed grains dressed in black, watching how the insects clambered over the burgundy rhizomes and ate up the leaves.

Eji's cloudy, dulled eyes moved from the buckwheat field to the mountain valley, then from the mountain valley to the river valley, then from the river valley to the little prairie village, nestled among the green trees and the mountain forest.

In this way Eji coughed and watched, from morning to noon and again from noon to dusk.

The village at dusk made Eji even sadder. The cattle hands hurried their herds down to the valley through the light of the setting sun; the shepherds swung their whips and walked down the mountain amidst the bleating sheep; the sparrows and crows rose and fell in the sky before settling down in their nests; shining white stones revealed themselves in the shallow bend of the river like many fossils inlaid into the green mountains.

The dozens of green-blue tiled-roof homes, crowned with curling kitchen smoke, were blanketed by deep green trees. Though from this angle she could only see the corner of an eave of her house flickering in and out of view, the household warmth carried by its thread of rising smoke still made Eji eyes stream with tears. Home. This home she had cared for her whole life, this village she had lived in her whole life, would it really disappear?

In this way Eji looked on for a while, thought for a while, grieved for a while....

In the blink of an eye, it was September. By September, a hint of cold came to Lamadi, requiring wearing woolen underwear when going out in the morning and at night. The buckwheat had already been harvested, but Eji still took time to sit there for a bit every day. Tana's dad and mom worried that it would make Eji's cough worse and would try to stop her going back there, but they failed. Eji said if she didn't go to the buckwheat field to look, she couldn't eat.

Eji's shortness of breath caused by coughing was getting worse. Now she couldn't do without her rosewood cane. Leaning on it and accompanied by Tana, she would cough and pant her way slowly to the buckwheat field. Tana had to pull Eji up the hillside with her cane.

Eji exhausted herself getting there, then exhausted herself again sitting down on a ridge every day.

Only the red stubble of the reaped buckwheat remained. The grass on the field ridges was almost all withered. Crows and sparrows spiraled down into the furrows, chirping as they searched for stray grains and insects stiffened by the autumn wind. The leaves of the trees on the mountain opposite the field had turned yellow. When the wind blew, the leaves fluttered to the ground like butterflies.

Tana, accompanying Eji, thought autumn was not much fun. She couldn't catch the sparrows, and she had no interest in the fallen leaves. All she could do was leave Eji and go gather beautiful pebbles on the sand along the river.

At noon Tana had a pocketful of pebbles. She went to get Eji for lunch, and found her sitting on the buckwheat ridge, straight as a stick, eyes wide open, and her expression unchanged, regardless of how loud Tana called to her.

Aba and Ama heard Tana screaming and wailing in the buckwheat field. They ran up the hillside and found Eji had already stopped breathing.

Tana's dad walked over to Eji and placed his palm on her forehead. Stroking down to close her eyes, he said: "Eji, are your eyes open because you're worried? Go in peace. I will bury you right here in this buckwheat field so you can watch over it every day."

Eji's eyes closed.

For a year afterward, Tana did not return to the buckwheat field. So much happened that year. Tana's family moved into an apartment in the banner town, and everything changed. Now they were truly city people.

And Tana started school. She didn't go to the Mongolian elementary school as Eji had hoped, but instead to a school where lessons were taught in Chinese.

Tana wasn't called Tana anymore, either. Written neatly on her notebook was the Chinese name Wang Xiaona.

One year later, Tana—no, Wang Xiaona—and her parents went back to their hometown to pay respects at Eji's grave.

The pretty little village on the prairie and the hills, resounding with human voices, barking dogs, happily calling cattle and sheep, was totally gone. The view was filled with rows of rumbling bulldozers. Construction workers busily dug foundations, laid bricks and mixed concrete. Heaps of steel bars and bricks lay everywhere. The only thing that hadn't changed was the three, century-old, elm trees, still standing proudly erect, striking the viewer with all the life they had weathered.

Tana's dad and mom took all this in with great excitement. Especially Tana's dad, whose happy mouth stretched into a smile that went from ear to ear. "Ha, so fast. This time next year the factory will be built, and this will be a busy plant. Then it will be connected to the city, and I'll work here."

Tana and her parents went around in circles until they finally emerged from among the bricks and rebar. They followed along what remained of the mountain path and came to the buckwheat field.

The field was overgrown with wormwood. There wasn't a single blade of buckwheat! It seemed the land they had sold was still waiting to be dealt with.

Eji's grave was not in the buckwheat field. It was in the mountain valley across from the buckwheat field. Her grave had a lot of wormwood growing on it. The wormwood shook in the breeze.

"Why didn't you bury Eji in the buckwheat field?" Tana asked.

Aba said, "We sold that land, so we couldn't bury her there."

Tears brimmed in Tana's eyes. "Then Eji can't see the buckwheat."

Aba lowered his head. "No, she can't."

Tana howled. She turned to Aba. "You promised Eji. You promised Eji!"

Tana sat crying on the ground before Eji's grave. No matter how hard he tried, Aba could not tear her away or pull her up.

8

Cat Tragedies

Lei Zhifen

The Xibo were historically known for hunting, so bows and arrows played an important role in their lives. As a result, when a baby boy was born, it was customary that a miniature bow and arrow set was hung on the door.

My father was the oldest son in the family. My grandparents were so eager to have a grandson that, even before I was born, Grandpa had gathered together red strings and bronze coins he would use to make the bow and arrow set for the expected male child. However, because I came along, Grandpa never got the chance to make it. He only hung a flag-shaped strip of red cloth on the door, the symbol of a newborn girl in the family.

Because my older sister was already on the scene, my grandma rolled her eyes when I was born. Mother was not treated favorably, either. As usual, she had to carry out her share of the daily work. No one would bat an eye at my cries of hunger pangs until Mother finished her chores.

Maybe I was innately more stupid than others, or maybe I was slow in my intellectual development because of the lack of nurture from the grown-ups. My earliest memory is that I was either laughed at for being ugly or talked about for being stupid. I was a child no one was fond of. Every day, I would stare into the faces of adults, trying to gauge their expressions. I dared not fawn or throw a tantrum, let alone try to get my own way.

By the time I was old enough to remember, my father had been working in the township government for many years. He would visit us every Saturday. Instead of coming to our room, he would go directly to Grandpa's and Grandma's room to drink, chat, and play cards. By the time he came to our room, I had already gone to bed. I only knew my father as a man wearing a suit and leather shoes. He had never held me in his arms or looked at me for a

Translated by Weihong Gao

second more than he did other children in our extended family. To me, Father was no different from any other family member.

For a short period, I found myself under Father's watchful eye because he found out I was left-handed. He was trying to correct me, but I always forgot. Whenever I used my left hand, he would scold me. I became so frightened that when he came home to visit, I would hide.

When I was six, Father, for reasons unknown to me, was sent down to a village to teach in its elementary school. Because it was too far from our hometown, we had to move away from our big, extended family, still bound by its traditions. My connection with my father began then, but because of the fear I had developed of him, I still felt very cautious when he was home.

Father became the head of our nuclear family. He no longer had to spend time drinking and playing cards with Grandma after work anymore. When he was free, he would play with us, tell us stories, make kites and kaleidoscopes, and blow soap bubbles with his tobacco pipe. Through these activities, Father and I became closer.

As my fear of my Father lessened, my mind developed. I began to have my own thoughts and my own desires.

Our real connection began with a kitten. A neighbor's cat gave birth to a few kittens. I wanted to bring one home so badly but was afraid Mother would not allow it. I went there every day only to see them taken away one by one. When there was only one yellow kitten left, I wasted no time bringing it home, hiding it in a bale of hemp straw, but Father found it anyway. He brought it inside the house, feeding it a small plate of rice congee.

What Father did make me feel proud. For the first time, I felt affection for him as a daughter.

Father not only taught me how to feed and train the kitten but also fed it himself sometimes. He explained to me how its whiskers worked and how it was able to catch mice in the dark. He taught me to observe its postures while it slept and the dilation and contraction of its pupils in varied light. With Father's support, I took good care of my yellow kitten. When we had to move back to our hometown because Grandma fell ill and needed my mother's care, the little yellow kitten came with us to join our large family.

Grandma owned a big, fat black cat, three times the size of the yellow kitten. On the windowsill sat a food bowl exclusively reserved for it. In the bottom of the door and the window, holes were cut for its exclusive use. It would walk in and out of the house in a calm and leisurely manner. When it got tired of walking, it would go back to Grandma to sleep soundly beside her. Maybe because it was so used to doing nothing but eating all day, it did not exhibit any hostility towards the yellow kitten, except for its arrogant, pampered attitude. In this way, the two cats lived in peace in separate rooms.

It is true that all tragedies are not alike. In the year of our return, right after the Chinese New Year, those who had come to wish the elders Happy New Year gradually departed, and the noisy household settled down. Second Uncle's Wife and my mother made use of the down time to take care of their own business. After breakfast, one was hand-sewing soles, and the other was making hemp twine with a spindle. My cousin and I were playing *galaha* (a children's game) on the edge of the *kang*, while the yellow kitten was joyfully jumping around, chasing the bean bag we were tossing. Who would have thought disaster was lurking in such a peaceful moment and that in less than a minute, the kitten would be dead?

We were having a great time when suddenly we heard a sharp crack from the kitchen. Second Uncle's Wife told me and my cousin to see what was going on. The moment I opened the door, the big black cat bolted out of the kitchen, and dashed onto the windowsill. With its head, it pushed open the cotton-padded curtain that covered a hole in the window and jumped out as quick as a flash. Inside the kitchen, a No. 3 clay bowl lay cracked on the floor, leaving an empty spot on the narrow table where the bowls were stored in order of size. Vegetable broth pooled slowly on the floor. My cousin shrieked, "The cat broke the No. 3 bowl!" Upon hearing this, Laoshu, my youngest uncle, who had been lying on the *kang* seething in his own private anger, leapt up and rushed into the kitchen.

The poor yellow kitten followed me to the kitchen. It was too young to recognize the warning signs of danger and to avoid it. Then I couldn't believe it. The little kitten stuck out its tongue, licking the vegetable broth running on the floor. Upon seeing that, Laoshu grabbed a gnarled stick next to the stove and smashed it right on the kitten's head. Instantly, the little kitten fell to the floor in a puddle of blood, half of its head caved in, its fur soaked. It struggled to get on its feet but it was no use. It lay on the floor, twitching all over with its legs flailing helplessly, and wailing through its sharp, clenched teeth. Eventually, it bled out. Its cries became weaker and weaker until they came to a stop.

This was the first time I witnessed death, a bloody unjust death. This was also the first time I realized that there could be such injustice in the world as that inflicted on the yellow kitten, the scapegoat for what the black cat had done. When I saw the dark look on Laoshu's rage-stricken, twisted face, I was so frightened that I did not dare to speak up on behalf of the yellow kitten, and yet I could not remain silent in the face of Laoshu's wrongful action, either. I went back to Second Uncle's Wife in the bedroom. Leaning on her, I cried. I didn't know if it was because I rarely cried that Second Uncle's Wife felt sorry for me, or because she took the opportunity to vent her long-held resentment against Laoshu that she whispered to me, "Don't cry. A cat has nine lives. It takes nine young women's lives for a cat to be reincarnated. He killed the kitten and he'll certainly be punished for it. May he never take a wife for the rest of his life."

Maybe in the vast cruel world, the mistake of killing the wrong cat was too trivial. The death of the kitten had no effect on Laoshu whatsoever. He had a wife and children just like everyone else.

I could not tell if it was because I had too vivid a memory of the yellow kitten when it died, or because that was the moment I lost my innocence. I only knew that I did not want to raise another cat after that.

The second time I owned a cat was purely driven by motherly love.

After I returned home from work one drizzling day, I heard "meow, meow" in the courtyard. Following the sound, I discovered a few black kittens next to the log pile. Moving closer, I saw the kittens crawling aimlessly, with their eyes still shut, legs too weak to stand up, and rain-soaked black fur stuck to their skin. I knew it must have been my naive son who brought them home. I asked him where he picked up those blind kittens, and he said in the vegetable plot in front of our house. I said, "Who would throw away healthy kittens in a vegetable plot? They're all blind. Send them back right away. Their mom must be looking for them." After a little while, I walked out of the house, but the kittens were no longer there. I asked my son where he had sent the kittens. He said he left them where they were before. Full of regret, he repeated what I said, "Those are blind kittens. Who would throw away healthy kittens?" I had become accustomed to the vicissitudes of life and lost much of my natural kindness, and yet the look on my son's face really made my heart ache.

Later, at the house of a classmate of mine, I saw a kitten with a unique pattern. It was white all over, but its tail and the edges of its ears were black. It was so beautiful that I begged earnestly to take it home. My son adored it and consulted me about a name for it. Given the fact that the yellow kitten died for its lack of intelligence, I gave the new kitten a name in Chinese *Boshi*, meaning a person awarded a doctoral degree. I also gave it a name in English, Doctor, because I was teaching my son an English word every day.

Doctor became my son's pet. Every day, it shared not only our meals but also my son's snacks. During the day when it got tired of playing, it would curl up in a ball and sleep on the embroidered bed cover in the warm sunlight; at night, it would sleep in any bed it chose.

Doctor got to know my son first. It often chased him around and played with him. Sometimes it even followed him part of the way to his daycare.

When it observed me, it kept a respectful distance at first. After a while, it tried to inch closer. Gradually, it became playful, naughty and flirtatious. When I was knitting, it chased the ball of yarn, batting at it one minute, pouncing on it the next. It was so cute and spirited that I couldn't help teasing it with my knitting needles. In response, it crouched, furrowed its brow, and focused on the points of my needles as I moved them this way and that.

As Doctor grew up, its curiosity towards us had shifted away day by day. Sometimes it crouched on the floor with a serious face, and then pounced as if it had suddenly discovered something. One minute, it was all stealth; the next, it leapt on its own tail or claw at the floor. Very often, it left scratch marks on the carpet and mattress edges. Sometimes when I saw the damage it had done I would scold it, but my son came to its defense, explaining that it was merely sharpening its claws in order to catch mice.

At some point, Doctor extended its playground to the outside.

In front of the house, there were a few apricot trees. Sparrows constantly flitted in their branches. I happened to discover that Doctor had grown interested in the birds. One day, I saw it sitting on the bed, gazing at the birds hopping on the branches. After a little while, it couldn't contain its curiosity anymore. It sneaked onto the windowsill, sitting still and watching the birds through the open window. The sparrows perched in the trees in twos or threes and then flew away one after another. Doctor could not resist the temptation any longer. With a nimble jump out of the window, it landed and crept forward. With a second jump, it sunk its claws into the trunk of a tree.

Shielded by the leaves, it crept up on a sparrow perching on a branch. Stealthy as it was, the branch sagged under Doctor's weight. The sparrow seemed to have sensed danger and immediately fluttered away. Doctor was undeterred. It hung its hind legs on the branch waiting for the next bird, but the sparrows either flew away or flitted onto another branch every time Doctor extended its paws near them. After quite a few attempts without catching a single bird, it reluctantly gave up and jumped off the tree.

I held my breath watching Doctor in the tree. I was waiting for it to come inside so I could tease it about its failed hunt, but with a brisk little trot it leapt up the wall of the courtyard, over it and out.

One night when I was sound asleep, I thought I heard an unusual noise in the house. I opened my eyes, saw the light on and my husband standing in front of me. I asked him why he was up. He said, "The cat caught a mouse." Startled, I sat up and asked him where it was. He said the cat was eating it behind the writing desk. When I asked him why he didn't get the cat out, he said he would wait until after it finished eating. He explained that every time he tried, it would scurry away with its prize in its jaws.

Sitting on the bed, I conjured up filthy images of cats eating mice, which gave me goosebumps, and I cursed the cat to myself, "It's true that nature exceeds nurture. What a despicable animal you are, unable to behave properly in your new domesticated life. You never have to worry about food, yet you refuse to be fed. Who told you to kill a mouse?" I was also wondering why there was a mouse in the house—the living room floor was covered with terrazzo, and the bedroom had wall-to-wall carpeting. While I was trying to figure out where the mouse came from, Doctor begged to come back to our bed and sleep after finishing its meal. It had no idea that we had associated its meritorious service with indelible filth. When it realized the door that used to be left ajar for its convenience was tightly shut, it let out miserable cries.

A chilly gust of wind brought me to the window just in time to spot a small whitish mass disappearing into the vast, silent world of night. Still upset, I offered the following complaint to its receding figure. "Your wisdom is too limited to be called Doctor. Don't you know that the civilization created by human beings does not require cats to catch mice anymore? The legacy of your ancestors does not apply to the modern world. The only role for cats in today's world is that of pets. Since you cannot change your feline nature and adapt yourself to your new life, don't blame me for falling out of favor with us."

Human beings are creatures that always put themselves first. When Doctor's tiny body disappeared into the darkness of the night, I became preoccupied with my own reality. As if suffering from paranoia, I felt the whole room was filled with mutated bacteria from the plague. I was so frightened that I couldn't sleep.

Just when I was drifting off, Doctor returned. Standing close to the window, it softly meowed for a couple of times. When it didn't hear any response, it meowed a few more times, as if urging us to open the window as we did before. When it realized no one was paying attention, it started to scratch the window frame with its sharp claws. Unable to open it, Doctor sat on the exterior windowsill, wailing again and again. Throughout the night, it sounded as if it had been angrily complaining about its own mysterious doom. Its lonely, frail, and anguished wailing added a sense of sadness and desolation to the night.

I got up very early the following morning, swept Doctor's little food bowl into the dustpan, and was about to put it in the storage shed. The moment I cracked open the door, Doctor, which had been waiting outside, wasted no time trying to force itself into the house. Quickly, I blocked its head with the broom, which was already sticking halfway in, and pushed it out. Doctor struggled, howling at the top of its lungs with a hoarse and tired voice, imploring the one that controlled its fate. Still, I kicked it out, shutting the door. Raising its head, Doctor glared at me with its angry brown eyes. The normally mild little creature showed its defiance with every fiber of its being, but there was no way that it could reverse its fate. I led it to the storage shed and locked the door.

I sterilized all my kitchen utensils and soaked my son's food containers and water bottles in disinfecting solution, but all my senses were telling me that the pervasive bacteria were still spreading through the house, as if I might get infected the moment I reached out for anything.

Since then, Doctor has never entered the house. Only when I disposed of my son's leftovers did I remember the cat's bowl in the storage shed. Human beings cannot live in fear forever. Time passed. No one in the family was infected with the plague. The apprehension lurking in my mind was unconsciously subsiding. One day, I saw sparrows fly onto the apricot trees almost bare of autumn leaves, and remembered the naughty Doctor watching the sparrows. I went to the storage shed and opened the door, but Doctor was nowhere to be seen. The leftover food I had put there that morning was still in its bowl.

No one knew when Doctor left. No one was affected by its absence, and we all lived our lives as usual. In the blink of an eye, another autumn had arrived. On my way home from work at dusk one day, I saw Doctor amid some wormwood plants in the ruins of a broken wall, wandering alone on the brown grass and fallen leaves. I got off my bike, wanting to call its name and see if it could still recognize me, but I just couldn't get the words out of my mouth. Instead, I stomped my feet. Upon hearing this, Doctor stopped, turned its head, looked at me, hesitated for a second, and continued on its way.

I noticed that Doctor had lost its youthful gait. It walked like an old cat, and even its once smooth hair had lost its gloss. I wondered under whose shelter it had lived for the last year, or if it had been drifting around like a stray in the cold, narrow streets and alleys. I also wondered if it had come to terms with human fickleness and learned to hate our cruelty.

Later on, I moved to an apartment building and never saw Doctor again, but in my mind, I occasionally see the image of an old cat at sunset, wandering on the dead grass in the ruins of a broken wall on a bleak autumn day.

9

Bitter Greens

MA JINLIAN

With a stiff neck, Li Fugui opened the door, walked down a stretch of level ground, then turned onto the road winding upward into North Hill. He never turned his head and his eyes never strayed from the path in front of him. The left side of the mountain path was lush and full with wild greens and flowers in full bloom. Butterflies danced in flight and beetles bustled by. One patch of green merged into another: wheatgrass, flax, and potato greens. He looked left, only left and never right. He filled his mind with thoughts of whose crops these were, whose families they belonged to. He looked at the wild flowers, the wild grass, butterflies, beetles, and bees. But not to the right would he turn his head. Nope, not the slightest glance. He was like a stubborn, old weed in the road; his heart and his mind were blowing in the wind, but he kept on. He kept going, and he never turned his head in that direction, and never looked over there. That must be avoided.

He wasn't brave, or not brave enough. Not to look in that direction. No, not even with one eye.

Sweat bloomed on his back, beads of it lined his forehead.

Step by step, his pace was slow and heavy. Inside, something deep and hard kept him going.

He was going to North Hill, going to dig *kongque* greens.

It was May, when the wild greens grew thick and strong, and at this time of year, he would always make time to dig. It was what he did, and he was not likely to change that now.

The hill rose up, repeating its twists and turns. As it climbed, the wind blew cool and refreshing. The village remained hot and stuffy, but not North Hill, where the wind seemed to come from all directions at once. The wind was like a cool, thin, comfortable outfit, surrounding him in the sound of its

Translated by Jesse Field

brisk swish. He took off his straw hat, fanned his head, and the wind evaporated the sweat. He sighed. Something loosened deep in his heart, a pressure that had built up for days slackened.

One more turn and he'd be entering the North Hill's rolling terrain. The village below would disappear from view.

Finally, he couldn't help it. He turned to the right.

There were old graves mostly, just below North Hill, most of the markers grown indistinct, but one was newer, still clear to the eye with a freshly made mound. Wasn't that just what he wanted not to see?

Scalding heat ran through his heart in a wave. His grief filled his whole chest. An unspeakable emotion, cold and hard, drowned him.

This was his son's grave. His son, Shemu, slept there under that mound of earth.

Shemu had been in the ground for a year now. Li Fugui counted on his fingers the days he'd had to endure that year. Shemu was dead, and he knew that. He had seen the villagers take the corpse, seen with his own eyes. Strange, then, that part of him still looked out for Shemu. He still felt Shemu would return, not sure when, but he would in the end. Shemu had been drifting in Shenzhen for years, and now he must be drifting somewhere, but he would miss home in time. He would get on a train and would come right back. One day, he would just show up and there he'd be, right before his father's eyes, scaring his old man something fierce, and then he'd probably die of happiness.

Shemu had just shown up like that, once, on a winter day ten years before. He had run away from home three years before that and never even called, just cut himself off. For three whole years, Li Fugui was almost crazy with worry. He'd watched and waited till he'd lost all hope. It was snowing that day, and the old man's heart was gray and crushed inside. Fidgety, unable to focus on anything he tried to do, he leaned against the window, watching the snow. And then slowly the door creaked open and in stepped a ghost, all white. It stomped its feet, put down its bags, and walked up to the window, greeting him with a "Salaam." Li Fugui's heart wrenched and leapt. This was his son. His Shemu had returned.

Changed and yet this was still his son. The boy had run away, fled to the outside world. At fifteen, still in the eighth grade he lost interest in school. Three years had passed and oh how that boy had worried this old man. The boy was tender still, just a baby sprout, really. Who knew what bitterness he may have tasted on the outside and what ills others might have done to him. Li Fugui had thought of this day and night—he really had. The idea of his innocent son in a hard world tugged at his heartstrings.

And now his son was back and Li Fugui was happy, so happy that that hot tears ran from his eyes. His son was taller now, but terribly thin, his lanky body as bony as a bamboo pole. A stiff wind could knock him over, or so it seemed. He looked just like his mother, so lovely in the eyes, eyebrows, and his skin was as pale as chalk. Judging by the face, you'd say he was prettier than any girl. He was girlish by nature, too, always shy and easily scared when he was young. He used to get bullied out there, but he would never tell the adults about it. He just hid alone and wiped his tears.

Li Fugui was forty-one when he had a son. He'd only had daughters before, never a son, and how he and his wife had loved their son. He was their jewel, their treasure. He would never forget the joy Shemu brought as he grew up, the happiness and satisfaction. Li Fugui's wife grew sick and died young. Because of his son, he hadn't remarried. The boy was always weak, and in those years, the family was so poor they couldn't afford to run a stove in the winter. At night, the baby boy would pee himself out of diapers. Afraid that his son would be damp, the father slept with the boy on top of him, the wet diaper underneath his body. In time, the boy grew and no longer wet the *kang*, but the situation gave Li Fugui rheumatism, and from then on he suffered from chronic lower back and leg pain.

He felt his son's well-being was worth the trouble. It was worth it at any price to be a father. Originally, he had hoped his son might study the scriptures and become an *Ahong* (Muslim teacher) some day. That would be good for him, and good for the old couple, too. After they passed on, there would be someone to pay their proper respects to the dead. But the boy wasn't interested in the scriptures, and so he was sent to school instead. Once again, he hoped his son would get into a good school, maybe even get a salary job. An iron rice bowl! But once again, the boy was a disappointment. He was just like the other children in the village. Mediocre. A bunch of ne'er-do-wells, the lot of them. Li Fugui learned to let go of his dreams and just concentrated on raising the boy to adulthood. The sooner the old man found a wife for the boy with as little fuss as possible, the sooner the old man would have a grandson to hold.

Who knew that after all those generations, they were all about to lose the peace and quiet of those hills? There would be no turning back, either. Nobody wanted to live off the land anymore or to watch over it. Instead, they left. They ran off to work on the outside. First the men and then later even the women. This occurred right when Shemu was at that age when boys were curious about things. The other young men were all heading to the outside, returning with their hair dyed blond, sporting tattoos of dragons and eagles over their arms and shoulders, big old earrings dangling from their ears. They carried around these little boxes they called cell phones, *wala wala* talking into those things, holding conversations with someone a thousand miles away. Which villagers weren't dazzled by it all?

Shemu saw all this and began to get a glint in his eye. Li Fugui saw it and grew uneasy. This was why he took the boy up the hill to dig *kongque* greens.

Kongque greens. He and his son had habitually dug them for years.

Li Fugui settled the basket on his back, grabbed a trowel, handed another to the boy, and they set out up the hill. Step by step. Father and son. North Hill had the most *kongque* greens. They were everywhere. Li Fugui put his basket down where they were really growing thickly. Then he bent low and started to dig. His son followed soon after. Li Fugui turned to look. His son's head hung low as he dug, clumsy and jerky with the effort, though he made no sound. His son was nicking the greens! Their milk bled out, squelched and stuck to his hands. Those hands. Just look at those pale, delicate girlish fingers. Li Fugui had to chuckle a little to himself about that, because he'd never managed to toughen the hands of his precious son with hard work. That's why they were still baby-soft and tender. Goodness gracious, he had spoiled the child! Well, if he won't study, then let him be a farmer. Let him be like his ancestors, those who staved off starvation because they could handle a spade and work the land. And then Li Fugui knew again what he was about. The road ahead was clear. He would do his duty and be a hard-working farmer. He would shoulder his father's burden and keep this household going.

But his heart wasn't in it. Look at him—all this time at it and all he had to show for it were a few measly *kongque* greens, and even those were weedy.

Li Fugui couldn't bear to watch any longer. He squatted down right in front of his son. He put his hands on the boy's head to stop him. Shemu looked up, puzzled. "Now look here, look at that, do you think that these are good *kongque* greens? Huh?" He picked up what the boy had cut and shook it in his face.

The boy just stared at him weirdly, awkwardly, completely at a loss.

"Now, I've told you before, *kongque* greens aren't weeds. They're greens, son. They could save your life. When your grandfather was alive—no, don't even go that far back. When I was young and the famines came, well, we owed our lives to the greens." Li Fugui looked serious, and his voice shook. "Our whole family depended on *kongque* greens."

"I know. You've said that before. You've said it dozens of times." His son mumbled.

Every year, when spring turned to summer and wild greens were ready to eat, he would spare a little time from the fields to bring his son up the hill to dig *kongque* greens, bringing up the past along the way.

True, Li Fugui loved the wild, *kongque* greens. These days were better so at least no one would go hungry. And yet, come May he craved *kongque* greens. All else seemed bland. Eating *kongque* greens meant returning to the past, to the days when they died of hunger, bitter days never to be forgotten. His brother and sister both died of starvation. Dear little sister, gone up the hill to dig *kongque* greens and there she'd breathed her last. And now his son must hear the tale, as they dug and ate together. Kids these days, they just got worse all the time. They wasted the harvest, some children simply dropped grain without batting an eye. Some children tossed perfectly good steamed buns on the ground. Yes, and rice, too. And they'd never picked it up. They walked on it, mashed it. Even dumplings seemed worth no more than dirt, to be tossed into the pond. He'd seen it many times. Smug kids who never tasted life's bitterness. No wonder they have no love for the harvest. He saw how they went bad when they were on the outside. They were lazy when it comes to farmwork, they couldn't tell one grain from another, and they just weren't like the decent folk who grew up on the land. But no, his son wouldn't forget his roots. That's why Li Fugui told him about the *kongque* greens, how good they were, bitter at first, sweet after. In times of famine it could keep us alive. We mustn't forget the bitter times past or we will never truly know how good the days to come can be.

Li Fugui couldn't remember how long he'd been trying to teach this lesson but he knew that they'd been going up the hill since his son could first walk.

"The greens, Shemu, the *kongque* greens." Li Fugui wished his son knew what these greens were really worth.

"It's not called *kongque* greens." Shemu interrupted him and said firmly. "They're called *kuku* greens. *Kuku*. That's what it says in the textbook."

That took Li Fugui by surprise, but it also brought him great joy.

"What's that? You say your textbook has something about hill greens from these parts? Tell me more! What does it say?"

But the boy was bored and sullen now, his brows curled in like dumplings in soup. "Oh, nothing much. It just says they are called *kuku*, *ku* as in bitter. It's a type of edible, wild green."

Li Fugui was pleased. "Ah! Yes, yes, yes, they are called *kuku* greens. For five generations, that's what we've called them. *Kongque*, you know, that's your name for them."

Shemu smiled, then, or at least a slip of a smile crossed his normally darkened face.

Li Fugui noticed his smile and it warmed his heart. Never mind his tall, wiry body and his mature look, he was still a child, his smile was still so innocent and tender.

His son talked funny when he was little. Maybe it was because he had lost his mother, but at ages seven and eight, he still swallowed his words. The first time he'd gone up the hill with his father, he'd pointed at the jade patches of bitter greens, clapped his little hands and called out "*Kongque* greens, *kongque* greens. Look! So many *kongque* greens!" Li Fugui laughed to hear the silly sound in his little voice, and so he took to saying it that way, too. *Kongque* greens. As time went on, his son had grown up, gone to school, and stopped talking funny, but father and son persisted in calling them *kongque* greens. This kept alive the pleasant memory of his son's childhood, and Li Fugui felt he got more effort out of his son that way. He hoped he'd never forget.

Now the boy saw his childish error and wanted to say it properly. Well, Li Fugui would say it right, too. *Kuku* greens, yes, that's the way you said it. Not that it mattered much what they were called.

Father and son were both tired when the sun started to set and they carried the *kuku* greens home. Li Fugui picked out the choicest ones. He blanched them in boiling water, sprinkled them with garlic paste and chili pepper oil, swiftly tossing a salad. It was delicious. His son had loved this dish as a little boy. Father and son sat in front of a lantern, chewing away. As Li Fugui looked on at his boy eating, he was filled with a sense of fatherly contentment. They finished and he patted his tummy and lay down without even washing the dishes. He slept and in his dreams he was happy. But tomorrow, he thought, tomorrow he would teach his son the work of the farmer.

The next day, Li Fugui arose but his son was nowhere to be found. He discovered that his shirt pocket had been opened and the seventy *yuan* he had put there was missing. He rushed outside, but there was no trace of his son. On the table lay a sheet of paper, but Li Fugui could not read. He took it to someone to read aloud. The words on the paper said, "I've decided to go off to find work, hold on to the *kuku* greens for when I come back." That was it. Li Fugui held the paper tight between his shaking fingers. His heart shook even worse. The thieving brat! So he's spread his wings and left his old man. Damn! What's so good about the outside? In his heart he cursed the boy. But he took up the remaining greens, lay them out to dry in the sun, and bundled them for the winter. If his son happened to come home, he would make a special batch of fermented greens. Bitter greens are delicious when preserved in this way.

Li Fugui wanted to go look for his son. He approached those young men who went outside for work. He wanted to know what the outside world was like, and where a person would go to find work. This might help him look for his son.

"How old is the kid?" asked one young man.

"Fifteen." Li Fugui said. Then he added, "He just turned fifteen in the spring."

"Hey, fifteen is a man. What are you worried about? Besides, he's not a woman, right? You still worried they'll drag him off?"

Several of the young men began to laugh.

It wasn't enough for Li Fugui. "I asked you where you go to find work. Tell me the place. I need to find the little thieving brat!"

The young men eyed Li Fugui in surprise. "What, you, old man?" One of them laughed. "Are you crazy? You've spent half your life in these hills.

And how would we know where your son went? Do you even know how big it is, on the outside?" The young man talking drew a large circle in the air, his hands stretched out. "It's like, this! It's huge! There's no end to it!"

Li Fugui watched him draw the circle and felt a little dismayed. If the world was so big, then how could he find his son?

One of the boys who was a little more considerate than the others urged Li Fugui not to go. "There's no telling where your son went. You'll never find him. Look, it's a whole other world out there. Not like you think at all. You won't find him, and you might even get lost yourself."

Li Fugui hesitated. And as it happened, work started to pick up and he couldn't get away even if he wanted to. So he put aside this thing with his son.

Shemu left and it wasn't until winter three years later that he returned for a visit.

But even on these brief visits, there was no question of the boy staying home permanently. Li Fugui would wait and wait for the boy to return, only to have him stay a few days and then run off again. It seemed that the boy's heart had grown wild and had forgotten these hills and his hometown. There was something important in the outside world that kept pulling his son away. Li Fugui's only consolation was the money his son sent every so often. At least the boy was filial in money matters. Li Fugui took the money, but he couldn't bring himself to spend it.

He kept on farming even though he was getting old and was no longer able to handle the physical demands of it. He left his plots up in North Hill to the weeds, and such good land it was, too, what a shame to waste it. But he was old. Time spared no man. If only he could pass the land on to someone else for planting. These days everyone's mind was on going outside to find work. Nobody was interested in farming, least of all up in North Hill.

There were patches up on the southern face of North Hill that had gone to waste. Nothing there now but patch after patch of brambles and thorn bushes. Even the *kuku* greens weren't doing so well up there. Just a few tattered, scraggly bunches here and there, none with the old freshness. Even so, he went up the hill to dig greens, tossing a salad with the first bit, then drying and preserving the rest. He stored it all up carefully. One year led to another, and the greens half filled the cliffside *yaodong* (cave dwellings). He was loath to throw them out or to use them for kindling, but they were more than any one person could use. So he bought an autumn lamb, and a particularly thin and weak one, to boot. To look at it just made you feel sorry for it. It certainly didn't like eating clover out in the cold. The bleating would go on all day. Li Fugui fed it *kuku* greens. The whole long winter, the lamb lay under the eave outside the door, chewing mouthful after mouthful. Li Fugui lay curled up on the *kang*, unable to sleep, listening to that lamb's chewing. It was unhurried, deliberate, slow chewing. Hours on end. Li Fugui couldn't help it and his thoughts got ahead of him. Suddenly, he felt that his son was back. The boy was as silly as ever. Out by the door, he grabbed the greens and stuffed them in his mouth like a sheep, *munch, munch, munch.*

He picked himself off the *kang* and opened the door. In rushed the north wind, carrying little flecks of snow that shot and whipped in the wild air. The lamb lay upon the firewood, eyes closed, head in the greens. The sky was heavy and gray; the wind was high; and the snow was coming down far out as far as eye could see. Li Fugui's heart was heavy and gray, too. Even the sound of his coughing seemed heavier. The lamb turned to look at Li Fugui with sleepy eyes.

That whole winter, Li Fugui sat at the window, gazing at the distant sky.

Then came May. Li Fugui once more went up the hill to dig greens, tugging the lamb along behind him.

He dug his greens and threw them in a small *yaodong* in which the lamb was tied up inside. During his breaks, he went inside to have a rest. The lamb was tied up at the gate, the *yaodong* behind it already half full of dried bitter greens. These had sat in the strong sun till they were thoroughly dried and still held the crisp, sharp scent of the sun, the pungent odor of earth, and the unique medicinal bitterness of the greens. Li Fugui took a deep breath and his thoughts got the better of him again. The combined scents were exactly the way his son smelled. His Shemu, who grew up chewing greens, just like the sheep by his side now. No matter how long Shemu was away, thought Li Fugui, no matter how much money he made or what kind of person he became, in my heart, he will always be my son, my Shemu.

Li Fugui began to hear what other families had been saying. He guessed they all must have known for a long while. Young and old, men and women had all known. Only Li Fugui had been in the dark.

The years passed, and Li Fugui got used to his days alone. His son came every now and again for brief visits. He always brought some kind of special food, something rarely seen in the village, and he would leave money, and then he'd rush off again. He said he was busy, said the outside world was not like here in North Hill, that people out there didn't take their time with things like they did here. Out there, they counted out time in minutes and seconds, and time was money. When a strong young man missed a day, that was a day's wages lost. If he wasn't careful, he wouldn't have that hard-won job for long.

Li Fugui didn't say much in return. All he could do was look at his son. There was a lot he would have liked to have said, actually. It was bottled up inside him. He had held it in all this time, waiting and waiting for his son to return. And now that Shemu had grown up he acted like a grown-up. Li Fugui looked on in silence. Joy and misery mingled in his old eyes. He felt a strong sense of longing and attachment whenever his son prepared to leave again.

His son was determined, though. He said goodbye, quickly packed his bags and lugged them off, disappearing into the distance without so much as a backward glance, much less a wave goodbye. If no one else was around, Li Fugui would let his tears fill his eyes. The little thieving brat. Growing up had turned him cruel.

Li Fugui turned and took stock of the place. Still the same old home, nothing changed. His son didn't really take much with him, but Li Fugui always felt it just wasn't the same without his son. He felt his very spirit was lost. There on the *kang*, amid the piled-up quilts and the rumpled pillow towels where his son had slept, Li Fugui's felt his son's absence keenly, that he had taken his heart along with him, away, to some place out there they called Shenzhen.

People saw Li Fugui passing his days alone, lonely and bored, and they remarked that he ought to "re-string his fiddle." A house must have a woman to be a home for all the months and days to have any meaning. But Li Fugui would just shake his head, stubborn as ever. "I'm long past the age to have any thoughts of women." His only hope now was that his son would marry soon and bring him a grandson. The sooner, the better. That's the only bit of happiness anyone can hope for when they're old, he thought.

Life on the outside changed his son. Every time he returned, Li Fugui would remind his son to get married and start a family. And his son would be silent for a while, and then finally he'd say, slowly and deliberately, "We can talk about it later, when I get a little money. I'm still young."

That was what he said. He sure put a lot of weight on money. He'd even let it slip that he meant to buy an apartment in the city. He planned to start a family there, and then to move his old father there, too. They would enjoy a good life. Li Fugui didn't see how that could possibly work. Why? He was only a farmer with muddy legs. For generations, his ancestors had scraped the earth to stave off starvation. Now his son wanted to take this wonderful earth and throw it away, run off to the city? Well, where was the sense in that?

His son viewed it another way. He wanted out of these damned hills and their poverty, and if he had to struggle his whole life to do it, well, so be it. To make his wish a reality, he would pour his life's energy into making money and accumulating money. He came home less. In time, even his phone calls dropped off.

The boy's still young, thought Li Fugui. He doesn't know the way the world works, or he wouldn't look down on these hills, his home. Damn little thieving brat! When the child finally grows up, lives to be my age, then he'll realize how great his home is.

Right around then is when Li Fugui started hearing the rumors, stuff about his son. It was Doghead who first said it. He ran into Li Fugui one day. Walked right up to him, and actually asked to borrow money. "How about a thousand?" he said. "Five thousand would work, too."

Li Fugui's blood went cold to hear it. "You idiot, is that your idea of a joke?" He waved the man off as he spoke. "My house is as tight on cash as yours. You know that! If you needed five or six I could spot you for a spell, but you ask for too much. I don't have it."

Doghead earned his name because for years he'd worn a cap made of dog's fur and didn't know better than to take it off during the summer. He would attack anyone who tried to make him take it off. Li Fugui could smell the stink coming up off of the man's head. Doghead stuck a finger up under the hat for a scratch. "Now, now, good uncle," he said with a laugh. "Don't be all cheap like that. Your family has got a money tree now, so don't try to tell me you're still poor. I know better!"

This left Li Fugui at a loss. He stepped up closer and confronted the man. "What are you saying, Doghead? What's all this, now? You say my family has a money tree? Where? How come I didn't know?"

Even as he spoke, he looked back at the house, the yard. Was there a money tree over there somewhere?

There were in fact several poplar trees in the yard, the wind blowing through them at just that moment, going *huaaaa … hua.*

"Uncle's playing dumb," said Doghead, breaking into a grin. "Well, don't give me the money then. But what gives, huh? What's the use trying to fool a fool?"

The grin on Doghead's face just got broader and broader. "Eh? Uncle looks like he's seen a ghost! Boy, you sure put a lot of weight on money, huh? Father and son are sure a pair, both got money on the brain. Mm-hmm!"

Now Li Fugui was actually frightened. Doghead was definitely not right in the head, but what he said just now rang clear and true. Li Fugui got the message loud and clear.

"What? Say that again." He seized Doghead by the collar. "What's that you're mumbling over there about, you? What're you talking about?"

Doghead let out a long-annoyed interjection. "Peh…. Hmph! So Uncle still won't admit the truth, huh? Everyone knows your Shemu trades his life for money. Are you trying to tell me you don't know?"

Li Fugui was even more puzzled. "My son trades his life for money? Where'd you hear that?"

He tightened his grip on Doghead, but he wriggled free and escaped with a wail.

To Li Fugui, it was as if someone dropped a stone on his chest. Nothing made sense in the world, and he wasn't sure he'd ever feel right again. Doghead couldn't make this up, of that much he was certain. He hadn't the brains for it. There was something to it. What happened to Shemu? What was going on?

Li Fugui realized that something bad had happened. His heart beat faster; he stumbled into a run and had not traveled more than a few steps before he bumped into one of his relatives in front of his house. The cousin didn't even wait for Li Fugui to speak—he grabbed him by the sleeve. "Look, here, Fugui, I need to talk to you, man-to-man. Are you going to stand for this? The shame of it? And he, your only son, too?"

Li Fugui still didn't know. He was in a fog, red-eyed, anxious. He roared back at his cousin, "Argh! What is it? What on earth happened? Tell me, tell me now!"

His cousin sighed to see him like this. "So, you really didn't know. Well, I was wrong to blame you, then. I'm sorry. But your Shemu. Idiot boy. It's a very stupid thing that he's done."

It turned out that Shemu hadn't been working construction all this time, like he said. Carrying bricks, puttying the walls. He tried, oh he had tried, but he couldn't take the rigor of the work, and the money wasn't all that good. The boy went dark, into a dark part of his soul and he fell in with a bad crowd. They told him he could make money off his blood. Fast money, no pain. So he began to draw his own blood and sell it. That's what he's been doing these past five, six years. It makes sense that he'd have saved a little money from it.

"You see how it is, Li Fugui? Sure, our people are poor—been that way for generations. But we take the bitter work, right? That's what real people do! If the money isn't easy, you just have to make it slowly. How could he soil his body like that?"

"You know damn well, Li Fugui, folks just back from Shenzhen were all talking about it. Yes, they said this child Shemu was a goner for sure, blood drawn to the bones, thin as kindling. Heavens! It hurt us to hear it, Li Fugui. We know he's your only child. We know you wanted him to keep this clan on going."

His cousin had grown old, with a large thatch of beard that flapped and rustled as he spoke and as he sighed, his watery eyes struggled to hold back the tears.

Li Fugui slumped to the floor. It took all his strength to stand up again. He stumbled like a drunkard out through his cousin's gate.

This was the last straw. He had to find his son. It would not matter if Shenzhen were at the other end of the Earth. He would find his son and haul him back. Clutching a scrap of paper with his son's telephone number on it, he packed up a large bag and hit the road.

Li Fugui could not read and he was long out of the village before he realized that in today's society, if you cannot read, you're no different than a blind man.

First he went to Shanxi. He had been there before when he was young. The hill people all gathered around the threshing markets. The strong, young men all got to know each other out in the wheat and barley fields. They'd earn a little money from their own sweat and blood to add to the family pot. He'd done it himself. As far as Li Fugui knew, the outside must look like the great plains of Shanxi, all spacious skies and amber waves of grain. But now that he was out there, Li Fugui found that things had changed. People lined up to find work in cities now, not wheat fields.

He spent a night in Xianyang Train Station, then boarded a train south.

During the whole trip he ate next to nothing. He had so much on his mind and his heart still felt weighted down by a stone. How could he eat? But he was thirsty, so parched it hurt, in fact. He saw other passengers carrying cups of hot water, so he followed the crowd back to where the water dispenser was. They were lined up, but he was too thirsty to wait. Hot water didn't slake his thirst in the slightest, so he filled an empty plastic water bottle with cold water. Five times, he filled it, downing each one in a single draft, leaving his stomach bloated, but at last he felt sated.

When they reached the terminus, the massive crowd filed out the train little by little, with their noise, confusion, and jumble of bags. Li Fugui found out from a young man with long hair that they'd reached Shenzhen. He grabbed his bag and followed the crowd out into the honking traffic outside. All kinds of dialects were being spoken, some were northern ones that he could understand, and others meant nothing to him. It was all a nattering tangled mass of humanity. Li Fugui lost his bearings, felt faint. There were as many people coming in as going out, and Li Fugui couldn't for the life of him get his sense of direction back. He tried to stick close to the others who had just gotten off the train, following along as they wound their way through.

Everyone seemed extremely harried as they went on their way. Li Fugui had eaten little in the days before and felt badly jostled on the train. Try as he might, he couldn't keep up with them. His soles began to shake. He forced himself to step forward and chase after them, but the last few northern dialect speakers were gone. Li Fugui was lost. In all directions there were more people and he couldn't see an exit. He tried just walking onward, but soon seemed to return to the spot he'd just left. He turned around in haste and walked the other direction, watching the long lines as he walked. Each traveler held a ticket, he realized. They were all taking other trains. He wandered back and forth scanning the crowd until he found the exit.

It was raining outside. Fine threads of it fell on his head and some of it stuck. The road was wet and cars sailed up and away in the rain. Li Fugui was dumbfounded. So this was Shenzhen. He thought of his son, then, and of what he must have thought and felt the first time he came to this place. What horrible things had his son had to have seen then, just fifteen carrying just seventy *yuan*.

Li Fugui faced this world with a completely blank expression. Dazed and confused. Shenzhen was not what he had imagined. It was not anything he could ever have imagined. People, cars, confusion. He did not know a single person and no one he saw was his Shemu. The tall buildings in the distance loomed dark and obscure. They made Li Fugui dizzy.

His need to see his son was much more intense. Only when he saw his son again could he settle his heart. The chaos of this world filled him with horror.

He found a phone booth, took the sheet of paper out of his pocket and dialed his son's number.

He heard a voice, but it wasn't his son. It was a woman's, cool and impersonal. *We're sorry, the number you have dialed is not in service.* "Eh?" Li Fugui felt clobbered by a beam, but he hardened his resolve and dialed again, and again the voice, *We're sorry....*

Li Fugui left the phone booth, the soles of his feet feeling weak and wobbly. He sat down by the side of the road, his hand pressed against his beating heart. Now what? He thought. He'd tried to anticipate things but never considered the phone number being out in service. He knew what "not in service" meant well enough. Either his son owed money on the bill, or he wasn't using this number at all. He just hoped it was the first one. Thieving brat, he thought. Please don't have changed your number.

The rain came down harder. Li Fugui stood under a large sign, standing back as far as he could go. His bag was soaked. Soon, his whole body was saturated. Then suddenly an umbrella appeared. A woman's face, her hands, gesturing and her lips moving but it was all blah blah blah. He couldn't understand. She switched to Mandarin then he understood. She was saying come stay in the hotel, only seventy for the night. Li Fugui shook his head and hardened his tongue to pronounce the Mandarin properly. "Too expensive."

"Fifty, then. Fifty's not expensive, you know." The woman shook her finger at him. Li Fugui's hunger had weakened him, his heart was heavy and the rain kept coming down. He didn't know what to do. The woman waved her finger again, told him it was almost nightfall, that the area wasn't safe, there were bad people around. Li Fugui felt there was no choice but to follow her.

"Fifty's not expensive. It's cheap, you know." The woman seemed to want to wag her tongue to show she wasn't happy with him. She drummed up more business as they walked, all travelers with luggage in tow or on their backs. Li Fugui felt a little better then. He wasn't alone. They all followed the woman, stepping through the puddles and rain, turning left, then right, again, and again, enough to leave them disoriented when they reached the "hotel."

They descended a wet and slimy staircase that seemed to take them into an underground warehouse. Inside was a dark room with several beds. The cement floor was wet and it stuck to their feet.

This place was supposed to be worth fifty *yuan*? Li Fugui muttered muffled complaints to himself. The others, though, took it all in stride. They all threw themselves at once onto the beds and went immediately to sleep. Li Fugui was tired, too. He took a few bites from his rations and got ready for bed. He hung the ration pack up on the bed. Since his big bag was soft, he put it under his head for a pillow.

Li Fugui was walking in the crowd when he saw Shemu. It had been two-and-a-half years and both were excited. The last time they were together they had been up on North Hill digging greens. "Look at the *kongque* greens!" cried the boy. "They're too big to dig!" Li Fugui turned to look. Wow, it was true, there was a *kuku* plant as big around as tree, and tall as his son. No wonder the boy couldn't dig that one. He hurried over to help. It was hard work.

Li Fugui woke up and saw that two of their party had gone. He turned and felt for the bag, but it was gone, too. The shock set his sweat going again. He felt carefully around his waist for the hard *yuan* coin in his underwear, and the money sewn up in his pockets. Both were still there. The bag was lost, but his ration pack wasn't. Li Fugui had to laugh, and only a little bitterly, shaking his head. Those two who ran off must have thought the bag had something expensive inside.

And he'd always been such a light sleeper, he thought. He'd had to stand the whole way on the train—he was just too tired.

Nothing in that bag, anyway, except for a sack full of dried bitter greens he'd brought for his son, thought Li Fugui, a little puzzled at the way he'd lost them.

He went out to the street. The city wasn't much altered by the passing of the night, but remained a wet, noisy mass of confusion. But there was no time for that now. He needed a phone booth, needed to call his son again.

Again he got no service, even after several tries.

Failure on the phone left Li feeling his only line to his son was cut.

He was out of ideas. He'd failed to find his Shemu.

Blank again, he walked the streets.

The scale of things here far outstretched his capacities. People, everywhere, buildings, everywhere. There was an order to it than he had first assumed but still a tangle of streets. Li Fugui tried to examine every face he brushed past, but none was Shemu's and all were strange and cold. He grew more uneasy as he went along until he was so worked up he had to stop. Better ask somebody. Some just shook their heads or gave him blank uncomprehending looks. Others waved him off impatiently.

No one said they'd seen Shemu. His Shemu was a water drop lost in the city. So many faces, but where was the one he sought?

Li Fugui stood in the road and imagined it was stream of water, not people, that roiled back and forth, turbid waves that pitched and fell, sweeping all away in the current, drowning them all, Li Fugui included.

Honking cars and their noxious fumes streamed through. Li Fugui forgot to be afraid, forgot where he was at all. He walked along the road in a daze. Would Shemu walk or ride in a car? How could he find him? What kind of place was this, anyway? What a mess! Was there any peace and quiet, like in North Hill where he was from? Back home, the most complex sound you ever heard was the wind blowing across different kinds of things, the whoosh of it piled into layers. But that was a pure sound compared to this. He'd never heard such cacophony.

Suddenly a strong hand caught hold of Li Fugui and hauled him over to the side of the road. A man's face, twisted with anger, screamed at him. About what, Li Fugui could not make out. He felt deaf from hearing too much noise.

His mind finally managed to piece things together. It was a cop cursing him, mad enough to bite the old man in half. "If you don't want to live, go off and die someplace alone. But stay out of the street! You do that again," the officer warned, "and you're dumpling filling, buddy."

Li Fugui turned back to look at the street with its cars rushing past and he broke out in a sweat again, scared half to death. He could have been crushed like an ant in that flood of cars.

His feet and heels went limp. Blankness filled his eyes. Not only had he lost his son, he'd lost himself, as well.

He could understand his son, he thought. And if his son really had sold his own blood and risked his life out here, well, he could almost understand that, too.

What kind of life must he have had here? Only fifteen, weak, skinny, and penniless. This place was so very strange. So the money had come from blood, every penny of it. And Li Fugui, frugal as he was, had spent some, too. He'd never thought the money could be traded for blood, traded by the drop. How many drops did it take to get to one *mao*? One *yuan*?

Blank, Li Fugui walked along the curb. He searched on, desperate for his son, desperate for a miracle.

Six days he kept this up, but when there was still no trace, he knew he had to stop. His rations were spoiled, sprouting green fur. If he was too hungry to walk, he steeled himself and forced a few bites down. Even then, it was almost gone. He asked around for Hui food, but there wasn't any. Water and moldy rations wouldn't sustain him long.

He knew he had to go. Any longer and he'd be lost forever, no place to rest his bones.

He went to the station and bought a ticket north.

The train departed in the middle of the night, filling his ears with a flat clacking sound against the tracks. Li Fugui curled up in a corner of a car, hungry and exhausted, aching all over, aching and tired at heart.

Outside the window, in the dark night, black shadows of trees brushed the sides of the train, then fell away without end. His son was lost, Li Fugui felt now. Not now, ten years before. Lost when he went to that city, lost, never to be found. The boy raised on bitter greens had lost himself in that southern city.

Li Fugui went back to his village dejected. For several days, he lay alone on his *kang*. The woman next door couldn't help feeling sorry for him and started carrying over hot meals. He couldn't eat and the meals went cold, but eventually he clambered out of bed and managed a few bites.

How did the world work these days, anyway? In his fifty years on this green earth, he'd never been depressed, never let his poverty keep him down. It was nothing to be afraid of. You grew your grain and ate your vegetables and that was that. Staying alive comes first. And nowadays? Well, people had enough to eat, at the very least. How come his son put so much weight on money? Why didn't he look after his life? Now there was all this money, money. He had no idea how much his son had, but what the boy sent back had all gone straight to the bank, and now there was a full twenty thousand in there. Li Fugui, who had tasted life's bitterness, never dreamed to have so much. But he was happy because the money meant his son could marry. Bride prices were up these days, way up, but this money meant that even securing a pretty girl would be no problem.

Now everything had changed. The money was all there, every last penny, but his son, the price he paid. Li Fugui had a pain in his heart, a pain that burned, that he couldn't express. Ah, what a world they had today.

It was another six months before Li Fugui got through to his son's phone. "Shemu…. Shemu … ughnnn…." Li Fugui spoke heavily into the phone. "My child, please come home."

"What's happened? Are you sick?" Shemu grew concerned from what he heard in his father's voice.

Li Fugui straightened up, spoke again into the phone. "Yes, I am sick. It's very serious. If you don't come home, I'm afraid I'll never see you again."

The line went silent. Li Fugui heard only the rough buzz of the current passing his ears. A long moment later, there was his son's voice again, softly. "Wait. Just wait okay? Soon. I'll have the money soon. Once I have the money, I'll come back."

That was it. The line went dead. The phone was off when Li Fugui called back.

Days in North Hill were always slow and quiet. After work, taking a break under a tree, Li Fugui let his thoughts get ahead of him again. He saw the scene at Shenzhen, suddenly, the noise, the gaudy lights. It was like a dream he half remembered, as if through a haze. Skyscrapers, enormous, oppressive, stacked one behind the other and blotting out the sun. The cars, so many cars, going here, going there, like an anthill. The crowds pressed in and left him dazed, faint. What kind of world was that? What kind of life? He had lived his whole life in the mountains. Wandering those streets just once, he practically lost himself. And Shemu, ah, his son, Shemu, Shemu only fifteen, Shemu with only seventy *yuan* to his name. What had he gone through? Did anyone know?

His child of North Hill was lost in the city.

Li Fugui changed, became taciturn, remote. He spent entire days out on his plots. Work done, basket on his back, he climbed the hill to dig his greens. Outside the house all the spare space was covered in drying greens.

It was another nineteen months before Shemu finally came home. There was a drizzle that day. He hired a car and had himself driven up to the village. Only later did people learn he wasn't showing off, he just really didn't have the strength to walk on the road. Li Fugui came up to his front door, unsteady on his feet. Someone was helping his son get out of the car. Li Fugui did not go over to help. He looked. The boy was thin as a bamboo pole. Li Fugui's face was blank as ever it could be.

Shemu said it was the end, and he just wanted to be with his father now.

His condition had deteriorated quickly. Li Fugui watch him die before his eyes, bit by bit.

The villagers all came to see Shemu, and everyone brought some food. It was all homemade, all good country food. Pea starch puddings and flaky pan-fried bread. Scrambled eggs and chive preserves. Shemu tasted them all, but he could only eat a little, and even then he could hardly keep it down. But he tried. He broke into sobs, a mewling, whining cry. "If only I could have eaten this well before," he said. "When I was small. Then I wouldn't have put so much emphasis on money. I put my life on the line because I was scared of being poor. I just wanted something better."

Li Fugui said nothing but watched his son in silence. After a long while, he took the dried greens out, picked some of the cleanest and best-looking ones, blanched them, and tossed together a small cold plate. And Shemu did eat, tears blotting his face with big drops. "Take me up the hill," he said. "Take me to dig *kongque* greens. It's been so, so long."

Li Fugui carried his son on his back up the hill.

Shemu was twenty-nine, but light as kindling sticks and carrying him hardly slowed down Li Fugui at all. Before they knew it, they were atop the hill again. It was March and the greens hadn't sprouted. A few frozen plants swayed in the wind. The boy scanned all around, then grabbed a bit of the muddy earth. Closing his eyes, he brought it to his nose and breathed in. He looked happy, then, happy to sleep once more on the hill, where the wind blew clean, and his family and townsmen around. It was good.

He told his father where the money was, told him to find the bankbook on the *kang* under the mat.

Li Fugui said nothing but listened in silence.

At sunset, father brought his son down from the hill.

Shemu took his last breaths on the road down.

They gave him a simple funeral.

Everyone thought Li Fugui would pass on quickly himself, now that his son was gone. But that wasn't what happened.

He lived on—thrived, even. He planted his land, took on a whole herd of sheep. Like everyone else, he planted in the spring, harvested in the fall, and in the winter he sat by the window and watched the snow. Every May, when it all began to grow again, he would take his basket and go up the hill for his greens.

That year, the village was going to build a new school. And the people were so happy, because now the children wouldn't have to travel more than ten kilometers to get there. A little less bitterness for everyone. The day construction started, everyone showed up to watch, including Li Fugui. He put down his basket, wiped the dirt off his hands, and fished a pale red bankbook out his pocket. He handed it over to the head man. Accepting the bankbook, the head man announced that the old man, Li Fugui, wanted to make a donation, that he was giving one-hundred-and-fifty thousand *yuan* and that he just hoped the school would be a little nicer for it, and that it could open a little sooner.

The people in the village were shocked. They had to see Li Fugui in a new light now. And to think that's how he dressed, in homespun clothes, so plain and so old. And already he's taken up his basket and headed up the hill again, spade in hand.

If they craned their heads, they could have seen all the way up North Hill, to its summit, to the belts of bitter greens along its slopes, to the way the greens met the wind, with stiff, strong waves of their tiny leaves.

A breeze blew and the green mountains responded with the cheerful sound of small hands clapping.

10

Wild Horses

Maidina Seyiti

On the wide-open prairie, I gallop, white mane waving in the
   wind, cool and graceful gazing at the far distant mountain
   peak, and even farther to the horizon.
What beautiful colors, what a beautiful landscape in a scroll.
Green! Green under my hooves, green in front of my eyes, green
   behind me.
Blue! Blue in the sky, blue between the mountains, blue in the
   water.
White! White on my body, white in the sky, white in my heart.
Knowing no fatigue, knowing no rules, not lacking faith, galloping forward courageously.
The master of this piece of pure and beautiful land is my only
   master, giving me free reign to gallop on the Pure Land.
Yes, I am a wild horse, trusting the new landscape master shows
   me, believing I will continue on—galloping in the next, un-
   restrained, unreined.
No matter if my hooves wear down and crack, they will still feel
   the solid strength of the earth.
No matter if the extreme heat beats down on my head, it will feel
   the brilliance of the sun.
No matter if the river water floods the road ahead, my body will
   still feel strong and alive with the life force that comes from
   the water.
Yes, when I gallop in the land I only need to remember that my
   master is in my heart.
I am a free wild horse.

Translated by Jennifer Young

11

Snow Lotus

Mao Mei

That day, we climbed Glacier No. 1 of the Tianshan Mountains.

As we neared its peak, the cluster of clouds that had tailed us our entire way up dispersed like a flock of birds startled by a whistle, revealing the glacier and letting the sun shine freely upon its surface. Like countless mirrors, the surrounding crystalline ice reflected my image ten thousand times in all directions, and all at once I was everywhere. In that moment I stood in the center of the world; the majesty of it thrilled me, heart and soul.

With my infinite reflection enveloping me, I thought of the beautiful young man from Greek mythology, Narcissus. It was said that he fell in love with his own reflection in the river and lingered by the water's edge until he ultimately fell in and drowned. At the place where he fell, all that the nymphs could find was a single flower: pure, white, and fragrant. They named this flower of death, narcissus.

This is a cautionary tale: avoid a similar fate on these snowy plains; avoid vanity; avoid my omnipresent image; and avoid these countless glassy surfaces. Even so, I clung to the belief that Narcissus fell in love not with himself but with the image in the river. Had not that image been distorted by the ripples in the water and altered by his own gaze? What was it exactly? Was it a face vanishing into nothing?

Every flower has its own true self. Once it falls into the river of myth and legend it can never be salvaged.

The snow lotus blooms year after year on the glacier, living and dying on its own. Botanists classify the snow lotus as a member of the daisy family, but for me it surely belongs to the realm of fairies and nymphs. I see snow lotuses as snow fairies; thinking, if there are water fairies, then naturally there should be dew fairies, frost fairies, ice fairies, snow fairies....

Translated by Wendy Mina Wang

There is a Kazakh legend about how the snow lotus came to grow on glaciers. It tells of a fairy who guarded the snow lotus atop the peaks. She was so moved by a love story told to her by a Kazakh boy who had come to pick the flower that she allowed him to take one. In doing so, however, she broke a heavenly decree and was locked away, condemned to spend eternity on that icy summit. The fairy's endless tears turned into the vast, sweeping glaciers.

The snow lotus grows on cliffs and in between cracks below the snow line. This environment is difficult for most plants to grow in. Only a few species of frost-resistant lichen are the snow lotus's companions. The climate in this region is volatile and unpredictable; sporadic spells of hot weather are followed by freezing conditions. Alternate days of snow and rain beset the land, wreaking havoc on all. The snow lotus must be a patient child, constantly adapting to its parents' erratic moods.

All that is noble thrives away from the public eye. Beneath the ice and snow, the delicate sprout of the snow lotus waits, developing in secret. The sprout must endure frigid temperatures, often dropping well below -20°C. Under these conditions, the probability of germination is naturally low, making propagation very difficult and new growth even slower. A young plant typically lives five years under the snow before it first blossoms. The life-cycle of the lotus blossom validates the saying: good things come to those who wait.

After a long dormant phase, the snow lotus must sprout, grow, bloom, and bear fruit all within a brief growing season. This mode of existence is a biological rarity.

The frigid habitat guarantees that the snow lotus is rare and precious, and it is also prized as a potent medicinal plant. During the Qing Dynasty, the medical scholar Zhao Xuemin documented this in his work *An Addendum to the Compendium of Materia Medica*, "on the frozen land where the snow mounts, lingering all through summer and spring, a plant grows amid the snow; single-stemmed like the lotus, it stands with lovely grace." He added, "Tianshan sits on that land where the snow accumulates summer and winter; in the snow, a lotus grows, the best specimens can be found on Tianshan's summit." He also mentioned that those growing on Bogda Peak near the Tianchi Lake were of high quality.[1] In the Kazakh legend, the snow lotus was sprinkled by the fairies when the Queen Mother came to bathe in the Tianchi Lake. It is said that drinking the dew drops on its leaves prolongs life and

---

1. The *Bencao Gangmu*, known as the *Compendium of Materia Medica*, is the most influential encyclopedia of natural medicine in East Asia. It was written by the father of traditional Chinese medicine, Li Shizhen (1518–1593) of the Ming Dynasty (1368–1644). The *Bencao Gangmu Shiyi*, or *An Addendum to the Compendium of Materia Medica*, compiled by Zhao Xuemin (c. 1719–1805) during the Qing Dynasty (1644–1912), is a supplementary work to the original masterpiece. The Heavenly Lake of Tianshan in Xinjiang, China is an ancient alpine lake known for its spiritual and mythical significance.

improves health. If a shepherd happens across this flower, it is always taken to be a good omen.

The snow lotus has black roots, green leaves, white buds, and red petals; it stands tall on the icy summit, much like "The White Lady" with her red helmet, green-and-white armor, and black combat boots.

The snow lotus has the power to heal wounds and alleviate pain. Legend has it, a giant snake that happened to be injured repeatedly circled the small plant, vigorously rubbing its wound against the stalk and leaves. With each pass, the snake's wound closed up and in no time it healed seamlessly.

For me, the snow lotus truly is nature's wild, untamed spirit, a gift from the heavens.

Most people do not know much about the snow lotus, and for the few who do it is hard to find. In *Notes of the Thatched Abode of Close Observations* by Ji Xiaolan, the most miraculous trait of the snow lotus was recorded as such, "beyond the Great Wall, the snow lotus grows, atop the lofty mountain, deep within the snow.... those who find this flower, may possess it if they approach it silently. If one happens to point and shout to alert others, it will withdraw, leaving no trace behind. ... The natives say this is because the Mountain God cherishes the snow lotus; indeed, it would appear to be so!"[2] The moment you point your finger at it, it disappears into the snow. So, never point at a snow lotus. How can the body touch the flower which only the spirit may touch?[3]

Exhaling in its own faint fragrance, its white blossom pointing skyward, the snow lotus sits undisturbed. Apollo's Garden is said to possess every flower known to mankind, but it does not contain the snow lotus.

When I see dried snow lotuses in pharmacies, so delicate and sheer like a cicada's wing, I can't help but sympathize with it, thinking, why don't you "vanish into the snow without a trace," just as Ji Xiaolan had said, instead of ending up in my hands like a dried cicada shell. This image of a withered husk of a flower could have been taken directly from Tagore's poem, "I try to grasp the beauty, but it eludes me, leaving only the body in my hands."[4]

Because of my deep love for the snow lotus, I have an inexplicable sense of belonging to the place of its origin: the northern slope of Tianshan Mountains. Only when you are on the same latitude, on the same frequency, and in the same climate as a given thing, can you possibly hear the same thing it

---

2. *Yuewei Caotang Biji*, known as the *Notes of the Thatched Abode of Close Observations*, is a nonfiction novel compiled of supernatural tales and stories about the weird and uncanny. It was written by Ji Xiaolan (1724–1805), one of the most prominent scholars of the Qing Dynasty.

3. The author references a verse from the poem "Spirit Touch" of *The Gardener* by Rabindranath Tagore.

4. Another verse from "Spirit Touch." Rabindranath Tagore, *Tagore: The Mystic Poets.* Sky-Light Paths Publishing, 2004.

hears, see the same thing it sees, take the same form it takes, have the same thought it has, and adopt the same course of action it adopts.

Over a thousand years ago, Cen Shen, a frontier poet of the Tang Dynasty who lived on the northern side of the Tianshan Mountains for six years, captured the soul of the snow lotus in his "Songs to the Utpala."

> You require no company,
> And it would be a shame
> To be with flowers of equal flame.
> You bloom in pride and solitude.
> You receive no admirers, why?
> Deep in the distant mountain,
> Enduring the bitter bite of frost
> You are lost.
> Secretly, I feel sorry for you.
> Though I can see the Yangguan Pass,
> I cannot bring you to the king,
> Nor make of you an offering.

The Utpala flower that Cen Shen spoke of is now known as the snow lotus. Because of its clear, pure fragrance, the snow lotus is often likened to the Buddha. The Buddha sees the snow lotus as a celestial being: compelled to live in this world yet unwilling to be tainted by its impurities, it blooms in snow.

I silently praise the snow lotus for it does not know of its own beauty, and for that it is even more beautiful. How come it blooms so indifferently in a place without any rulers, laws or people? I can't help but speculate: if the snow really is as cold and distant as it looks, without any inner beauty, strength and fervor, how can the snow produce such an ethereal flower?

People like to visit Xinjiang at harvest time with the scent of fruits and melons in the air. But I trust that the best time to go is on a brisk, snowy day. In winter, climbing up Tianshan, it is not the frigid cold that brings you chills, but the majestic tranquility that makes you gasp in awe. In that untainted frozen world, you don't want to spoil it with your own footprint.

The day I climbed Glacier No.1 was exactly like this. The snow that day was great: shimmering blue and not at all sticky. I climbed with powdery, dry snow beneath my feet. Unsure of how long I had climbed, I was suddenly stopped in my tracks by the simple smile of a snow lotus up ahead.

Just as someone happening upon a treasure would stay quiet, I too crouched down and kept silent. The snowy mountains surrounded me with silence.

The snow lotus appeared full to bursting. It was as if it wore layers and layers of silk garments and each layer was wrapped in pure light. Its inner glow bathed me. I sat down next to it. With the snow lotus as company, for an hour I was the Snow Queen.

A flower vendor once told me that all white flowers are very fragrant; the more colorful and radiant the flower, the less aromatic it is. People are the same in that, the simpler and more unadorned a person is, the more inner strength and character that person has. All who are decent and moral are worthy of the snow lotus.

Before coming across the snow lotus, I never knew that life could blossom in between broken rocks and on cliff tops. The snow lotus is the epitome of beauty in bloom; the very evidence of its existence supports those in hardship, giving them the strength to pull through and live meaningful lives.

Year in and year out, when I am in Xinjiang, the snow lotus comes to me with music and fragrance. If one day I were to receive a flower crown, it would most definitely be made of snow lotuses and it is the only flower for me. No matter who you are, I would never present you with snow lotuses; it must stay where it grows, as a flower in the wild.

Up to the day I said goodbye to the glacier, to Tianshan, and to Xinjiang, the snow lotus was the face I could not forget.

Zhu Guangqian asked, "Why did Tao Yuanming love the chrysanthemum? Because he saw in its wispy, frost-resistant stems, the unrelenting character of the outcast official; why did Lin Hejing love the plum blossom? Because he saw in the fine shadows of its branches and smelled in its gentle fragrance, the profound attainments of the recluse."[5]

I think I love the snow lotus so deeply because, paying no regard to the "priceless peony, prized lotus" of the outside world, it lives as a hermit in seclusion—humble, yet high above everything.

---

5. Zhu Guangqian (1897–1986), a noted expert on philosophical aesthetics, published several influential works on literature and art from a psychological perspective. Tao Yuanming (c. 365–427) was a Chinese poet from the Jin Dynasty. He served as a civil servant for over a decade before he resigned out of disgust for the corruption and disorder in the royal court. He spent the rest of his life in recluse, writing poetry about life in the countryside. It is well-known that he admired chrysanthemums and wrote many verses praising the tenacious flower. Lin Hejing (c. 967–1028), a renowned recluse from the North Song Dynasty (960–1127), was a poet, calligrapher and painter. He spent most of his early adult life travelling before finally settling down in seclusion by the foot of Gu Mountain in Hangzhou. Having never been married, he is famous throughout Chinese history for his ardent love of plum trees and cranes, especially for treating them as his wife and children.

12

Qinghai

NAYE

We have left
And yet the sky is still there, blue

And yet the eagles are still there, soaring

And yet the rapeseed flowers are still there, blooming—
Swaying golden in the Tibetan field
Honeyed in the halo of Buddha

And yet the memory is lying there
When will the moon be clear and bright?
Me and you, oxygen-deprived, sleeping bags side-by-side

You hand me a Salem: history cannot be assumed
I hand you a cigar: time does not rewind

We are long gone
And yet the meaning of life remains
If life has any meaning at all

Translated by Seth Wiener

13

A Houseful of Birds[1]

NURYLA QIZIQAN

It was around 1967. Once when I came back home, our house was full of birds: two eagles, one falcon, one peregrine, a white-headed vulture, and two crows.[2] The eagles and the falcon were in the main room; the others were in the antechamber.

---

1. "A Houseful of Birds" and the next story "We Have Surpassed the Bears" are from Nuryla Qiziqan's *Hunter's Stories*. Nuryla Qiziqan is an ethnic Kazakh writer, poet, and folklorist from Xinjiang Uyghur Autonomous Region in Northwest China. She was born in a small village in Altay in 1951. In 2009, she published *Hunter's Stories* to commemorate her hunter father Qiziqan Ahman. Since then, she has been active in archiving pastoral and hunting knowledge, folktales, experiences of hunters and herders in Northern Xinjiang. During the collectivization era (1953–1980), state power infiltrated Kazakh social space and appeared as institutions like "pastoral production cooperation commune," marginalizing local chieftains and clan leaders, disrupting indigenous mobile pastoral social administration on the steppe. The legacy of collectivization still lingers in the Kazakh regions today, reflected in the terms of socialist power hierarchy such as pastoral office, the First Brigade, the Second Brigade, etc.
2. This story is the author's reminiscences of her younger self returning home to the winter encampment after working at the Women's Federation in Altay city for a year. She remembered how she was young at that time and had begun to favor urban living over rural life, which seemed unsanitary to her. Nuryla's father was an experienced and skillful hunter who worked for the commune along with his hunting hounds, eagles, and falcons. During the collectivization period (1953–1980), pastoral work was organized by the production unit cadres. Just as in this story, the Kazakhs herded their livestock on the pastures and lived in yurts in the summer, then moved to settlements along the foot of the mountains to get through the winter. Note the differences between collectivized farming in inner China and mobile pastoralism in Xinjiang. Collectivization in the pastoral regions of China was crucial in changing Kazakh pastoral way of life and knowing as well as altering their social fabric and values. As the story shows, since the People's Republic of China was founded in 1949, urbanization and sedentarization of the Kazakh herders through state-organized employment and education gradually began. Many Kazakhs like Nuryla became cadres, workers, clerks, and moved into the cities as demobilized soldiers, recruited as state employees, or they converted to agricultural work after leaving their pastoral villages. Cooperatives or commune production teams replaced the original pastoral society organizations. The herders became organized in the vicinity of the reclaimed farmlands and brigades and then formed larger settlements.

Translated from the Kazakh by Guldana Salimjan

At that time, the average standard of living for herders was low. Everyone lived in mud-brick houses with only one or two rooms. Sometimes dirt would flake off from the walls and roofs of the houses. Private ownership of the house was not allowed. A cadre of the production team decided which house we would live in any given year. People considered it unnecessary to fix up houses of others, as they would just move again, anyways. In the winter, only the main room would heat up, so a family had to cook and sleep in that same room. Sometimes a skinny little calf or a lamb that was too weak to be left outside was also kept there. Half of the room was occupied by people and the other half was practically a livestock corral. If city people nowadays saw it, they would certainly think it "primitive."

Our house was also like that, but the main room was bigger, about thirty square meters. Two or three pillars separated the bed from the door, and the bed base was piled up with two-*suyem* high clay bricks.[3] We layered it with dry reed and straw on top, then covered it with black-and-white patterned felt rugs to make it soft and comfortable. As the saying goes, "home sweet home."[4] Although we didn't have any shiny wonderful things, our home was clean and tidy.

Maybe because I had become used to the sedentary urban life, when I entered my old home that time, I was a bit startled by the scene, and I immediately smelled the stench of the animals. Two calves were tied next to the doorframe of the main room; a peregrine and a falcon rested on the pedestal in the corner with their hoods on. In the two corners near the windows were two giant eagles. It seemed that they took up most of the space in the room. The antechamber was even fuller. A white-headed vulture as big as an eagle was tied by its talons next to the corner closet. In another corner, two crows were also carefully tied to a stake on the ground so they wouldn't get tangled up. In order to survive, the crows had already started getting used to humans and had been pecking at the feed in front of them. In the middle of the room, some fox and wolf meat for feeding the birds hung on the pillar. Next to the door of the antechamber lay two hunting hounds named Tuyghin and Ushar. They used to be as fast as stallions, until they got badly injured felling a wild beast. At the moment, however, they were "retired." My father had been taking care of them, and he wouldn't send them off on difficult tasks. The dogs recognized me immediately, came up next to me, and started whining. No longer the home that I had been missing day and night, it had become a nest of birds and animals in my eyes.

"What are these? What is going on with you all?" I asked my mother, wrinkling my nose.

---

3. *Suyem* is a type of measurement used by Kazakh people, one *suyem* is the distance between the tip of the thumb to the tip of the index finger stretched out.
4. This Kazakh original is "'*öz uyim, öleng tösek.*"

My father was sitting on a stool in the corner next to the window, cutting fox meat into a wooden basin to make bird feed. It seemed that he had been busy for days in order to feed the birds well. He picked up the tone in my question, and answered sternly, "what else could this be? My child, are you new to this now? These are Altay eagles called *aq-yiq*.[5] This is the ferocious falcon, that is a peregrine over there."

My mother and my young brothers couldn't wait to tell me all the stories about how they captured these birds at the same time. My mother contributed with her net-knitting skills. My brothers caught crows. I was a little impressed.

"How did you catch all these?" I asked.

It turned out that originally only the falcon and peregrine were the targets, and the other birds all fell into the traps by accident. They had set up the net again and again, and finally caught an eagle. My brother was going to give it to one of his friends. The other eagle at home had been there for a while already.

"What are you going to do with them?" I said.

My father answered, "The vulture is wounded in its shoulder and cannot fly now. I will set it free when it gets better. I was commissioned by some people to capture the peregrine and the falcon. Dungan people love falcons, they train them to catch rabbits. Hunting with peregrines is a great pleasure too, when it's trained, we can go hunt ducks and geese with it."

---

5. There are more than forty different names for eagles in Kazakh language, as Kazakhs name eagles according to their physical features and their places of origins in Altay regions. For example, the Altay mountain eagles are called *aq-yiq*, which literally means "white shoulders" because this type of eagles have white feathers on their wings; Ural mountain eagles are called *zor-taban*, which means "huge talons"; Khovd regional eagles are called *qarager*, referring to its unique dark brown feathers; Ili regional eagles are called *quwzghinmurti*, as they have whiskers besides their beaks; and Sawur mountain eagles are called *sabalaq sarisi* for their longer leg feathers.

14

We Have Surpassed the Bears[1]

Nuryla Qiziqan

The brown bears in Altay have gained their freedom. It has been fifteen years since they heard a gunshot or got their paws stuck in traps. If the bears have any consciousness, they are probably happy with our government.[2] They should have followed our unspoken rule and not messed with humans. However, the bears didn't change their ferocious nature when we stopped hunting. Now the bears have increased in numbers and started attacking livestock in the corrals everywhere. And not only livestock, once we were shocked to hear that a bear even ate a passerby. It seems that the relationship between human and nature has always been unstable and arbitrary and will not be peacefully balanced for a long time to come.

A few years ago, a herder's livestock corral in Kishtay Valley was ransacked by brown bears.[3] Three or four households usually herd together as one unit of a pastoral village. At midnight, the shepherd dogs started barking, and the sheep panicked, pushing each other and cowering in their pen.

---

1. From Nuryla Qiziqan's *Hunter's Stories*.

2. During the collectivization period from 1953 until 1980 in China's Xinjiang, the socialist development ideology saw wolves and bears as pests that would harm pastoral production and should be eradicated. Hunting was to serve its purpose for protecting the commune's livestock and increasing sideline production. The 1956–1967 National Programmes for Agricultural Development Article XVII writes: "starting from 1956, within 12 years, substantially eliminate the most serious hazards animals that can damage production in all possible places." Hunters were politically mobilized in teams to eradicate predator animals to protect the livestock. Many times, they had to bend their indigenous ecological values to fulfill the hunting quota assigned by the commune cadres, otherwise, they would be denounced as "counterrevolutionary" and persecuted. In 1988, China passed and implemented the Wildlife Protection Law. The hunting and killing of wildlife were prohibited. In this story, bear population rose and many pastoral villages and livestock were threatened.

3. The author confirmed that this incident happened in 2005 (personal communication, July 2017).

Translated from the Kazakh by Guldana Salimjan

Knowing that wild beasts had come, the herders jumped out of their beds and looked outside: four bears—as big as oxen—were standing in the middle of the flock raising hell. In the hazy, dark summer night, people looked on as the bears clumsily grabbed the sheep around them and threw them out of the corral. A dozen people in the neighborhood quickly gathered and lit fires nearby. They banged on their iron pots and pans, shouting at the top of the lungs trying to scare off the bears. However, the bears weren't bothered at all and kept freely tearing through the flock. In the darkness, the poor sheep jolted and crashed from one side to another, not knowing where to escape.

In that moment, it was impossible to get help from outside. Nobody had a club or any kind of weapon so nothing could be done. The bears threw around the sheep as they wished for a while, until finally one of them grabbed a fat bleating goat under its arm and retraced its course back into the mountains. The other three followed in no hurry.

The bears didn't care at all about the fire, the banging metal sounds, or shouting. It seemed that they only left satisfied after finishing what they needed to do. The goat that was under the bear's armpit bleated "baa baa" as if it was crying "Help me! Help me!" The sound could be heard until the bears were far away, and it sent shivers down everyone's spines. Eight sheep that were thrown out by the bears died on the spot, and many were injured to various degrees. An elderly woman in the neighborhood kept knocking her brand-new pot with fire-tongs until dawn and cracked it. She was infuriated and complained, "These God-damned bears, look what they have done to my pot!"

The next day, those four brown bears again attacked another corral. It was outrageous how rampant and out of control they had become! The herders who had seen the bear attacks were terrified and couldn't sleep for nights, so they quickly reported the increasingly urgent bear situation to higher authorities.

The higher authorities concluded that they would allow the hunting of one bear. They organized a team of eight people from the relevant sectors. This news was immediately spread all over the summer pasture. The cadres from the local pastoral office cheerfully welcomed the bear hunting team. On the day the team arrived, the office cadres sacrificed a sheep for the banquet, and gave the team the best blessings reciting "*Allahu akbar.*" The next day, the First Brigade cadres also performed a blessing ritual and sacrificed a sheep for the team. In the end, they arranged the Second Brigade cadres to treat the hunting team on the following day. Gradually, the eight-person team became larger and doubled two or three times. With the help of a local guide, the hunting team searched all the possible whereabouts of the bears in the mountains, until their legs were sore and their steps were shaky. Still, there were no traces of the bears. The team was so exhausted that they could barely walk to their next banquet.

At first, when they heard, "the bears have increased in numbers in the summer pasture," they believed that as soon as they got there, they would find the bears. They boasted, "what if we encounter two bears at one time? We can definitely get one down!" Then the days were passing by and it turned out those ideas were merely fantasies. In frustration, they finally realized that bear hunting was not as easy as they thought.

The team was given five days to do the job. It took two days to get there. The third day also passed by quickly; it was spent wandering in the mountains, searching in vain. The scheduled date of mission completion finally came. To stay would be to defy orders. The hunting team had to prepare to return empty-handed.

The best season of pastoral life—summer—had arrived. This is a time when livestock put on their fat and the herders can take a break and entertain themselves, a time when robust young men gather together once they hear cheers for games. For people in the rural pastoral area, the hunting team from the city were the most distinguished guests, and their presence added more liveliness to the already lively summer pasture. Both sides found it hard to say farewell to their new friends. A herder found the excuse that one of the team members had in-law kinship relations with him in order to cajole them to stay as guests a bit longer. The hospitality and generosity of the Kazakhs touched the team members and they couldn't say no. The host earnestly prepared traditional Kazakh cuisine: nectar-like mutton in fragrant broth, and fermented horse milk poured straight from the churn which looked as if it were also bowing down to serve the guests. In between, alcohol in small shot glasses was passed around, playing its own significant role as well. Flattering compliments and delicious cuisine filled up the guests to the brim, and the churn that was full of fermented horse milk was slowly flattened.

When most people were tipsy, the team leader took this chance to express his sincere gratitude to the herders. In the end, he asked, "how many sheep have the bears eaten around here recently?"

A herder answered, "four sheep were eaten by the bears."

The team leader's smile froze on his face, "then we have surpassed the bears. Since we got here, we have eaten five sheep. Dear brothers, please don't make us stay longer. You see what we have done. We came here as humans, let's stop eating like the bears."

15

Daliangpo: Egg, Water and Milk

Patigül

1

> "Like an egg Daliangpo sits
> On the points of an ellipse
> With a crater in its midst."

These are a few lines from a children's ditty in Daliangpo, an egg-shaped village. My family lives on the highest crest at the southeast corner of the village, the tip of the egg. Behind my home extends the Kazakhs' sheepfolds. In front of it, across an irrigation ditch, is Hui-town.

A large river flows between my house and Little Stone's. When the snow melts, I run back and forth along the old, high dike, but it is difficult to find a place where I can cross the river. But even if the river is at a normal height, the dike is still long and high. One can smoke a pipe in the time it takes to travel down its length and back again.

Where the river is shallow and marshy, the water just covers the feet. Where it runs deep, its bottom cannot be reached. The water gurgles up from a spring in the river's depths. It is black and brackish; even donkeys turn their noses up at it.

Beside the dike, just opposite our yard, the family sunflower field stands silently guarded by six poplar trees. The sheepfold sits behind the house. By a short wickerwork gate, sheep dung piles up high, as if waiting for someone to shovel it up and transport it to the fields.

Beyond the sheepfold, a parcel of lowland sits like a large crater, but serves as a communal vegetable garden. Low-rise houses spring up around the crater like mushrooms. My house is on a high ridge at the southeast edge of the village. No matter which direction I go, it is always downhill. The

Translated by Dong Isbister, Xiumei Pu, Stephen D. Rachman

ground tilts outward and down. Water dumped from the doorway will flow away and not one drop of water will gather at the base of the house's foundation. Guests must crane their necks just to get a glimpse of the house, and even flies and mosquitoes aviate on a slant.

The weeds on either side of the dike are lush. Reeds, plantagos, tamarisks, sophora root, achnatherum splendens, camel quine, and dandelions all writhe in a wavy dense carpet. The tallest reeds are taller than a house and their stalks can be used for building houses.

In summer, the bank opposite the dike is full of sunbathing kraits, coiled and braided like hand-pulled noodles. Some are about as thick as the reins on a horse; others are as thin as licorice whips. At noon, nobody ventures there to disturb these spirits, except for us kids who steal watermelons while the grownups doze.

Seeing us creeping along, the snakes are not alarmed, but lethargically ignore us, dreaming their snake dreams in the sun. Occasionally, a few snakes not yet fully asleep, eyes half-closed, shift their bodies in the warm sand to make a path three-fingers wide for our bare feet, and then slither away to coil and sleep.

In winter, the banks of the river are covered in a blanket of white. On moonlit nights, you can hear the hungry cries of foxes and wolves. The rabbits have all been chased away by hunting dogs.

2

In Daliangpo—"Eggville"—the new neighborhood occupies the easternmost edge just beyond the old Uyghur neighborhood; this would be where an egg is widest. Over a dozen Han families from Henan and Gansu provinces live in the new neighborhood. The whistle from a small school there blows and its modern sound in this rural community catches everyone's attention.

Daliangpo's houses are all built peripherally, where the egg whites would be. Private plots and small gardens sit centrally in the yolk. Between the houses and the garden plots, there are extensive tracts of farmland radiating outward, making for a large egg white. The five hundred-odd people who live in this egg-shaped world, enjoy this arrangement, getting by through the strength of their hard-working hands.

On a daily basis, the people of the village determine its future growth: where to grow trees to block the wind and sand; where to plant beans and melons; where to sow alfalfa and cotton. But no matter what they grow or choose to do, the people of Daliangpo always manage to maintain—intentionally or unintentionally—the village's egg-shaped appearance. People marry, have children and grow old; these egg-people lead their busy, eggy, self-contained lives.

Daliangpo is a strange egg; it seems to have an elasticity. Whatever people do, they are surrounded by its flexible, invisible, eggshell-like boundary. Even if they die, they are all buried beneath Daliangpo's yellow earth. Very rarely has anybody ever left the village.

The same people seem to have lived in this village forever. Occasionally, bachelors come from the outside world and they are quickly Daliangpo-ified into its egg white. They are allotted a parcel of land for growing vegetables in the yolk, and can also use a few acres of uncultivated land not far from the village; then they marry, have children, and pass their days, living off of Daliangpo's water and land.

The Han neighborhood has a new area and an old area. The new part has the small school and the Xu, Guo, and Wang families from Gansu and Henan provinces. The old part has been left behind in Daliangpo. Fifty Han families or so from Jiangsu, Sichuan, and Shandong provinces live there.

Looking from my family's yard to the northwest, one sees the few Hui families that live closest to the crater, mostly with the surname of Ma. There is only one Hui family named Wang. When I was little, I often got ill, and my mother invited an old couple named Wang to be my godparents.

When I got a little older, the school moved from the new neighborhood to an area behind the Hui neighborhood. On my way to and from school, I would pass the vegetable garden in front of my godparents' gate. My godfather would size me up, and my godmother would feel my head, hold my hands, and speak to me with a Qinghai accent that I found difficult to understand. I would just nod or shake my head, not really knowing what they were saying. They would seem satisfied with my response and then deftly pull a radish or pluck a tomato from their garden, wash it in the nearby irrigation ditch, and give it to me to quench my thirst.

Everyone calls the place where my godmother's family lives Hui-town. They call it Hui-town, but it's really just a place where the Hui are in the majority. In reality, Hui-town has diverse ethnic groups. That crater where the Ma families live is on a gentle slope. The slope is bisected by an oxcart path. At the bottom of the slope live a few Uyghur families from southern Xinjiang Uyghur Autonomous Region and there is even a Kazakh family squeezed in at the top of the slope.

Heading away from the crater, up the gentle slope and then down the other side, one climbs up again to the Uyghur neighborhood. Actually, a few Kazakh families live in the Uyghur neighborhood, and there are two Hui families surnamed Su. The Uyghur people do not live as close to each other as in other parts of Daliangpo. They like to set aside space in their yards for grape trellises and melon sheds. This neighborhood stretches out in a long thin shape because of all of these grape trellises, and then it curves around, from the north end of the village, extending to the eastern part of the village where it heads south. Two Kazakh sheepfolds stand on the edge of the Uyghur neighborhood. Earthen walls enclose the rectangular pens.

The road to the Kazakh sheepfolds is lined with waist-high weeds. Those two sheepfolds house everyone's sheep and the two Kazakh families take care of all the herds. When the sheep are driven home in the afternoon, Uyghur girls enter the folds with large bowls and milk pails.

From my house atop the slope, I can just make out the headscarves of the girls walking down the grass-covered country roads. From the style and color of the headscarves I can tell who is going milking. If I go to her home in the evening, I know there will be aromatic milk tea on hand.

3

In the past, Daliangpo had no mosque. My father would go to the homes to offer prayers from the *Qur'an* when a new-born was named, or to officiate the *nikah* of a bride and groom.[1] We children were never allowed to go with him, but we could always tell the latest village news by the stuff he brought home.

Each towel we collected was a record of a death. If my father brought back a towel, someone in Daliangpo had been called to Allah.

If a person had been called to Allah, their family or neighbors would, regardless of whether it was day or night, come to see my father and have him perform the *janazah*—clean the body, change the water, and convey the deceased to the burial ground.[2] When it was over, he would bring back a new towel.

If we used the towels until they were black, we knew that the village had gone a long time without someone having been called to Allah. The more worn-out the towel, the longer it had been since that person had died. We had to wait for the next person to go before we could have a new towel.

Once, one of these towels became rubbery like a cow's stomach as my younger brothers and sisters and I repeatedly wiped our faces with it. We thought that this time we would have to use this one until it was in tatters. Then, just in the nick of time, a notice of death came.

Naibiyuela had died, and with him went the several thousand *yuan* he owed our family. As usual, my father brought a towel back from Naibiyuela's funeral, but with this difference: we used Naibiyuela's towel for many years,

---

1. The Nikah is the Islamic marriage covenant.
2. *Janazah* is Arabic for "funeral."

until it was bald, so that all that was left was a thin patch of vertical and horizontal strands, and a big hole would form at the slightest tug. Everyone would carefully dip the towel in water to dampen it, make a gentle pass over the face, and then hang it back on its wooden peg.

Every time my mother saw the holes in the towel, she would remark, "Look, Naibiyuela's family towel is really durable."

"This towel is worth thousands! What do you know?" This was how my father would talk about it. It sounded like he still wanted to use it for several more years. Actually, when villagers borrowed money, that debt would go with them after they passed away, and to chase after their children for it was simply not done. Even if you wanted to collect, they wouldn't necessarily be able to repay it.

4

There are two ethnic groups in my family. My father is Uyghur from Kashgar in Xinjiang, and my mother is Hui from Tianshui in Gansu. People make fun of mixed-blood children as *erzhuanzi* or "two turners." Hearing this, I became angry. I came home and complained about it to my father. He said, "With four or five ethnic groups from four or five provinces in the village, it isn't surprising that there are a few 'two turners,' and even 'three turners.' Not all the eggs under one old hen are from the same rooster, right? Your mother and I aren't the same ethnicity, but aren't we sharing the same spoon in the same pot for our whole lives?"

My parents do not share many habits in common. The Han people have a saying, "You can't pee in the same chamberpot." As soon as it was dark, my mother would place the chamberpot in the little recess under the *kang*. My father disliked it and maintained that it was totally inappropriate for my mother to urinate in the same place that she ate. No matter what my father said, my mother never moved it. Even if he secretly placed the offending object outside before going to sleep, in the middle of the night it would be returned to its usual place under the *kang* by my mother. She listened to his reproaches for her whole life, and he listened to the sound of his wife using the chamber pot for his whole life, so that in the end they called it even.

Father couldn't change Mother and so he led us to resist her. At night, before getting on the *kang* for bed, Father would take my little sister, four younger brothers, and me into the yard to relieve ourselves. Solemnly, as if holding a ritual, we stood in the garden watering the sunflowers. Boys standing in the front, girls squatting in the back: a symphony of pee.

Actually, it was a fun thing, peeing freely in one large sunflower patch. Father would point to one spot and we would pee there because he knew which plants needed fertilizer and which plants our urine would scald and wilt. I remember one funny incident in which my little brother took a dump and before the turd could hit the ground, our family dog swooped in with his yellow maw and lapped it up. Seeing this, Father joked that we couldn't lose because the poop would end up in the garden one way or another.

Still, we didn't dare do this in front of Mother.

5

Many ethnicities live together in Daliangpo Village. People come from all over, each ethnicity speaking its own language, eating its own cuisine. Over the course of many decades, we came to realize that we could understand each other. Father says, "If a swallow and a sparrow live together long enough, they learn each other's songs."

Father and Mother were a swallow and a sparrow living in the same house, except that Father understood what Mother said, but Mother couldn't understand what Father said. This made things difficult for us children, speaking Uyghur with Father and speaking Hui dialect with Mother. Outside the home, all our neighbors were Kazakh so we needed to learn Kazakh as well. In this way, we learned three languages.

People come from all directions to Daliangpo. They all drink the same water, eat food grown from the same soil, and gradually begin to smell the same.

The Sichuan people learned from the Henan people how to make *miangeda* (dough balls); Sichuan *malatang* (numbing and spicy sauce) was mixed into Gansu pots; Shandong people took Gansu's pickled vegetable flavors, Shanxi's mature vinegar, and the spices of Sichuan and mixed them into one pot. The Jiangsu people tasted it, thought the flavor was pretty good, and then followed suit. They in turn sprinkled some sugar in it and ate it with relish. When Daliangpo cooks, a thick hybrid aroma wafts through the Han neighborhood.

In this multiethnic village, Qasim families stir-fried peppers and eggplant; Hanifa families stir-fried string beans and eggs; Osman families slow-cooked potato and onion in a stew; and Hui families made cabbage, radish, and potato noodle stew. Although the dishes were prepared in different households, what is mine is also yours. One family's meat ends up in another family's dishes; another family's spices find their way into our dishes, and everyone shares salt and oil. This food is what we have come to call "multiethnic."

Among the ethnic minority families of Daliangpo, very few of them have all of the ingredients for any given meal—oil, salt, soy sauce, vinegar, tea, milk, or eggs—on hand. Everyone is busy doing this and that during the day. The farmers farm, the herders herd, returning home in the evenings to cook and finding their salt bags and oil bottles empty. They pick up their bowls and head over to the neighbors. They say they are going "borrowing." A small bowl of salt here, a half bowl of oil there, but for the most part, they borrow but nobody expects them to pay it back. When your family is low on salt and vinegar, you carry the bowl to anyone else's kitchen and "borrow."

When a sheep is slaughtered, everyone gets what they need, meat for some, bones for others, and this goes on naturally, without formal arrangements. In this way one sheep might feed many families. When a cow is slaughtered, it is the same. Everyone is welcome and no one is left out. It stretches as far as it can, even if all that might be left is a bowl of beef soup.

The village elders say, "Where man has been unfair, Allah will be just." In Daliangpo, the cooking pots magically stretch as needed. If a family has made just enough food for its five members, and while they're eating, three or four guests happen to show up, the pot will provide enough food to feed eight or nine.

In Daliangpo, nobody minds when someone drops in for dinner. In fact, they enjoy it. The elders say, "Your true friends arrive just as you sit down to supper and those who come after dinner talk behind your back." If you really want someone to know you are their true friend, you show up just before mealtime.

Naturally, the place of honor is given to the true friend, and they receive the finest meat from the wok and richest noodle soup. If a host serves a thin, watery dish to the point where a guest has to go to the pot to ladle something substantial into the bowl, or if the skin on the milk tea has no body to it, or is thin to the point of translucence, these are considered serious breaches of etiquette. A guest will eat, but think the host is a boor. The whole town laughs at such housewives.

Three-fourths of the year, the crater in the middle of the village is filled with vegetables, but in summer it really booms. The verdant pit becomes Daliangpo's massive wok. The Hui, Uyghur, and Kazakh fields are all in the crater. One family grows string beans, another family grows eggplants, and yet another family grows chili peppers. The crops that ripen first are harvested and eaten first. Today you might pick my peppers, tomorrow I might pick your eggplants. Each family grows one type of vegetable and a dozen family's vegetables come together to make a feast.

It is fascinating the way people share. When a baby is born, the Qasim's bassinet is borrowed. When the baby grows, the Tursun's crib is borrowed. Over time, every Kazakh and Uyghur child in the village will have slept in that bassinet and crib. They pass from one family to another, until the actual owners have another baby, and only then will they be returned. Even then, one can be sure that there is another expectant mother counting the days until the bassinet and crib will pass to her and her soon-to-be born child.

The village maintains a few horse-drawn carriages. The number of carriages depends on the number of horses we happen to have at the time. If you want to use a cart, you hitch your draft horse in the lead, then my horse in the middle, and another neighbor's in the back. If a horse is missing the trip will not take place. No one would ever think of hauling without three horses.

The village's dairy cows are also milked in turn by everyone. When a cow has calved the milk is shared until the calf is weaned. At that point, perhaps another family's cow will have given birth and the process repeats itself. In this way, Daliangpo has fresh milk throughout the year. Similarly, if a new mother's breast milk is insufficient, another nursing mother will breastfeed the baby.

Many ethnic groups have lived together in this village for generations and have come to rely on one another. It is said that harmony comes from the blending of milk and water. The healthiest child drinks the milk of many mothers, and here, in the healthiest of villages, health and harmony can be found in the blend.

16

Dalema's Sacred Tree

SANA

Dalema wakes up. She hears the little steam train in the forest open its enormous mouth and bite her, then scream hysterically. She opens her eyes in a daze, extends her right arm out from under the bed cover made of roe-deer hides, and stretches it towards the sky. In the dim light, her small, coarse palm looks like a black wood ear on an elm tree, listening vigilantly to any sound or movement in the distance.

She tucks her hand under the cover again. She pinches the other arm, feeling worried. The pinch hurts. And yet, the pain is no different from her usual pains. Somehow, she senses the pain is not as piercing and sharp as before; it is like a dense fog hanging over undulating mountains. Obscure. Directionless. She is old. She is surely old. In fact, she is so old that even her physical pain has felt weaker and indistinct. If one spot aches, the entire body hurts. It is a sign that she is getting frail and, if life is like the cycle of seasons, her life journey is about to head into the dead of winter.

This is exactly what Malu, the deity, tells people: life is cyclical. Now that Dalema's life cycle is falling back into the dead of winter, she needs to prepare herself to enter another world, and get on another journey of an itinerant soul.

Dalema is not sure what time it is. Is it three or three-thirty in the morning? Light peeps in through the seams of her tent, quietly and unfathomably, like an angry hunting dog. She blankly fixes her eyes on the light. It diffuses and forms a stream, slowly crawling its way to surround her tent. But she refocuses her thoughts on the first thing that comes to her mind every morning: she is old, surely old. She wakes up every day, wondering where in the world she will be buried after she dies. Of course, people die when they are old. But it's up to her to decide where to be buried while she is still alive. After all, her sons need to listen to her.

Translated by Dong Isbister

And she wants a tree burial. When the day comes, she hopes her sons will lay her to rest decently on an elevated bier, let her rest peacefully under the sun. Her soul will then follow the sunlight and float on the blue, clear, and ancient Angelin River until it reaches the paradise Malu describes.

How will her sons react? Dalema can perfectly imagine the looks on their faces. They will say, "Ewo, you must be out of your mind." They will also say, "Ewo, you may as well be buried in a grave. Otherwise, with only a couple of tries, those crazy chainsaws will have you plummeting to the ground. Then you will come to bug us in our dreams."

She should not bother her sons.

Dalema developed a heart problem when she was young. Many others in her tribe also have issues with their hearts, but nobody cares about it. Living in the forest, they know frigidity and humidity could get at their hearts any moment, just the way fruits get snatched. A short while ago, Dalema was hospitalized because of a relapse, but she told her sons to get her out of the hospital as soon as she could sit herself up. The hospital does not have a decent tree in sight. Not to mention its lifeless surroundings; it also has that diffusive suffocating smell of medicines. Before leaving the hospital, she conveniently packed a white porcelain bed-pan into her dog-leather bag, hoping to use it at home when she is unable to move around. For what she did, the hospital charged her sons a fine. But she pulled the pan out and threw it down into a gully when she was midway to home. If she had to pee and poop in bed, it would be time to do something about herself. She would not trouble her sons. The oval-shaped thing is neither fish nor fowl; it definitely should go.

Dalema can only tell Yesiga about all that is weighing on her mind. She packs some cheese her daughter-in-law made and heads to his house. He must have some sort of brain fog; he gives his full attention to the cheese and tries it in his big mouth with missing teeth. He does not even bother to ask why she comfortably sits on the pad made of roe-deer hides not saying a word. The younger Yesiga was shrewd. He knew exactly where a deer came from and where it would go. He could tell you all about it coherently. Look at him now. Drooping, sagging, thin eyelids. Not a single word of greetings has come out of his mouth.

Dalema is annoyed. Although she has missing teeth, she still spits out words sarcastically, like when she was young. "Hey, it's the sun that has been up, not the moon. Wake up! Stop being a muddle-head. Whoever sees you like this will be angry."

Feeling wronged, Yesiga says, "How dare I speak before you start? Whatever I say is not right. I'd better say nothing, so you won't wear yourself out by saying anything back."

Dalema, also feeling wronged, keeps her mouth shut. This old fella has no sense of humor. Can't he tell that she means to pick a quarrel to cheer herself up? She misses the days when they were young. At the time, neither would give in; they would get into heated arguments. If they had stopped doing that, life for the entire tribe would have been less interesting. They had brought a lot of cheerfulness to the tribe. They set their minds on beating each other and refused to compromise. Because of this, the Love Deity Umai flew away after flying around and watching over them for a long time. She abandoned the young couple meant to fall in love with each other. Not knowing what she would actually get into, Dalema got married, and so did Yesiga. He got married quickly, determined not to be outdone. Perhaps, they held onto their grudges and neither did anything to quell their temper. Whenever they met, it was still like a cat seeing a dog. Think about this. Over the years, the words spit out of their mouths could have formed two Angelin Rivers. People in the tribe would even laugh in their dreams whenever they thought about those encounters of the two bickering at each other without backing down. They would laugh so hard in their dreams that they had to sit up in the middle of the night. As a matter of fact, Dalema and Yesiga knew exactly what was going on, but had to swallow those bitter pills. They knew nobody felt sorry if they had tied the wrong knot. Had they been a married couple, they would have spoken all those funny words in bed and had nothing left to entertain other people.

Without even asking, Yesiga knows why Dalema comes to him, panting. It must be about the same topic: if dead, where is she to be buried?

Dalema's problem has become a real problem. More than ten years ago, a plague hit the forest by the Argun River and took five of those staying at a hunting camp. The survivors barely managed to get to their feet and elevated the dead bodies of their loved ones onto the high bier. They made a vow to the bright sun and the sacred mountain spirit: when it was their turn, they would lie flat on the bier and let the breeze fly their souls to paradise so that they could join their loved ones. Dalema and Yesiga were among those who made the vow. She had lost her husband. He had lost his wife.

Dalema desires a tree burial. It is the only way for her to see her dead husband. She does not want to be buried underground. What a horrible thing to do! She will be buried deep under the dirt, like a grey squirrel. If that happens, how will her soul get out? Will it just sob while being suffocated underground? Whenever she thinks about this, Dalema blames herself for living too long. If only she had died earlier. That would have given her peace of mind after she leaves the world. She would have left before the railways crawled into the heart of the Angelin forest; before the arrival of those roaring chainsaws fed by gas; and before green canvas tents (the color of a green snake skin) were set up all over the forest. How nice it would be if she could leave the world without worries! Back in the day, her sons could easily find four big straight trees for the scaffolding, mark the trunks at three meters above the ground, saw off the part from above the mark, ensure the four trees together form a square-shaped foundation, and then tie the plank tight. Things would be easier afterwards. They would elevate her body, place it on the mighty bier and wrap it up tight with branches. Look! her body that labored all its life will at last be lifted by towering trees and laid halfway to the sky. When that time comes, the Mountain Deity won't blame a dying person for any request and will generously offer her four large trees. He has seen it all. She has lived on the high mountain and the lofty hill her entire life, but not once has she cut a living tree. Like the others in her tribe, she only chooses to use dead trees as firewood. Now that she is dying, she deserves an exception. Lying on the bier will make her feel contented. What could be more dignifying than dying a natural death? She has lived her life conscientiously and gracefully. She will leave the world without any sin, but with a steadfast life behind. What regrets will she have?

But look at the mess that has become of the forest. Those gas-sucking saws screech and shriek like devils, day in and day out, and cut down towering trees, one after another. Those giant monsters with eight wheels are on the move, day and night. They carry the trees down the mountain and load them onto the train so that they can be delivered to different places. A town named Moerdaoga has been established down the mountain and is crowded with loud *waidiren* (outsiders). They have the audacity to do anything without fear. They pick mountain delicacies, catch fish and birds, and hunt and kill animals. They cut down good and healthy trees and take them home as firewood. *Tenŋgeri*, the Sky Deity! These people will scare us to death. Whatever they do, they do it cruelly and daringly. The only thing they haven't done is to set the mountain on fire and burn up everything.

No wonder Dalema keeps talking about her nightmares. She dreams of animals walking into her tent, one after another, bidding farewell in tears, and then vanishing into the deep forest. Where did they go? She counts numerous disorderly animal footprints and sadly wonders. They must have been forced to run away to the forests in Siberia. Poor animals! Will they fare well there? The temperature is minus forty to fifty degrees in winter and thick snow can fall as deep as a meter. They will be frozen to death. Dalema's tears for the miserable animals are followed by dreams of her own misfortune. In her endless dreams, her three sons go from place to place to look for a spot to build the burial scaffold. At last, they find four birch trees in the bare mountain, and make do with them to build the scaffold. Oh Malu! She climbs up, hoping to give it a try, but falls right down to the ground before she sits up properly. When she falls, she sees this clearly: chainsaws are gnawing at the roots of the birch trees.

Dalema describes her lengthy nightmares over tears. "Yesiga, I don't want to go underground. Dirt will clog my ears, cover my eyes, and soil my hair. I won't be able to listen to leaves drift and fall or birds return to their nests; I won't be able to listen to the Angelin River burble and gurgle after snow melts in spring. Don't you know how pleasant those sounds are?"

Yesiga listens and then cannot hold himself anymore. He makes an effort to change the topic and focuses on the present, "Don't feel upset. Come live with me. You won't die any time soon, not by a long shot. What would I do if you died? Selfish old woman. You never think about me."

With her mouth wide open for a while, Dalema says angrily, "You have lost all your teeth, but your mind is still whirling with that. Aren't you afraid the deity above will slap you?" With that, she rises from the mattress pad made of roe-deer hides, holds up the hem of her roe-deer hide dress, and walks out of the tent. Yesiga doesn't want to stop her, because she loses her temper at nobody else but him. Since the age of thirteen, she has learned to find fault with him and frequently criticized him however she expresses herself. She also proudly turns her head away from him, a common trick she uses to ignore him. Just wait and see. Before a pipeful of tobacco is done, she will forget she has just pulled a long face. Some ideas will come to mind. Then she will go to his house again and complain to him over and over. Mountains have mountain ridges and waters have waterways. When they were alive, Dalema's husband and Yesiga's wife believed that separating the lovers would be like splitting a river. It was as if those two bastards had made a plan and died together, leaving the two living lovers behind to mourn and regret. From what Yesiga remembers, Dalema decided to ignore him after she buried her husband, Kuke. Her look seemed to tell him that he had killed Kuke. But it was Kuke that had brought them together again. On a drizzling afternoon, she walked up to him saying hesitantly, "Kuke came to visit me in my dream and also asked me to say hello to you."

Kuke, a tall, sturdy, and handsome hunter, was the best in the Duoleba clan. Yesiga had a grudge against Dalema, thinking that she disregarded his deep love because she was fond of Kuke's physique and looks. But only after death settled the old scores between him and Kuke could he speak of the dead fairly. He admits that Kuke was a real man. Of course the pretty and capable Dalema had chosen to marry him, just as cotton clouds naturally float in the blue sky. Now that Kuke has appeared in her dream and told her to say hello, he would need to live up to his trust. So, he is happy to let her do as she pleases when she acts like a young girl. Just let her believe she is like a flower bud that is ready to blossom.

Dalema leaves the tent, walks for some distance, but doesn't hear Yesiga call her to return. She pauses in dismay, hoping to see his long, square face, but she is disappointed. She has to head home on the road that has taken her to Yesiga's. Tsk! Tsk! It serves her right.

A squirrel bounds by right before Dalema's eyes, its large golden tail high. It jumps onto the bushes and stares down at her. Dalema chortles. This clever little thing has recognized her and now tries to entertain her. She is happy to see that the squirrel has grown a lot since last fall. It has grown into a beautiful big girl. Time to get married.

Last fall, the little thing hadn't grown much. It forced its way into Dalema's tent and jumped around as if it owned the place. Tumen, the hunting dog, started to growl to intimidate the squirrel, but Dalema patted the dog's head, telling it to mind its own business. The squirrel stopped by a couple of more times and looked for food in the tent. It even hopped and stopped in front of Tumen, using its wheat-ear-shaped tail to provoke the dog. But Tumen showed good manners like a grown-up and treated it kindly. Later, the squirrel stopped showing up. Not only did Dalema feel something was missing, Tumen also looked unhappy. Perhaps it, too, missed the mischievous little squirrel.

"Heartless creature. Come and go as you please. Tumen cares more about friendship than you and has been thinking about you." While scolding the squirrel, Dalema grabs some cheese crumbs out of her pocket and leaves them on the grass. Sure enough, the squirrel bounds off like a golden ball, and moves closer to sniff about. This little fella is out of the ordinary: it has a curious appetite and puts everything into its nimble mouth to taste. All of a sudden, Dalema gets goosebumps. Not caring if it understands her, she says, "Hey, you should never, ever enter the green tents. If those inside the tents catch you, you will lose your life. They will definitely push an iron stick through you and grill and eat you." Seeing it busy eating, she sighs and walks back slowly. Perhaps it won't be long before squirrels won't even have pine cone seeds to eat. She looks at the vast meadows that have had trees felled and, filled with worry, slaps her forehead a few times.

Outside the tent, Daughter-in-law is igniting a pile of damp willow twigs to repel mosquitos. The mid-summer dusk takes on the soft light of the setting sun and, like the quiet golden river water, extends to every corner of the forest. A dozen or so fat mosquitoes and horseflies buzz around her head, waiting to land and bite her. Occasionally, she has to free her hands to smack the bugs on her face. Her clumsiness while she is busy doing all this reminds Dalema of a pregnant bear. Daughter-in-law will give birth again. Her big round belly is now up against her chest, but it does not hold her back from getting up early to do household chores every day. Daur women are just like this; they will keep their hands busy until they have to give birth.

Dalema looks at Daughter-in-law's belly with sorrow and pride. Her mood is softening, too; like the sunlight, it grows warmer. She hopes her youngest daughter-in-law can give the Duoleba clan one more real hunter. The life force is strong in the clan: she gave birth to five children; two died very young; her husband also lost his life to a pestilence, but she has been blessed with four grandsons who have all grown as powerful as bull calves. It is not hard for her to see that the young ones, like all the Duoleba men, can never change what runs in their blood; they will grow into real men, no matter how much suffering they undergo.

Dalema is over the moon when thinking about all this. Her steps are even light and spry. She carefully walks around Daughter-in-law and enters the tent, fearing she might touch the body that is carrying her grandchild. Through the smoke swirling up from the fire, Daughter-in-law sees her quietly stuffing something under her robe, as if pregnant. She holds back her laughter and asks: "Ewo, it's almost time to eat, how about me setting the table?" By tradition, the young should never ask one's elders about their whereabouts, so she can only hint at it. Besides, Daughter-in-law knows that Mother-in-law has just come back from Yesiga's. Perhaps, the two of them have already figured something out.

Keeping her hands on her belly, Dalema replies somewhat evasively, "It's still too early. Why don't you lie down to rest a bit? Give the baby a little room to move. He wants to stretch his arms and legs." After she finishes, she totters away, keeping her hands on her belly. Although she walks on for some distance without looking sideways, she feels Daughter-in-law's gaze fixed on her back, which is rather uncomfortable. She can't help but blame herself for revealing her weakness. It's no surprise, then, that her mind wanders and she sends it off on flights of fancy. But seriously, it is the hatchet under her robe that makes her feel giddy, and, yes, there is also that sturdy idea, an idea as strong as a tree. When it is formed, the idea is not even the size of a mushroom, but it has grown into a huge tree in just an hour and it has taken root in her mind. She is nervous, but also feels very excited. She has led a good, clean life, as clean as the bright blue skies, but at this advanced age she will be doing things for people to gossip about. She can't help but feel embarrassed.

Dalema tries to let her hands go, but the lawless hatchet she has tucked in her deerskin belt is so heavy that it almost falls off. This makes her feel somewhat discouraged. Expanding her diaphragm, she exerts all her strength and lets out a birdcall. The quiet surroundings fill up with bird-calls and the echoes linger for all their kind to hear. The hatchet also seems enchanted by the birdsongs. It begins to calm down and stays attached to her body without moving a bit. With satisfaction she snorts, "That's right; no need to make a fuss. I am counting on you to whistle in the dark; we can't do without each other."

There is an indistinct whiff of small animals in the air. Finding it strange, Dalema pauses, sniffs hard a couple of times, and determines that a fox cub is slinking along the forest floor not far from her. She is right. Those wily foxes have run far away, but this little kit, driven by curiosity and having seen little of the world, dares to stop by where it should not. It takes guts. She begins to worry about it. It strolls around at its pleasure, not seeing the tents belonging to the team of lumberjacks on the edge of the forest; traces of fox scent turned into dancing footprints, flashing from her eyes with soft, sparkling sounds. Evidently, while the sun still shines, it will not go home.

Dalema walks on and soon finds herself approaching the team of lumberjacks' tent site. Between the trees, she observes a few green tents. A moving shadow appears from behind a tree. She can tell from a distance that it is a man peeing right there. She turns her head to take a look at the road she has just travelled. She blames the little fox's mother who fails to live up to its reputation for being clever and cunning. It is indeed a blockhead, not knowing how to care for its child. This little kit doesn't know any better and, who knows, may be lured into a trap. My Malu! It is so tiny!

Worried, Dalema shouts at the top of her lungs: hoo-hoo-hoo…. Her voice is resounding and piercing. It penetrates into the forest and the forest responds with loud, shrill echoes, which actually startle her. The man who is peeing shows his head from behind the tree, grumbling and swearing, "What is that shout all about? Are you losing your senses?" Dalema is even more annoyed. How can he carelessly pee on a tree? Trees are living beings and deserve respect, just like humans. Will it be okay to pee on people? This guy is a *waixiangren* (outsider) not knowing right from wrong, ignorant of all taboos, and yet he has the gall to shout at her. Luckily, the little fox is gone, and it is surely gone. It won't return even if you ask. It understands her warnings and knows something is not right. Its instincts will help it remember a truth: keep your distance from humans.

The hatchet tucked in her belt once again wants to fall smack dab on the top of her feet. Dalema holds it down, making it behave and stay where it is. Now is not a good time to be angry and create disturbance. While she walks, she hears footsteps behind her. The man walks fast and soon passes her. He even holds a bright red tool in his hand. Her heart starts to pound: she smells a distinctive foul odor released from the tool, an odor not normally detected in human or animal bodies. In no way is it the same as anything she has ever smelled in her fifty-seven years living in the forest. She feels an old urge to vomit. Whenever she smells something like this, her stomach churns as if she were intoxicated. She looks down, hoping to find some wormwood or *tianmang*. She wants to chew them so that they can help quell her feelings of weakness after she vomits. Seeing a few small, light purple baikal skullcaps sway gently, she picks them and puts them into her mouth. The flower's scent drives off the suffocating stench and the writhing, stifling odor stumbles off and stays away.

All of a sudden, the man stops to wait for her. He asks, "Who are you looking for?" Glaring at him with her red swollen eyes, she tells him that she wants to see the person in charge. With no hesitation he replies, "Follow me then. It will serve your purpose to meet our *banzhang* (crew chief)." Dalema stays quiet for a moment and asks again, "Is he in charge of the chainsaws?" The fast-talking man blurts out, "Yes, he is in charge of everything, even dead bodies."

The man continues to walk ahead of her, pouring out words into her ears. Dalema has to exert herself to follow him. From his nonstop complaints, she somewhat gets what he wants to tell her. He says that lumbermen working in the Greater Khingan Range area lose a few lives to the falling trees every year. He also says certain large trees are not meant to be touched at all; divine spirits are certain to be hiding inside. The thing is, before a tree is felled, lumberjacks need to determine the proper direction it should fall and that should unquestionably be downhill. When a tree falls across the slope, it crushes and kills the loggers standing there. Even more appalling yet is a type of humongous tree. This type of tree has lost its roots to cutting, has nothing inside, and yet it stands stiff and straight, but you can never tell when it will collapse. Just when lumbermen lose hope and walk a few steps away, the giant tree will topple with a big bang, flattening everyone into the snow. He says the lumbermen have constant nightmares at night. When they are ready to fell trees during the daytime, they make sure to secretly kowtow to the trees they have selected and plead for forgiveness before turning on the chainsaw. They are scared half to death every day. If it were not for all the mouths to feed at home, who in the hell would want to do this work?

Dalema sighs at what she hears. She says as she walks, "Poor man. He should have known that the Mountain Deity has a temper and will take revenge if you touch his body. Even if he pokes you gently with a finger, you won't be able to stand it."

The man lowers his head to stare at the chainsaw in his hands, speaking quietly, "I am scared; I am really scared. I am scared that I won't see my wife again. She has been waiting for me to return home with my earnings." Slowly, his voice cracks and breaks into a sob.

Shaking her head, Dalema talks to herself, "It's good you now know you are scared. Everything on the earth has a soul. If you provoke someone, they will remember the harm you do to them. If you provoke the innocent grass, you may not think it's a big deal. You would think it won't have any physical strength to seek retribution, but each delicate blade of grass will remember your wrongs, which means you will soon get what you deserve."

"Isn't this what you people believe?" The man looks nervous, but asks somewhat curiously, "I have heard that you practice shamanic dancing to prevent misfortunes. Does it work?"

Nobody will be spared. Dalema hesitates for a moment, but continues by following her train of thought, "As the divine spirit advises you to be virtuous and cultivate *wuxing* (insight), it also remembers your foolishness. It has no desire to be perfunctory by simply giving you advice. Foolish people are unable to see this. Oftentimes, in order to gain something, they forget being watched by another pair of eyes."

Listening to the old woman speaking gibberish, the man becomes impatient. Whenever these natives open their mouths, they will urge you to believe in gods. They believe in so many gods: those flying in the sky and running on land. They even humbly venerate stones, rocks, rivers, air, wind, rain, and rainbows as their divine spirits.

He walks ahead of her, fast. Hearing the old woman behind him huffing and puffing, he heaves a sigh of relief. Thank goodness! She has at last stopped running her mouth. If she continues with her stories of gods and ghosts, it will be quite an ordeal for him.

He enters a tent and speaks loudly to the person in bed, "*Banzhang*, an old woman wants to see you." After he says this, he places the chainsaw at a corner of the tent, knocks the dust off his hands, and steps out. As soon as she enters the tent, Dalema notices a dozen or so chainsaws; they huddle there like a group of monsters with snarling teeth, which makes her angry. *Banzhang* looks up slothfully and says, "State your business. Hurry up! It's almost our time to eat."

Dalema's eyes hurt. It is a sort of twitch, as if warning her of something. She smears a finger with spittle and applies it to her eyelids, speaking to herself, "No jinx!" She takes a couple of steps forward and says seriously, "The thing is, you are a *waixiangren*. You are from somewhere else, but we have lived in the forest for generations and buried our loved ones up in the trees after they died." Seeing him nod, she becomes excited, and speaks more smoothly. "Our people have been buried in this part of the forest. You have been cutting trees and are now closing in on their resting place. For years, they have rested in the forest peacefully, and Malu keeps a record on behalf of those who are still alive. The sun above the Angelin River is kind and fair; it shines on the living world and the dead people as well. Souls don't die. For humans, living is one form of wandering and death is another. Young man, your eyes are like the dark clouds, trying to stop me from speaking. Ah, I must have forgotten that you are a *waixiangren* and you won't understand me. You won't get it even if you hear what I am saying. Bear with me if I am rambling; I am almost done. What I am saying is, leave the forest and go somewhere else. Don't cut trees anymore. What a sin! One big tree after another. All of them have grown almost tall enough to reach the sky. There was no human trace when they first stuck their heads out of the ground."

Dalema suddenly slaps her own face. Now the body of a dead mosquito is sticky in her hand. While she was talking, it buzzed around her. A greedy, pesky sucker. Don't blame her for killing it.

At first, *Banzhang* was completely confused because her Chinese was full of errors, but he finally figured out the purpose of her visit simply by making a guess. She comes to tell them to leave here and go somewhere else. She babbles on and on, the words pouring out of her mouth like a river, but it all boils down to this key point. He kicks the grass under his feet, but the grass would not let go of his rubber shoes and loses no chance to crawl up his calves, planning to make their home there. There is no place the damn grass cannot reach. Like converging waters in the valley, grasses have gone wild. Eyes open or closed, he sees them throw themselves ferociously at him. If the team members don't make efforts to kill the grass whenever they can, the wild grass can unquestionably drill into their bones. *Banzhang* kicks the grass under his feet, and gets bitten in return, it is undoubtedly a grass bite. Believe it or not, he is the one taking the bite. The old woman is right about one thing, that is, plants in the forest are all spirits. Like humans, they won't stand for any nonsense. He stares at the window in his tent. It can't be wrong. He pulled out the wild grass approximately a couple of days ago, but they have grown again, ready to lean their bodies in through the low window or simply make their way inside. He pulls a handful of the grass off the window, uses them as a wipe, and tries hard to remove gasoline off his hands. He has just filled up the chainsaws but lost his appetite because of the pungent smell of gas. Who would be there to listen to his complaints?

"Okay, Ma'am, it's not up to me to decide if we should leave. Even the township leaders don't have the final say." He does the best he can to comfort her while she glares at him with her small, stubborn eyes. "We all need to do what the higher-ups tell us to do. All of us on the team have to work our socks off; we will be scolded for not making the quotas. Ma'am, you don't need to worry about the kind of life you and your people will lead. I have heard that new houses are being built in town for you, and you will soon move down the mountain."

Dalema looks glum. With a heavy heart, she walks out of the tent. It is obvious that nobody would be willing to leave here simply because an old woman pleads. She knew it would be like this, but the stubborn side of her insisted that she come, even if only to be rebuffed. There is one thing she can do now. She can enter the tent when nobody is around and use her hatchet to chop the chains off those saws. Then those toothless funky-mouths won't even have a chance to gnaw the trees.

Dalema walks around in an open space not far from the tent, waiting for *banzhang* to leave for dinner. The sky slowly loses its color; the trees in the distance fade in the dusk and turn into looming shadows; and a thin mist hangs near the ground. It won't be long before the entire forest is wrapped in the thick mountain fog, as if hiding underwater.

Someone comes into view and walks toward her at a brisk pace. Dalema has a big smile on her face. The quick-tempered Yesiga hasn't changed the way he walks, even at his advanced age. Look, he thinks he is still a young man who is walking fast to get somewhere. Dalema is in high spirits immediately; she also keeps her back ramrod straight. She has someone to lean on and Yesiga is the one. He always comes to her in a timely manner whenever she is lonely and helpless, and whenever she deals with thorny issues. It seems that he has been sent to her by divine providence.

Yesiga walks ahead with wings on his feet and moves his thick lips to make fun of her at the same time. He says, "A silly roe deer walks back and forth, going round and round in one spot, but fails to see anyone. Then it begins to wonder. How come I was timid and scared of everything, including moon shadows. I had no clue I could be so powerful. It seems those ferocious animals don't deserve the fame they have received, because they run away when hearing my voice. From now on, I won't be timid anymore; I will stand on my dignity like the ruler of all animals. When the sun rises, the roe deer realizes that it has fallen into a trap and has also dreamed all night of becoming the ruler."

Holding back her laughter and showing due respect for his feelings, Dalema nods her head and responds, "Yes, you have got it right. I am that silly roe deer. Before dawn breaks and while the sun is still asleep, why don't I have a dream of being the ruler?"

Yesiga opens his mouth, but not a single word comes out. Dalema is the ruler even if she admits she has lost. She is surely not wrong about this. If she is determined to be the ruler, she won't be subdued by anyone.

At last, *banzhang* leaves the tent. Seeing his dark back disappear into a different tent, Dalema becomes happy and loses no time to tell Yesiga to look out for anyone coming. Yesiga puts on a gloomy face after learning about her plan. Feeling annoyed, he mumbles, "I didn't sign up for this. I never do sneaky things."

Dalema is also angry. She involuntarily yells out, "Hey, is that how you speak to another person? Go gather all of them here, and I will do it right before their eyes. They will praise me, 'Look, she is one hell of a brave woman!'" She stalks over to the tent without Yesiga. He stands there, as if in a trance.

Soon Yesiga hears the pounding, ringing clang of metal on metal. He cannot stay there any longer and runs to the tent. He stands in the door and looks at Dalema in surprise. She must be crazy. She holds the hatchet high and strikes with hateful force, and then saw blades screech, as if there were hand-to-hand combat in the tent. At a glance, Yesiga knows that her frenzied passion has overtaken her, and she has lost her concentration. So she strikes aimlessly, one time flailing near her own leg. Luckily, her big, loose robe shields her from the blow. Otherwise, she would have become Dalema, the Lame. Wow, she is amazing. She continues to wave her hatchet without groaning once. Yesiga feels excited, grabs the hatchet out of her hands, holds it above his head, and then smashes down on the saw blade firmly and force-fully. The blades shatter into bits and pieces with a satisfying crunch. He is very satisfied when hearing the blades crumbling into bits and pieces. "This is not the place for you to make a show," he says disdainfully, teaching the blades a lesson. "You'd better go back where you belong; you are not needed here."

Seeing this, Dalema is pleased as punch. Yesiga is indeed a capable man. He neatly chops off all the chains, taking care to leave them in their proper place. Afterwards, he leaves the tent, followed by Dalema. Feeling content, they completely forget that they should have been cautious, and make their way back home as if nothing had happened. Soon Dalema feels that her body is heating up, like a hot iron bar. Carried away by their success, she says, "Now the forest is quiet; it is as quiet as the frozen winter riverbed. When you whack those chains, I can hear my bones crack and creak; they would not cry uncle, you know; I could have done the work."

When Yesiga learns that Dalema leaves things unfinished to simply make him look good, his happiness instantly evaporates. No matter how nicely things are done, he is not up to par in her eyes. If she were a man, he would like to teach her a good lesson. But for now, he can only respond angrily, "Hey, have you no conscience? You can hear the cracks of your own bones, but not the curse words I have reserved for you inside me, right? I think of you every day and rely on you, but you always get on your high horse when you are with me. Will there ever be one moment of regret in your life?"

Dalema looks around, panicked. This old man doesn't think twice before complaining in a loud voice. Why so loud? If a passerby happens to hear this, everyone in the hunting camp will hear about it tomorrow. Even the unborn baby inside her daughter-in-law's belly will laugh and roll. But she cannot blame him this time. Evidently, he is truly, seriously angry. He walks ahead, puffing and blowing. His feet and the flourishing wild grasses he steps on are locked in a ridiculous trial of strength, pulling and dragging noisily. Before long, he leaves her far behind.

Dalema starts to laugh. She can't help it. She laughs for a brief moment, and then her eyes well up with tears that slowly roll down her face. Thank goodness it is already dark. Thank goodness the stubborn old man pushes forward with all his strength and can't see her tempestuous tears. Look at old Yesiga! His body is as strong as a rock and he will definitely live a long life. You never know, he might create a miracle, and become a legend for his descendants to talk about. As for her, she is old. She sees more clearly than anyone that her days are numbered, because her heart is like a bird-nest with holes and damage. It will be blown off and dropped onto the ground by the flashing winds of life and time. Recently, Umai, in the shape of a bird, has frequently flown into her dreams. She has been waiting for the exhausted heart to plop and leave the body. She will fulfill her duty to fly over and hold it in her mouth before it drifts and enters the mundane world. Then she will fly across the border between the nether world and the world of the living to return the heart to Dalema's dead husband.

What could she promise to Yesiga, this old man who can't tell right from wrong?

"Stick wooden poles into the ground and erect it, use roe deer tendons to make a rope, and dry meat strips under the bright sun. The strips will dry quickly and thoroughly and won't attract maggots."

Dalema repeats these words to herself, quickly sits up on the sleeping pad, and gets dressed in a hurry. Then, from under the pad she pulls out her sharpening stone that is broken in half. She wastes no time sharpening her knife. Afterwards, she cuts a whole piece of roe deer meat into long thin strips and hangs them on a rope to dry.

Her youngest son came back from his hunting trip around midnight yesterday. The moment she saw the two big leather bags on the horseback, she knew he had made a large kill. He shot two roe deer, dressed them by the river, left their bones there, put the clean meat into the leather bags, and brought them back. Before going to bed, she kept telling herself to get up early to dry meat, but it was already broad daylight when she awoke. As soon as she opens her eyes, she holds her breath as usual and listens for the noise of those chainsaws in the distant forest. But it is very quiet over there, only white clouds leisurely roaming the sky. No screams of chainsaws can be heard—the kind of scream that could drill a hole in your skull. It's no wonder that she slept so comfortably for so long.

Happy and cheerful, Dalema rises invigorated. While leaving the meat strips to dry, she amuses Daughter-in-law and tells her not to forget to smear some bear oil on the newborn's butt. That way, the baby will grow up to be as strong, brave, and fierce as a bear. She also tells Daughter-in-law to feed the baby a little flower juice on his first-month birthday, hoping he will be someone who sees the finer points so that girls will be attracted to him. She sums up by saying, "A man must have these two qualities. Your Dad was such a man; I am dead set on being with him all my life."

It is then that the chainsaws screech without any warning. Dalema's right hand involuntarily jumps, slashes a finger on her left hand, and blood gushes out of the cut. "Ouch!" whispers Daughter-in-law looking on, and she runs into the tent and grabs a roll of birchbark. She tears off the soft, film-like inner layer and wraps the wound firmly for Mother-in-law. Dalema looks up at the meat strips on the rope. They are busy suckling under the sun, taking in whatever the burning sunshine can offer, their colors shining bright and ruddy. They will certainly be the best food, all the more tasty, crispy, and delicious.

Dalema doesn't even feel like saying anything. She stops what she is doing, holds the wounded finger up, and slowly walks back to the tent. She sits herself down on the sleeping pad that her son has prepared for her, feeling throbbing pains in the wound. She has also started to experience a dull chest pain, and overwhelming fatigue has subdued her entire body.

The observant Daughter-in-law can tell that Mother-in-law is not feeling well. She puts in a birch bark bowl some dried blood from deer hearts, adds some warm water to brew it for a moment, and then holds the bowl to help her drink it. Dalema listens to Daughter-in-law and finishes half of the medicine that tastes acrid and puckery. Soon she feels her heart rate stabilize. It is unlike a moment ago, when she felt as if someone were tapping on her chest with a small hammer. "Go and do what you need to do. I am fine." She says to her son who is standing in front of her looking worried. A few moments later, she talks to herself while shaking her head, "It's caused by anger. I am furious. I'd rather those disgusting chainsaws chopped off my head first. I have had enough of this kind of life."

Weak and weary, she lies down and is immediately overcome by an irresistible sleep. Then it's a world of endless, serious dreams—one dream after another squeezes in. Her son is walking laboriously in the forest and can't find his way home. Walking in line behind him are those animals: wolves, foxes, deer, roe deer, wild boars, and bears. They follow him, looking for a road that will lead them to survival. Their eyes are gloomy and cold like the winds of fall. She waves her hands and calls him to come over, but he leads the animals deeper into the forest at a slow pace.

A sharp pain in the wound wakes her up. She sits up and hears the sound of her son and his wife doing things outside the tent. For a moment, she wonders if she is still dreaming. She thinks that she only dozed off, but then realizes she took a long nap. She looks outside the door and notices that the light has dimmed. Her eyes are swollen. Even her lips feel fat, bee stung. Frightened, she extends a leg and presses a finger to the lower part. A dimple immediately appears. Like an eye that has a cataract, it stares at her blindly. It seems she will need to go to the hospital again.

Dalema feels an urge to wail but also thinks it will be like throwing caution to the wind to do so. In the shrine, Malu will be upset. It will probably warn her by saying, "You'd better be quiet. Many people have suffered but have endured quietly and said nothing, even on their deathbeds. Why are you the one wailing?" As she thinks about this, she forces back the tears that well up in her eyes, walks out of the tent barefoot, strolls around in the yard, and finally, exhausted, sits down by the campfire. The campfire is roaring under the hanging pot in which roe deer meat boils. She enjoys the aroma and says to Daughter-in-Law who is tending the fire, "I'm hungry again. I am always hungry. How useless I am! Your father-in-law is worry-free. He doesn't ever need to eat anything where he is now. He just strolls around every day." While talking, she plunges a butcher knife into the boiling water, stabs a piece of meat to determine if it's well done.

Her youngest son sits on a pile of firewood, counting his bullets in the leather bags. Two bullets fall out of one bag and disappear in the blink of an eye. He drops to one knee groping for the bullets for some time. In the end, he finds them, the two smooth little play things. He sits back on the firewood and focuses on his mother, looking worried. She indulges herself and chews the meat. She seems to fully enjoy it, but the mass fills her mouth as she chews and chews, unable to swallow it. This is a sign of a deficiency of *qi* in the spleen and stomach, but she wants to show her son that she is strong; she can still eat a lot and he doesn't need to worry about her. He holds his feelings in check, walks over to the pot, and picks a piece of well-done venison. He tears it into little pieces and puts them in the birch bark bowl for his mother to eat. Now is not the time to show emotions on his face, not a face etched with worry to say the least. Tears of deep sorrow must be kept inside; they should never appear on the face. Sweat is the only thing that should openly roll off the face.

Dalema feels that she has regained her strength after eating her fill. She grabs an empty leather bag and leaves home, heading for the tent of the work-team. She presumes that they will throw away the broken chains and carelessly leave them outside the tent, allowing them to corrode in the rain and wind, and she is right. The broken chains cannot kill or inflict wounds anymore; they have become useful things in her eyes. She carefully picks up the broken chains, places them into the bag, puts the bag on her back, and walks slowly into the forest.

A tree stands in her way and an exposed root trips her up. She sets her bag down and bends to pat the root. Feeling sorry for it, she says, "Young man, you need to learn self-control, go as deep as you can, and make sure not to stick out." She puts the bag back on her back, zigzags among the trees, and comes to a halt before a verdant pine tree. She wraps her arms around the tree, but immediately pulls her hands away, as if burnt. Some power inside the tree is transmitted to her arms. It must have been the Tree Deity telling her that he resides in it.

Dalema gets four or five broken chains out of the bag and hammers them, one after another, into the roots. She believes that the wild chainsaws, when hitting the broken chains, will instantly be silenced and the power saws will break. Everything has its vanquisher. Motivated by her own smart idea, she implants metal teeth into the tree roots, one after another, so the trees can protect themselves from being wounded or killed. Once she exhausts all the broken chains, she will talk to her son about purchasing nails. They can use the money that has been put aside for her hospital visits to buy nails down the mountain. The more, the better. How she wishes she could help all the trees to have their own teeth! Her son will surely acquiesce to her request. Why shouldn't he when she is doing a good deed? He is very understanding and kind, and his heart is as pure as gold.

Dalema hears footsteps not far from her. Those are human footsteps; actually, they are Yesiga's. She can recognize those footsteps even with her ears covered. She is so happy that she stands up straight, arms akimbo, shouting, "You have found the right place. I am dead tired. You will need to take over."

Yesiga pokes his head out from among the trees. He says mischievously, "You were making some loud noises. I thought it was a woodpecker drumming around for worms."

Dalema coughs before replying, "Shut your crow-mouth, you jinx! You want to make me mad, right? I'm not falling for it. Now that you are here, it's time to work."

Yesiga circles around the big tree that has just received Dalema's broken chains and says admiringly, "What a capable woman! You should be our Mokunda. If you were the chief, we men would have all unswervingly helped you, but you were born at the wrong time."

Dalema softly smiles, as if bees were busy making honey in her throat, "You are far too modest, Yesiga. Don't you see that I always go to you, baffled and panicky, whenever I have to deal with something. All my plans are in fact yours; I get them every time I pick a quarrel with you."

That almost brings a big, radiant smile to Yesiga's face, but he manages to suppress it. In all the time that they have known each other, this is the first time that Dalema has praised him to his face. He is touched but also feels a bit sad. Taking the hatchet that she hands him, he mocks himself half-jokingly, "I feel more comfortable about the words you use when you pick a quarrel with me. When you speak normally, I am at a loss for words." He forcefully drives broken chains into the tree roots, and the bag quickly becomes empty, which makes him feel utterly dejected. "There are far fewer broken chains. I haven't used many and now they are all gone. Where can we go and buy some nails tomorrow?"

Dalema pats the tree trunk contentedly and says, "This is not bad at all. One tree saved is one life kept. Look! The trees we have protected show their loyalty and their leaves are smiling at us. Tonight, they will certainly get a good night's sleep without having a single nightmare."

Yesiga listens quietly for some time and then turns to Dalema, speaking seriously, "I have heard the footsteps of the sun that is going down."

Dalema stands up straight, holds her breath, listens, and then whispers, "I have heard them, too. The Sun Deity is going down. Its footsteps sound like dance-steps. They are music to my ears."

They stand still, face-to-face. They listen to the sun revolving, dancing as it sets behind the mountains; they listen to a bird alighting in a tall tree reaching up toward the sky; and they listen to a few green leaves lazily falling from the sky. Two leaves happen to gently meet, softly kiss each other, and reluctantly bid farewell before quietly diving to the earth of infinite passion. The earth, on the other hand, is letting out slurping sounds similar to those of children drinking water.

Yesiga laughs merrily, "Look, the earth is drinking water." He pauses to think for a moment, and then emphasizes, "the earth is a child. It has had too much sun today, and must be dying of thirst."

He hears a soft sob. It's Dalema. For a moment, he can't believe his ears. He must have a problem with his hearing, he thinks. Then she sobs a little louder. He senses that she has been sad. Seeing him peer into her face, Dalema simply goes ahead and cries, "I want to live; I really want to live my life. What will you do when I am gone? You will be alone. Who will you turn to if you want to talk about things? It won't be long before you get sick. Children are after all children. They don't think the way older people do."

Yesiga lowers his head. A gloomy hand seems to have got hold of his throat, which makes it difficult to breathe. This stubborn old woman appears to be casual and says whatever is convenient for her, but she doesn't actually speak her mind. Instead, she hides her thoughts in a cocoon. Feeling the light of her life growing dim, she opens her stubbornly closed mouth and reveals her deepest secrets. He is not wrong about his guess: he has been in her heart. That is enough, because it is exactly what he wants. Let heaven be his witness. In his lifetime, he has had nobody but her in his heart. He has not truly cared about anything other than this. He has devoted his heart to her. Yesiga raises his head and says regretfully and happily, "Hey, show that old courage of yours again. You need to do your best to live on. Don't you dare to have any more of those silly thoughts. If nothing else, you need to live for my sake, right? I will go home to tell my children that Auntie Dalema has relented at last and wants to be a member of our clan. They will be very happy to hear that. They have been waiting a long time for you to move into our house."

Dalema listens, her heart filled with longing, bouncing with delight. She now has a vague smile on her face where there were tears a moment ago. But when she turns her eyes to the woods in the distance, a thought strikes her, together with the night-wind. Slowly she shakes her head. From the way she does it, Yesiga seems to hear ever so faintly wild fruits sway; they hang from branches and sway in the grave fall winds. Dalema is on the verge of tears again. She says in sadness, "A good woman should not marry two men in her lifetime. I am Duoleba's wife in this life and I will live up to my name. Let's wait for the next life. I will marry you then and pay you back for all the good things you have done for me."

Filled with heartache, Yesiga drops his head.

Those chainsaws continue to screech but suddenly come to a halt, as if placed in a choke-hold. Her heart singing with joy, Dalema gets down on her knees by their campfire and respectfully throws a big piece of fat venison into the roaring fire. The joyful flame sticks out its red tongue, licking the meat with relish, and soon belches. The sun is still bright and beautiful as usual. Everything looks vibrant; even the Fire Deity takes an unusual liking to food. Look at its hot tongue! They dance around the hanging pot and the savory aroma of the venison porridge emanates from it. It seems that the porridge is about done.

A long buck-grunt comes from the woods. Finding it strange, Dalema pricks up her ears. The buck seems to know that she is listening attentively and grunts non-stop. Dalema can't help but laugh. This old man, Yesiga! He can even think of using deer grunts to tell her that their labor was not in vain and the lumberjacks' chainsaws have been destroyed because of the hidden broken chains. The grunt coming from his deerskin whistle is loud, like a rutting buck calling a doe. It is August right now—the dog days of summer. How likely would it be to see rutting bucks grunt about? They usually come into rut in September. Bucks, in particular, don't elegantly hide themselves in the woods singing lovely ditties when they are in rut. Their tempers flare like a raging fire. Not even worried about losing their lives, they leave their herds and stand on the mountain slope, grunting and calling out to young does for love. This old man, Yesiga! What's his deal here?

Teasing should only be taken as teasing in the end, but Dalema enjoys listening to Yesiga. Days filled with his playful teasing have come to an end, though. When those chainsaws open their wild, big mouths again, trees in the mountains fall one after another. Those are trees that are hundreds of years old. Whenever they fall with crashes, the entire land trembles. Dalema's family tent also shakes and the statue of Malu swings like a clock pendulum. Dalema looks up at Malu one time, when she kneels down and prays before the statue, but only sees that Malu keeps shaking its head without giving her any guidance.

Dalema has no choice but to go to Yesiga again. She admits defeat. She admits that she is utterly defeated. Yesiga is a man and, after all, men are smarter than women. Women's brains normally can handle odds and ends fine, but will become hopelessly muddled when it comes to important matters. With all the disorderly words coming out of Dalema's mouth, Yesiga only remembers one sentence: he is a man, and a real man should have a plan.

Of course Yesiga has plans. The plans in his head are as many as the headwaters of the Angelin River. He tells Dalema one plan after another until she picks one: digging pits on the road to trap logging trucks. Those trucks with rubber tires are so annoying. They take thick, strong logs down the mountain to the town all day long. They are like lumbering pregnant animals with bulging bellies. Someone needs to bust their legs or something, so that they will know how to behave.

They both leave home early in the morning. After getting together, they make their way on the logging road. They stop here and there, looking for the best spot to dig a pit. Heavy tires have ground away the pavement and left deep rutted tracks on the road, as if lightning had heart-wrenchingly etched its surface.

They stop at a bend. Dalema thrusts her shovel down into the dirt and decides to dig the trap right there. She has every reason to do so, as thick bushes obscure the view there and others will not see them easily.

Yesiga is now ready to take over the show. He says Dalema needs to look out for people and he can dig the trap by himself. After he holds the shovel up and waves to her, he starts digging, but immediately feels weak in his arms when the shovel hits the metal-like surface. And yet he doesn't want her to shake her head behind his back when she thinks back to the old days. How powerful and strong he was then!

With mixed feelings, Dalema watches him. Like a diligent ant, he uses his skinny arms to dig unyieldingly. Indeed, his spirit is willing, but the flesh is weak: when he fiercely jabs his shovel at the ground, it instantly bounces off the rock-like soil with its own power of resistance. At the same time, his arms, legs, and back look clumsy and heavy. Dalema walks over, stands by his side, and firmly extends her shovel. Now that they are old, they, more than ever before, need to work shoulder to shoulder. She firmly digs her shovel in at an angle but all the same, the soil firmly resists her. Its temper has become short. It is not the same soil that used to be loose and easily dug even by hand. Now it confronts everyone head-on and shows its determination to remain stubborn until the very end. Dalema does not dig long before she starts to breathe heavily. "You cannot tell right from wrong. What will you get by confronting me?" She spits and then goes on exasperatedly, "Don't you use your brains? So be it. Let trucks run on your body. Let them take away all the logs."

They just finish digging a decent sized pit before cars are heard coming in the distance. Yesiga rushes to cover the pit with branches and then covers the branches with a layer of dirt. He takes Dalema to the roadside. They totally forget to hide themselves and stand there without any camouflage, like two slow-witted roe deer.

A logging truck suddenly comes into view. This huge, gas-sucking monster has its belly loaded with logs, and vrooms along toward them. Seeing the truck body whose color is as red as blood, Yesiga recognizes right away that the truck is a Scania, a foreign model. The hunters along the Angelin River know everything about it inside and out. When it appears on the road leading to the forest, it means the era in which hunters rely on hunting for survival is coming to an imminent end and a new era is beginning. What will the new era look like? Nobody can tell.

The blood-red, fast-moving Scania truck approaches, hurtles at them like a conqueror, but it dips into the trap in no time. It grunts a couple of times before popping out of the trap. Its eight huge wheels easily support its chassis and it jumps out as quickly as it went in. Before they can get their minds around what has happened, the large logging truck is already gone, leaving behind a cloud of dust filling the sky.

Yesiga is enraged. Dalema has never seen him insanely mad like this. It's true that he stands motionless over there. No sound. He breathes evenly, like a clock with a pendulum. But Dalema knows that he is extremely angry.

Yesiga lifts his hands up to the sky and mumbles, "*Teŋgeri*, the Sky Deity! Please bless me with unlimited power! Please bring my young blood back so it can flow strong! Please make my bones renew their rock-like strength!" With these prayers, he holds the shovel and jumps into the pit, digging strenuously. Dalema also holds a shovel and jumps in, standing side-by-side with him and digging as hard as she can. The shovels remove clusters of lush grass roots. They have grown luxuriantly, as if pushing up through the depths of the earth's crust and spreading to every corner of the land with unimaginable speed. The white juice from their wounds mixes with the dark soil, emitting a smooth, sweet scent.

Dalema sneezes while working hard to remove the grass roots that protect the soil; she digs out the wet dirt at the bottom and throws it out of the pit. Fresh, sweet grass roots attract a large group of fat ants. They busy themselves crawling around. A few are careless enough to fall into the pit. Then they panic and scatter in all directions. Dalema even senses that some ants are crawling on her sweaty back, because it feels cool and itchy. She can see from his back that Yesiga is digging hard. The clothes on his back are soaked with sweat, like birch bark in the rain. The pit is getting deeper. They don't sweat for nothing, Dalema thinks to herself with pride.

Yesiga makes it. He sticks the shovel forcefully into the dirt and shouts, "Good. Those metal monsters run pell-mell, and it's time to teach them a good lesson." It takes him a few tries to get out of the pit, but he doesn't make a scene. However, it's funny when Dalema tries to do the same thing. She goes on all fours and falls back into the pit. Yesiga has to jump in and push her out.

After he gets out, Yesiga carefully covers the pit with tree branches and then layers this with more dirt on top. Hearing a car approaching in the distance, he says confidently, "this time it won't get away."

A *Jiefang* truck is vrooming closer, but Dalema and Yesiga forget to hide themselves again; they crane their necks to watch while standing in a meadow not far from the road. In the blink of an eye, the giant monster is trapped in the pit and the sound of the tire explosion almost gives them clogged ears.

The massive blast swells into a huge mushroom cloud in the sky, followed by echoes in the mountains, which bang loudly like holiday firecrackers. The couple feel elated and laugh their heads off. Dalema laughs and turns her face toward Yesiga, like a golden yellow sunflower blossom. She can only see a big, black, hollow-mouth on his smiley face. Look! He is overjoyed; this is more exciting than his wedding.

A short man leaps out of the cabin and furiously dashes at them. Another man gets off and stands on the left side of the road, waving to stop the log tractors coming up.

Dalema is a little bit scared. She stays close to Yesiga and says, "We'd better take off." Fixing his eyes on the man running towards them, Yesiga says unyieldingly, "I am not a rabbit. I'm not going to run away. I didn't plan to do that when I came here. What can he do?"

The short man charges over, grabs Yesiga by the collar, and ties his arms with a rope. Dalema doesn't even have time to see the man remove the rope from his waist. It appears to have shown up unannounced. Dalema stretches her arms, staggers along to Yesiga, and pulls the damn rope as hard as she can. The short man rudely pushes her away, swears loudly at the three men running toward him, and then, as if jinxed, he turns his anger inward, sighing and talking about his woes.

With some effort, Dalema keeps her feet on the ground. She then regains her strength and walks over again. Yesiga can read her mind. He cries out to her, telling her to halt and maintain her dignity. Seeing him care for her dignity while he himself has been taken by force, she bursts into tears. Yesiga is right. One should have dignity. He doesn't want to see her fight and curse like a shrew. It will be a disgrace if she does that. She obeys him, stands motionless, and tries hard to hold back her tears. But he frowns and gives her an angry look. Seeing this, she immediately lifts her hands, wipes away the tears, and also makes sure her face is dry and clean. Then she holds her head high and proudly stands in front of those men. She is certain, without another glance, that he is content now. He used to say that he liked her integrity.

The four men put their heads together to talk things over and then split up, each taking up a separate task. They pick up the shovels and dig a slope in front of the stuck tire. A driver parks a tractor in front of the truck, gets a steel rope about the size of a big pine cone in diameter, and attaches it to the tow hook on the front of the truck. Then he starts the tractor engine. Its bright and shiny tracks clatter forward for a short distance before the car grunts along and gets back to the road surface.

Dalema hangs her head in sadness. All they have done is to no avail. They have just taught that monster a lesson, but it only grunted a couple of times and then made it out. The pit behind it now looks like a collapsed mouse hole. At most, it can hold two birch-bark buckets of cold water. Just at the moment, Yesiga bursts out laughing. He lowers his voice and tells her, "I have figured something out. We will do a better job next time. They will certainly think they have run into some mountain spirit!" With a heavy heart, she takes a look at him and the men. They are replacing tires by using an iron tool of magic that can lift the body of the truck in a breeze. It won't be long before the truck grows a brand-new leg and is turned loose to run amok everywhere again. It deserves to die.

Two men come over, clamor at Yesiga, and shove him into the truck. They will take him with them; they will take him to the township where someone can discipline this old creature. They call Yesiga "old creature."

Yesiga gets into the cab, triumphantly, as if he were on his way to receive a prize or something. He makes an effort to turn his head and look at Dalema. Something is obviously wrong with his neck; perhaps it has been sprained. He shouts out loud, "go home. I will be fine."

The men laugh out loud. One of them even whistles to show his ridicule and mockery. The driver backs up the truck, runs over the two mud-covered shovels, speeds off, and disappears without a trace. The tractor also purrs away, leaving behind its stink.

At long last, Dalema cries quietly. With nobody around, she cannot hold it any longer. She let her teardrops fall like autumn leaves. She feels her heart has been taken, leaving a void as deep and boundless as an abyss, and this abyss is shrouded in a desperate, dense fog. She has never felt such despair, just as she has never known that a human body could become an abyss.

Dalema takes a step, then a few more steps. The sunlight stretches itself and crawls over in a calm and collected way to bite the top of her feet. She cannot remember how long she stands there. She also appears to be in a trance. Time to go home. A voice whispers in her ear; a hand gives her a gentle push. She turns her back and walks slowly into the forest.

She walks for quite a while and stops again. Before her eyes are three smaller diverging roads. For her, it is like coming face to face with three identical leaves. Feeling unbearably hot, she takes off her scarf and holds it. Cold morning air in the forest can chill one to the bone, so, when leaving home, she wraps a scarf around her head in case she should catch cold. She stands at the crossroads but is unable to see well because of the intensely bright sunlight. She takes one road and walks some distance but comes back, then she takes another. The tall bird vetches pull the scarf out of her hand without her noticing it. The weather-beaten scarf lies buried in the grass and, sad and worried, watches her walk farther and farther away.

Dalema sets foot on the road to the deeper forest and keeps walking. Her feeble heart reminds her to look for her final resting place. The smell of the forest is getting stronger, and again she starts to cry. Her father and her husband are resting in the deep Greater Khingan Range. Their spirits have been kindly accepted by the vast forests; nobody will be able to disturb them over there. Thank goodness, they are where humans don't have the power to reach. They float freely every day, following the mountain winds and bathing in the golden sunlight. What a wonderful world! The sufferings they underwent while alive have been transformed into blessings, helping their souls find eternal peace.

Without the bier holding up her body, Dalema will not be able to meet them.

Deadly, overwhelming fatigue attacks her whole body. Dalema slowly closes her eyes. A thin layer of oil-like sweat covers her back, then the entire body. She is nearing the end of her life. She remembers clearly her loved ones with this type of deadly sweat before they passed away.

"I am tired." She groans and, staggering, sits down on the ground. Around her are approximately ten or so white stumps. She would not want to sit on them. Everyone in the tribe also bears in mind the saying that nobody should rest on a tree stump. Even if the body of a tree is cut, the roots still sustain lives granted by the earth. How can humans place themselves above the Tree Deity?

Dalema reaches out and runs her fingers affectionately over a tree stump by her. It is like a large round table. It must have been an old tree. The fine growth rings are like ripples, presenting themselves in front of her. She counts ripple after ripple of the rings but quickly becomes confused. The tree must be over a hundred years old, to say the least.

Dalema gradually lowers her head and sets it against the tree stump. Sleepiness has overtaken her. It is like tree sap applied to her eyelids. After she closes her eyes, she slowly falls into the dense fog. She hears a bear call her name and sees Wusen, the mother bear, walk slowly and then stop in front of her. It gives her a few hard pushes, stands up to roar to the sky, and fades into the white fog, again slowly.

Dalema immediately opens her eyes and rises to her feet. All she can see are trees and meadows. It is quiet and deserted around her, but she believes that Wusen, the mother bear, has absolutely been here.

Dalema got lost in the forest once when she was seven. On the third day, she fell asleep against a large tree root. She was sound asleep and, unquestionably, would have never woken up but for that growling she heard. She saw it, Wusen, the mother bear. Scared, she wet her pants and cried, both hands covering her eyes. The mother bear waved its black palm, turned its gigantic body around and walked away. She looked at it, eyes wide with fear. But it didn't look back, not even once; its broad back gradually vanished into the deep forest. She ran a few steps downhill, miraculously found a small path, took it, and walked back home.

Later, Yesiga's grandfather went hunting and shot Wusen. He returned to the campground, looking sad, and asked for some help to carry it back. By tradition, people in the tribe gathered to eat bear meat. In awe, they cawed and cawed while swallowing the cooked meat, hoping to make the bear spirit believe it was the crow that was violating its sacred body. As for the bear skeleton, it was the hunter's job. It was not done by one hunter, but all hunters. All of them remained quiet. They kept their hands busy, looking solemn. They dare not carelessly leave a single, solitary bone anywhere. While it was still bright, people in the tribe carried Wusen's skeleton into the deep forest and buried it following the tree burial rituals. As long as its spirit finds its bones, just as the river finds the valley and the white clouds find the sky, it won't even think of giving the hunters any trouble.

Dalema refused to eat the bear-meat, as she believed firmly that Wusen had saved her life. She had never forgotten the grandeur of Wusen's burial. When the people in her tribe laid its enormous skeleton on the bier, a downpour suddenly arrived. In a few minutes, the rain stopped, and two beautiful rainbow arcs appeared in the sky. It was a sign of good luck, which is rarely seen. Looking up at the miraculous, celestial arcs, she believed the spirit of Wusen, the mother bear, had followed the rainbows all the way to paradise.

Dalema has kept a secret. She could not marry Yesiga because of Wusen, the mother bear. She married her husband also because of Wusen, the mother bear. The daring bear is the totem of the Duoleba clan, and, of course, she should marry a descendant of the bear.

Holding her breath, Dalema listens, and then walks deeper into the forest. She can't be wrong. It is Wusen, the mother bear, that calls her from afar. Her husband heard a bear calling his name the night before he died. The bear is the ancestor of the Duoleba clan. Since they are the descendants, naturally, they need to go back where they came from and Dalema is no exception.

Once again, Dalema feels that she can barely walk. Her vision is getting blurry; and yet not a single decent tree has come into view. Stronger trees have been felled and transported elsewhere, leaving behind some smaller trees that haven't grown to full size. Dalema staggers on for a short distance, supporting herself along the way, careful not to lean against the smaller trees. They are inexperienced, and their bones are still fragile. There is no way for them to withstand the weight of her old bones.

But she has to lean against a tree, panting heavily. Her days are indeed numbered, she thinks ruefully, but it is not time to collapse yet. She exerts herself to get a firm foothold, and the tree also does its best to support her. A few tender leaves fall off the top of it, softly touch her face, and then land on the ground. The tree is bending, which is not a good sign. She is worried. Bending at such a young age means it won't accomplish anything in its lifetime. With some effort, Dalema straightens up. The young tree also stands upright again, like a tall, handsome teen. She caresses it, unwilling to walk away. She feels a torrent gushing inside the tree and the vibration is forceful enough to make her palm tingle. Now Dalema gets it. It is the earth pulse pounding in its body, pounding in the body of all living beings. She also feels life bouncing over her head; it is an eagle hovering in the blue sky. She smiles, admiringly. In the sky of the Greater Khingan Mountain Range, only steppe eagles are able to soar freely under the sun.

At long last Dalema finds a towering, colossal tree. It seems to have presented itself to her. Dalema walks around it three times. She can barely believe the magic before her very eyes. The tree is old; even those chainsaws have passed it by, leaving it where it is. Perhaps they are intimidated by its grandeur and mysteriousness, or there are other inexplicable reasons. The bark has splits in it but new bark has formed. Thick limbs, like numerous strong arms, stretch skyward. Bright sunrays stream through the leaves and scatter over the grass. Soft breezes caress the land. Speckles of light float elegantly in the forest like enchanting, lingering voices.

Dalema kneels down before the tree and piously kowtows to a dark hollow in the heart of the tree three times. Bear smells are somehow still released from inside the cavity that has been hollowed out over time. Dalema has figured it out. It is Wusen, the mother bear, that calls her over. It has found the final resting place for her. Humbly, she arranges herself, enters the hollow, and, following the spirit's order, sits in an upright position. The space kindly accommodates her, offering just enough room. Dalema feels the sacred ancient tree is holding her tenderly. It feels as if her mother were hugging her childhood self. She slowly closes her eyes, takes a long breath, and at last hears the sound of her suffering heart returning to the earth. The sound carries far but is tranquil; it leads her into another world. She falls asleep. She dreams that she and the ancient tree become one and will never separate.

17

Mokuqin the Cow

Su Hua

In my childhood, our family raised an extraordinary cow. Upon hearing her story, you may feel she is not a cow but a sort of spirit.[1] Actually, the cow did not grow up with us. My grandpa raised her from a calf.

Me, I spent most of my childhood with Grandpa. He was tall, muscular, with a gray, curly beard. He was also hawk-eyed, and one look from him could turn someone into a nervous wreck. Grandpa loved raising cattle. Every animal reared by him was tough, indomitable, and top-notch for all kinds of work.

Grandpa's house and ours sat front-to-back, separated by a willow wattle

---

1. In the source text, the Chinese character "它" is used for all animal characters. The English equivalent of "它" is "it." I have chosen to vary the use of "she" and "it" to reflect the story's plot development and allow better readability. The story has three main animal characters: the animal protagonist Mokuqin, the red heifer that is Mokuqin's mother, and the black baby calf that is Mokuqin's son. I use "she" to refer to the red heifer, and "it" the black baby calf. The reference for Mokuqin is more complex. I use "it" when Mokuqin is a *tuokulie* (what a one-year old calf is called in the Daur spoken language) and a *yiteng* (what a two-year old bovine is called in the Daur spoken language). I use "she" to indicate a clear transition in the plot development when Mokuqin becomes a mother. Of note is that the Daur spoken language does not have words that are equivalent to reference pronounces in the English language; the use of reference pronounces for animals is even considered to be disrespectful for them (Dong Isbister's communication with the author on October 3, 2019). Because the author wrote this story in Chinese, a language without the equivalents available in the Daur, "它" was used to distinguish non-human animals from humans. This usage does not ascribe any gender to a non-human animal. The use of "she" is a hard choice for me to make, given that the translation takes place in a time when gendered pronouns are subject to scrutiny and contestation in discourses of diversity, equity, and inclusivity. Are the pronoun problems in a social context and the ones pertaining to animals the same? Should they be the same? What gets lost when the signifier (the cow) and the signified meanings of animal identity in Chinese, Daur, and English do not match? These are the questions I wrestle with in the process of translating this story. For more discussion around the difficulties of translating animals' identities, see the introduction, "Ecomemories: The Tasks of Translators."

Translated by Xiumei Pu

fence. We grew vegetables in our front yard; they grew theirs in their back-yard. At the east end of the fence was a small gate. Outside the gate, along the east side of the fence, our footsteps had compacted the earth into a hard, smooth trail. Layers of my childhood footprints were left on that trail.

In Grandpa's house I had adorable calves to play with and yogurt, milk skin, and milkfat, for me to enjoy. Every time I visited Grandpa, I wished I had an extra tummy. I ate so much food that I ballooned like a stuffed piglet; the corners of my mouth were white with foam. Grandpa would look at me with a soft and gentle glow in his eyes, lightly knocking at my head with the bowl of his pipe. Words of love slipped between his teeth, "Look at you, you are bulging like a piglet, like a dumpling!" Grandpa's teeth were regular and very strong.

Grandpa was so good to me, but so cruel to cattle. I could hardly bear watching him punish them.

All of Grandpa's cattle were native-bred. European breeds were rare at that time. The majority of Daur people raised cattle to produce milk for their own family. Very few people sold milk on the market. Although native cattle had low yields of milk, the milk that was produced had a stronger taste, unlike foreign cow milk that tasted as bland as water. Grandpa owned a red, quick-tempered, small-boned heifer. Her tail was very beautiful, long, and fluffy at its end, hanging down to the ground. In summer time, the tail made for an elegant flyswatter, swinging like a girl's ponytail, drawing countless curves in the air. But the heifer was difficult to harness and received quite a few beatings from Grandpa for not being cooperative. She often ran wild and willfully, or stopped short.

I still feel unbearable pain when I replay in my head the scene of Grandpa punishing the heifer. It is as if the swish of the whip fell not on her back but on mine.

When Grandpa was about to discipline the heifer, he would bolt the gate of the open-air cattle pen and shut her in there alone. He tied a rope through her nose ring, wrapped the rope around his left hand, held it tight, then he grabbed a whip in his right hand, raised it high, whipped it down hard. The cow would bellow miserably with every lash. She dodged desperately in the pen, but that only infuriated Grandpa. The more the heifer did that, the harder Grandpa whipped her. Dark red blood oozed out from around the nose ring.

I hid at a distance from the scene. The heifer's heart-rending cries terrified me. My heart was thumping, and I wished the punishment could end shortly. Seeing Grandpa had no intention to stop, I would run to the gate of the cattle pen, and with tears welling in my eyes, I would plead: "Grandpa, Grandpa, stop beating her, please? Stop. She is bleeding."

The dark red blood made me nauseous and scared. I was afraid the cow, out of rage, would knock over Grandpa, or Grandpa would unintentionally beat her to death.

Grandpa ignored me, and continued beating the hell out of the heifer. She tried to break free by running around Grandpa. Grandpa was spinning like a top, gnashing his teeth with rage. Crisscrossed welts appeared on the heifer's back and even her hair stood up.

"Down!" Grandpa commanded in a stern voice. The heifer knelt down reluctantly, looking at Grandpa with pleading eyes. "Up!" Grandpa shouted like a thunderbolt. The heifer stood up deftly.

"Down!"

"Up!"

"Down!"

"Up!"

Grandpa repeated his command over and over again. Only when he believed the heifer's spirit completely yielded to his control did he toss the whip away. He untied the rope from the nose ring, wiped away the heifer's nose blood with his big rough palm. The cow timidly licked his hand with the tip of her rough tongue. Grandpa caressed her back, smoothed out her hair, touched her horns, then went to fetch a barrel of soybean water he had already prepared and fed her. But the cow would be beaten up again in less than half a year. She was too stubborn.

This was the mother of Mokuqin, the cow we raised from a calf.

Mokuqin was born at the river bend.

It was early spring. There was still a chill in the air. Snow that had accumulated on the sunny side of the slope started to melt, leaving vertical stripes on the ground; snow on the shady side still maintained a cold, lifeless face.

One afternoon, several girls from my neighborhood and I sat on the warm *kang* playing *hanika*. (Hanika are paper dolls traditionally made by Daur children. The dolls' can be made into men, women and children, and painted with different faces. Typically, hanika dolls can stand up and many Daur girls play house with them.) A cowherd rushed in, panicking. He wore a hemp rope around his waist. His face was weather-beaten, and looked like a net knitted with lines of latitude and longitude. The news was the red cow had gone into labor at the river bend. If not taken care of immediately, the newborn's umbilical cord would be exposed to the cold, and it would cramp and die.

The news put Grandpa's house in a frenzy.

Grandpa and a few folks brought the calf home until after the sunset. Hearing the bustle, I went out to watch. Four men moved a little wet thing from a hay-cart to a piece of gunny sack cloth, and then two of them grabbed the corners of the cloth to carry it inside the house. Grandpa rushed in front of them to open the door, shouting, "put it on the warmer end of the *kang* first, put it on the warmer end of the *kang* first."

In the dark, I was not able to tell the color of the calf. I could only see its legs stretching out as straight as sticks as it gasped for air. Its mother followed behind, making low, sad moos.

The adults stretched its legs, force fed it a few painkillers, and inserted sewing needles into some acupuncture points. They also gave it an injection of amidopyrine. I covered the calf with Grandpa's roe deer robe and worried it would die. I kept asking Grandpa,

"Grandpa, Grandpa, is it going to die?"

"Who knows," Grandpa's face was a gloomy sky. He spat out some curse words and continued, "It was moving when we put it on the cart. It knew to raise its head when the cart jolted along the road, how can it be that…?"

I reached out my hand to touch the calf's mouth. The mouth was wet. The teeth were chattering. The body was barely warm.

"Grandpa, try feeding it with warm milk." I proposed.

"It is in such a bad shape. Is it able to even drink milk?" Grandpa filled his pipe with tobacco, struck a match, and started to smoke. Wisps of blue smoke rose in the room.

"Give it a try." I did not give up but kept at him.

"All right, warm up some milk." Grandpa agreed.

So, someone started a fire and a small dish of steaming milk was served. I rushed to it before everyone else. I reached out my small hands to test its temperature. Grandpa told me that it wouldn't work if the milk was either too hot or too cold. "Ok, just right." I spoke as if I were a grown-up.

The adults forced open the calf's clenched teeth. I used a small spoon to pour milk carefully into its mouth. At first, milk dripped out from the corner of its mouth, slid down its neck, and stained my sleeve. Finally, it managed to gurgle down a mouthful.

"It drank! it drank!" everyone shouted with excitement. "Thank goodness. Now we can hope to have *wali lali*." The more milk it drank, the more I fed it, spoonful after spoonful. (In Daur, *wali* means bovine colostrum. The Daur use bovine colostrum yogurt to braise millets, flavor it with cream and sugar. It tastes very aromatic and sweet.)

The calf was very beautiful. Its body-type was different from its mother's. It had long legs, well-formed bone structure, and thick hooves. Its head is rounded. Its ears stood out like two pieces of tender tobacco leaves. Its tail was not as beautiful as its mother's, but it reached below its hind knees.

Grandpa said the calf was a mix-breed. Its father was a foreign bull. A mix-breed cow can produce about the same amount of milk as a foreign cow, but its milk tastes like that produced by a native cow. Grandpa twirled his curly beard with joy for having bred a mix-breed calf.

The calf's eyes were extraordinarily large. They were blue and translucent. Its coat was smooth, soft, and shiny, like satin. It did not give up easily. The moment it caught its breath, it tried to prop up its hind legs and chest, attempting to stand on the *kang*. But, it was very weak and fell heavily. Still, it tried again and again, refusing to give up. Grandpa had no other choice. He put some hay on the floor and moved the calf to the floor. Like a drunkard, it stood up unsteadily and stumbled. Its front and hind legs forked, like the Chinese character "八." It moved its hooves forward feebly, sniffing every so often.

Grandpa pushed the calf to the cow's teats. The udder was full but the calf did not know how to latch on and suckle. Neither did it know how to use its strength properly to move forward. When Grandpa pushed its butt, it backed up with a bursting energy. Grandpa was sweating, trying really hard to get the calf to suckle. He put his index finger into its mouth. The calf latched on, suckling with gusto—"*patza, patza, patza.*" Grandpa walked in front of the calf. The calf followed. Step by step, Grandpa led it to its mother's udder. My goodness! The calf sure loved the taste of the milk. It wagged its tail jubilantly. It suckled and suckled and suckled. The corners of its mouth were soon dripping with milk foam. The milk was abundant and came out fast. The calf couldn't swallow fast enough, its throat making a gulping sound.

The calf was very clean. It always slept in the same place, the spot where it first bedded down, and it never soiled where it slept.

Most of all, I enjoyed feeding it milk at noon.

The mother cow was allowed to stay at home and rest for a few days after she gave birth. She was then sent to join the herd during day. The new-born calf was too young to eat grass. If we did not feed it milk at noon, it would go hungry and lack the strength to raise its head. For Daur cattlemen, the priority was to save sufficient milk for their calves. The surplus milk was then used to make yogurt, milk skin, and butter.

As soon as the school was over at midday, I went directly to Grandpa's to compete for the opportunity to feed the calf. I made sure the milk was the right temperature for feeding, then I funneled it into an empty bottle, covered the bottle with a rubber nipple, and secured the rubber nipple with threads. If the rubber nipple was not secured, the calf would easily suckle it off. The milk would spill; and the calf would choke.

"Wo-wo-wo," I called to the calf. It was resting on its dry hay bed, with its eyes closed. Hearing my call, it immediately got to its feet, and trotted my way. Its big eyes were filled with excitement. It recognized the milk bottle and latched on to the rubber nipple, blinking its clear blue eyes, moving its hind legs in rhythm, wiggling its little tail joyfully. It just wouldn't let go of the nipple. The moment it drained all the milk from the bottle, it lowered its head to butt me as if it were butting the mother cow to make the milk come faster. The calf was sure strong. The first time it did that, it almost knocked me over.

I had quickly learned about its behavior. When the milk bottle was nearly empty, I gradually backed up toward the kitchen door, and then suddenly pushed the calf away from me. Before the calf knew it, I was already in the kitchen and had closed the door. From the glass door, I saw the calf trotting anxiously. It could not figure out how the milk disappeared all of a sudden. When it saw me grinning on the other side of the glass, it clip-clopped toward me and looked at me intently, with a hungry expression on its face, and traces of milk on its tongue.

Once its umbilical cord dried up, the calf was sent to stay in the backyard of my Grandpa's house. The yard was fully fenced. In one corner were bales of hay for the winter. Frozen cow dung piles were lined up in rows. At first, the calf was very happy. The air was fresher, the space was larger. It ran around and around, bouncing and leaping like an arrow shot from a bow. Sometimes, bouncing and leaping were not enough and it climbed on the hay bales to watch what was going on in the distance. A truck drove into sight. The driver honked the horn. Scared, the calf leaped down from the bales and fell heavily to the ground. "Moo," it got to its feet and started to run again. Later on, it came to realize that it was rather lonesome to spend an entire day in an empty yard all by itself. It mooed and mooed miserably until someone showed up at the gate. Then, it stopped mooing, walked quickly to the person, raised its head, begging for love and consolation. If the person did not walk away, it would bounce enthusiastically, hold up its tail, then stretch it straight out.

It was not quite sunset, but the calf couldn't wait. It would stand at the back window, mooing as if it were begging for attention, "please don't forget me. It is getting dark. Isn't it time for me to get inside the house?"

While still a calf, it did not have its own name. Everyone called it Tuoku-lie. The Daur call any calf of any sex Tuokulie, similar to how they call their kids in gender-neutral names.

One summer evening, Mother came home wearing a red armband, but Father did not have one on his arm. In a fury, he went in their bedroom, grabbed his belongings, and moved them to the small room. Ever since then, Father and Mother had slept in different rooms. Mother sighed in secret. She wanted to talk with Father but their talk soon devolved into an argument, scaring my elder sister and me. Father often drank himself into a stupor. When he was not sober, he would cry, complain, throw and smash things. Our home was shrouded in darkness in those days. Before long, Father was detained on charges of being "the child of rich peasants," and "a descendant of the Kuomintang."

Even elementary schools cancelled classes in order to participate in the Revolution. Because of my father, my elder sister and I were disqualified from becoming Little Red Guards. Sister cried for a whole day. Her eyes were red and swollen. Her hair band came undone, leaving her braids loose and untidy. I cried for a whole day, as well. Not for myself, but for my sister. She wanted to be a little red guard so much. Me, I did not care. I'd rather go fishing in the river.

Grandpa was taken ill but no one knew what his sickness was. He coughed up blood a few times. He went to Yaoquanshan Mountain to drink mineral water for a cure, but he didn't fully recover. Uncle came back home from his job in another city. Even though he cared for Grandpa at the hospital and concocted herbal remedies for him everyday, Grandpa passed away. Grandpa's funeral took place on a very hot day. The funeral procession had ten horse-pulled carriages. Paper money was tossed in the air, and fell like snowflakes to the ground.

Before Grandpa passed away, he divided up his cattle and gave them to Mother and Uncle. Mother received the quick-tempered red cow and her calf Tuokulie. Uncle sold his cattle, and went back to where he worked and lived. But Mother made it clear that Grandpa's cows shouldn't be the end of the line in our family; they should be passed down generation after generation. Herding Tuokulie turned out to be a head-scratching challenge for us. Initially, we let it go with its mother to join the herds of cows. We strapped a porcupine-skin muzzle over its mouth. The spines on the muzzle allowed it to graze but discouraged both mother and calf from suckling. To our surprise, this old method of weaning did not work for Tuokulie. The calf returned home every evening with the muzzle dangling along one side of its face. The mother cow? Her teats hung dry and flat. As if they committed a crime, mother and calf stole a glance at us but pretended nothing had happened. They extended their horns and let us fasten them, with no resistance at all.

Then, I became an unusual cowherd.

In the morning, after breakfast, I put a few *xiaorenshu* (illustrated storybooks) in my pocket, grabbed some steamed buns or similar types of food, joined a couple of friends my age, and herded our calves to the river's bend.

The calves were grazing on the banks. We were catching grasshoppers in the grass. We put them in a fishnet to use as bait for catching hook-snout carp.

Skylarks often shot out of the grass into the clouds like arrows. They flapped their wings, singing their lark songs high up in the air. When you raised your head to look for them, you would only be able to see mere black specks until your neck grew sore. The willows swayed with the breeze, emitting a sweet fresh scent. The river rolled leisurely and tirelessly, carrying aquatic plants and fallen tree twigs along with it. In the distance, the mountain peak was shrouded in mist.

That summer in the sun, I got as dark-skinned as an African child. The horns of Tuokulie grew almost three inches, like two daggers slanting up to the sky.

A cold spell from Siberia swept southward. Before the first snow, Mother had become the "wife of a traitor and a follower of Soviet Revisionism."

Little Sister was only seven months old at that time. Thanks to the clemency of the revolutionaries who condemned Mother during the day, Mother was sent home late at night. Whenever Mother stepped into the door, the first thing she did was to unbutton her shirt to breastfeed Little Sister. Mother's chest was terribly bruised. Her breasts shriveled. Little Sister soon suckled Mother's milk dry. Still, she was searching blindly for milk on Mother's chest, squirming and screaming. Mother was in great pain; she grimaced, frowned, gasped. Later on, we decided to feed Little Sister with cow's milk.

Night after night, Mother sat at the table to write letters of appeal.

I recall that during that period we had no money and were in debt. Mother had resolved to sell the mother cow but kept the forlorn Tuokulie.

Our situation was getting more desperate. We got the news that Father had attempted suicide. Mother was hospitalized for lymphadenitis and the mumps and was not able to eat or drink for over ten days. I stayed at the hospital and took care of Mother, while Elder Sister stayed at home to take care of Little Sister.

No one had time for Tuokulie.

That year, Elder Sister was thirteen years old. I was ten.

Tuokulie became a stray calf. My heart aches when I think about it even today. How did such a tender life survive the bitterly cold winter? Where did it get water? What did it steal to fill its stomach?

Occasionally, Tuokulie came back home. It lay quietly next to the stacks of hay, chewing its cud with its eyes closed. Its coat was long, but it had lost its baby shine. A breeze swept past and rippled its coat. Usually, Tuokulie would disappear the next day. We did not keep hay ready for it, or remember to give it water. Eventually, Tuokulie disappeared completely. Nobody knew where it went, and nobody cared if it was dead or alive.

Early spring in the following year, I saw a stranger leading Tuokulie eastward. At first, I could hardly believe my eyes, but it slowed down. Its blue eyes locked on mine. It recognized me before I did. Its eyes were filled with surprise, joy, and a plea for help. Seeing me dumbfounded, it mooed at me.

Tuokulie, is that you? You are still alive? Why are you so thin? The bones in its shoulders and back bones looked like mountain ridges. Its coat was messy and twisted in little dirty hair balls. It looked like skeleton draped in leather hide. Its butt was bony and pointy as an awl. On its rear thigh was a deep scar where no hair grew. Half of its beautiful tail was lost. The apex of one ear was cut off by god knows who. The horns were the only decent-looking parts on its body. They were one palm-length longer than before, curving inward like a crab's claws. One horn was pointing a little bit to the front, the other pointing in the opposite direction, just like a crab using its pincers to clutch at something.

Excitedly, I dashed toward it and the stranger. My negotiation with the stranger startled Mother. She paid the stranger some money in exchange for an animal that actually belonged to us. Tuokulie had already outgrown its baby look and become a *yiteng* (two-year-old).

It did not show any joy or surprise to be back home. It had become a cautious creature. Whenever anyone came close, it would scrutinize them, studying their eyes for any signs of danger. If it determined there was no threat, it would resume chewing its cud, with total indifference to any touch or caress.

Ever since then, it had a new name Mokuqin that means "suffering" in the Daur language.

Mokuqin became crafty. When no one was looking, it pushed the yard gate wide open and rushed to the haystacks. Eating to its heart's content wasn't enough, it would lay down on a thick layer of hay to get a full night's sleep. Our neighbor's pigs also took the opportunity to sleep in the haystacks, snoring the whole night through. The moment when you appeared at the gate, Mokuqin would get up quickly. Before you got near it, it had already dashed out of the gate like a sneaky cat. If you stood still, it would do as you did from a distance, staring at you vigilantly with its clear blue eyes.

Father was infuriated, swearing to kill it, but Mother absolutely forbid it.

How did Mokuqin open the gate? How did it unfasten the rope tied to its horns? One time, I paid special attention to watch it and find out.

When it was time to tie Mokuqin to the wooden hitching post, it shook its head unwillingly but would allow you to rope its horns and tie it to the post. When it noticed nobody was paying attention, it shook its head, neck, wriggled its horns. Its hind legs, in alternation, kicked the rope. And to my surprise, Mokuqin freed itself from the bondage of the rope with just a few attempts. Then, it snuck out like a thief, checking all the while to see if anyone was looking. Quietly, it inched her way to the gate. It tilted her head and used one horn to lift the iron door latch. Its horn was as deft as a hand. Quickly, it lifted the latch. With the other horn, it pushed open the gate. Now, the road stretched before Mokuqin, free of any obstacles.

Mokuqin used the same tricks to open the lid of the vat and get at the distillers grains, or open the door of the storehouse to steal large frozen scallions or dried vegetables. Occasionally, it broke into our neighbor's yard.

Complaints from neighbors were commonplace.

"Devil," Father ground out between his clenched teeth. We apologized to our neighbor and knowingly called it "Mokuqin."

To correct its pilfering ways, we replaced the locks with hefty ones and put a heavy old iron wok on top of the vat. We tried our best to satisfy its hunger for food: millet congee, salted soybean feed cake, or distillers grain.

I often gave it a good scratch with a wooden stick. It would stand still with great enjoyment, bringing its attention to the itchy spot in perfect corporation with me. It blinked its eyes slowly and chewed its cud with a "gu-lu, gu-lu" sound. The muscles in its neck, moving in rhythm.

I found out that Mokuqin had a fear of twelve- or thirteen-year-old boys. Whenever it saw boys of that age, it tensed up. Its ears stiffened and its eyes widened. Watching out for the boys, it tread softly, and avoided the direction from which they were coming. Even when no longer in the danger zone, it kept walking fast, turning around to keep an eye out for them. Poor Mokuqin! Probably its soul was driven halfway to heaven by those teenage boys, as mischievous as the Monkey King.

The grass at the river bend yellowed and greened three times.

Mokuqin had grown to be a robust and beautiful cow. The slender and strong legs supported the body firmly. Her hooves made smooth and even tracks on the ground. She walked with an air of calmness, pride, and peace, like a queen of the herd. Even bulky bulls humbled themselves when they passed by Mokuqin. If she signaled annoyance with cows or bulls crowding around, one glare and a shake of her lowered head and horns, would drive them away. In that moment, my heart was filled with pride. Mokuqin was pregnant. The baby bump was getting bigger and bigger day by day. Her hide and coat had developed a sheen. She mellowed and walked with great care.

An outsider came to live with our neighbor. It was said he was a rightist removed from his job post and sent back to his ancestral home. He called the head of that household, Elder Brother. He wore a faded coffee-colored cotton army coat with a hemp rope belt tied around his waist; he was splitting firewood in the yard all day. As time went by, he started to drop by our home to chat with my parents.

He was not tall. His broad bean-shaped eyebrows were set far apart from his eyes, making his soybean-like eyeballs appear to be wide-open all the time. His eyes were bright, without a single trace of melancholy. He often told us jokes, or his peach-blossom-luck love stories that always had no end. He stuttered, but it did not hinder his ability to express himself. Every time he came to our home, we would rock with laughter at his jokes and stories. He said he felt uneasy depending on his brother and sister-in-law for support, and he wanted to find something to do. My parents suggested that he become a cowherd. The monthly salary for a cowherd was three *yuan* per head. Herding ten cattle a month, he would earn thirty *yuan*; herding forty or fifty head, he would earn quite a lot of money. Back then, one *jin* of pork cost eight *jiao*, one *jin* of beef six *jiao*. Even better, working as a cowherd required neither a background check on one's political status and conduct nor approval from the personnel department.

So, he became a cowherd.

A few days after he got "back in the saddle," Mokuqin became a mother. She gave birth to a black calf with a shiny coat and hide. Mokuqin could not be torn away from her son for a single moment. She kept licking until the coat became wavy like permed hair. Watching that, I came to a deeper understanding of what it means to be "*tian du zhi qing*," to love shown like a cow licking her calf (parental love).

Whenever we sent Mokuqin to the herd, she would sneak back home. Before she got to the front door, she would moo loudly on the street. Her voice was deep and sharp, like that of a trumpet. One could hear Mokuqin from a great distance.

She seemed to call to her calf, "Son, I'm home."

The little black calf would prick up its ears in excitement, responding in its babe voice, "Mom, I'm here!"

My mother asked the rightest cowherd to watch Mokuqin like a hawk.

Mokuqin was a pain to the rightist cowherd.

Mokuqin took advantage of the rightist cowherd's unfamiliarity with the place, and often eluded him, taking a detour to get back home. If she was closely watched, she would lead him through a labyrinth of side streets and lanes where the rightest cowherd would soon lose his sense of direction.

"Si-sister, your cow is truly really not, not, not easy to lead! Her behavior is re-really bad, such a rebel! I, I can't stand it."

All of us were rolling with laughter.

Soon the rightist cowherd hit a setback, his throne in the cattle kingdom was toppled.

A red-letterhead document was issued, forbidding workers and cadres to raise cattle. Daur families were allowed to raise only one head per household.

Mother argued with local officials. She said that it was a Daur tradition to raise cows and drink cow milk, just as Han Chinese living in the Northeast love their soybean paste and pickled napa. But Mother was alone in her protest; she could not change the policy or turn the situation around. To avoid running against the wind and getting hurt, mother sent a message to her cousin who lives in a mountainous area over a hundred *li* away from us, asking him to come over to take the cattle and take care of them for us temporarily.

One day in July, my uncle tied Mokuqin to the back of his wooden wagon and let the calf run behind them. With the soughing sound of cart wheels rolling on the dirt road, they left Nierji.

Mother resumed writing letters of appeal.

The rightest cowherd resumed his job of splitting firewood.

In winter, Uncle came to Nierji to shop for the holidays. I couldn't wait to ask him how Mokuqin was doing. Uncle mumbled, "Don't mention it. I have never seen any animal like that. You remember that time when I came here to take her home? She just lay down on the road halfway, and refused to get up. She lay there like a stone no matter how hard I whipped her. No shame. I eventually realized she behaved like that for the sake of her baby calf. Only after I put the calf on the wagon did she get up and walk. You see, she...."

How I missed Mokuqin! How smart she was! I longed to throw a few bundles of dry hay to her, watching her swallow them; I longed to scratch her hide with a small wooden stick, and watch her chew the cud peacefully; I longed to fetch her a bucket of soybean feed cake, and hear her throat making a glug-glug sound. I imagined her hooves clip-clopping toward me like when she was a calf.... Was her calf a *yiteng* now?

I wanted so badly to go to Uncle's village with him, to see with my own eyes how my Mokuqin was doing. But Mother said no. I insisted. She gave me a box on the ears and said, "Tossing on a wood wagon for over a hundred *li* just to see a cow. You're talking nonsense, aren't you?"

Before we even knew it, spring came. One evening, I squatted down in front of the stove with a book, feeding the stove for cooking while I read. Suddenly, I heard a low moo sounding like Mokuqin. My heart missed a beat, then I thought that couldn't be Mokuqin. That might be a cow passing by the street. Another moo, deep, high like a trumpet, very close to me. The head of Mokuqin appeared at the kitchen window, her eyes looking into mine.

"Oooh, the cow is back!" I dashed out. Everyone followed.

Mokuqin's eyes were bloodshot. Standing against her body was her exhausted son. Uncle was nowhere to be seen.

I quickly realized that the cow came back on her own. She got homesick when spring came.

This fine spirit, how come she was not lost? Did she encounter any wolves on her way home? I wrapped my arms tightly around her neck and put my face on it, ignoring the dust there. "You miss home, don't you? I miss you, too!"

As if she understood what I said, she made a deep sound from her throat, licking my hand extended to her mouth. Her tongue was rough. Every lick stung my hand, but I let Mokuqin do that and liked it.

The next day, Mokuqin was anxious. It was still too early to send her to the herds, but she mooed incessantly to urge us to get on the road. I had no choice. We left earlier than we should have. She walked very fast, cutting three steps down to two, without even waiting for her son, went straight to the river bend where the cow herds used to gather. I actually did not know the gathering place of the cow herds. To satisfy her will, I followed Mokuqin. I would follow her and protect her wherever she wanted to go. When she was still some distance from the river bend, she raised her neck and called to show an animal's attachment to her home. Her sincere, full, and open feelings moved me so, my nose stuffed up, the corner of my eyes became wet with tears.

She stopped when she reached her home. She took a good look at the opposite bank of the river bend, glanced around, her blue eyes were filled with great satisfaction. When she realized herself and her son were the only living beings at the empty river bend, she panicked. She mooed loudly in every direction. Her voice got louder and longer with each moo, as if she were calling her pals "Where are you? Why is no one here?" Her voice vibrated at the river bend, spreading out through the willow tops, across the river, across to other bank, across the sky, fading out in the icy distance.

Mokuqin did not die of old age, nor was she sold. She died because a nail got into her stomach.... I don't want to talk about it anymore. I just hope that everyone should be careful when they feed cows, I hope even more that their cows are able to live a normal cow life, not like Mokuqin who had to go through such turmoil.

I always regretted that I was too young at the time to know the significance of documenting such an epic story, otherwise, I would have taken lots of photos of Mokuqin. Now, I can only write about her with my clumsy pen to commemorate her.... May her spirit in the other world know that I, her little cowherd from long ago, still miss her....

18

Shujuan the Black Bear

YE GUANGCEN

1.

Shujuan was a black bear—a female. Twenty years ago, she had been picked up deep in the mountains by the members of a geological exploration team.[1] At that time, although not yet one month old, she had been abandoned by her mother, for some unknown reason, among the scattered rocks of a small stream. Terrified and helpless, she was mistaken for a peasant's black cat by the team's cook, Old Sun, who took her back to his tent and tied her up near a sack of flour in hopes that she might keep the mice away. At dusk, people came over to play with the "black cat." As soon as the "black cat" bared her teeth, however, everyone realized she was no cat, but rather a bear. Appearing quite sick, she weakly curled up into a ball, unable to raise her head. Later, once Old Sun had fed her some porridge, she regained her vitality and capered about adorably. So, it became clear: the bear hadn't been able to raise her head because she had been hungry, not sick.

Within half a month, the little cub already weighed more than ten *jin*.[2]

---

1. A central theme of this novella is the humanity/animality of its eponymous "character," the black bear Shujuan. Given the bear's gender and female name, this translation opts, following common English usage, to refer to Shujuan with the female third person pronoun "she." In the original, however, following Chinese convention, which very rarely uses male/female pronouns to refer to animals, Ye Guangcen deploys the neuter third person pronoun throughout her text. Note: the simplified system of Modern Standard Chinese writing distinguishes three forms of the third person singular pronoun, corresponding to the English words "he," "she," and "it." In the spoken language, however, the three different characters for these words are all pronounced the same. Scholars date the graphic distinction of gender in the pronoun system of Modern Standard Chinese to the early twentieth century and credit it to Western influence.

2. *Jin*: a Chinese measure of weight. One *jin* is roughly equal to 1.1 lbs.

===

Translated by Daniel M. Youd

===

No longer was it so easy for people to gather her up in their arms like a small child. The soft downy fur on her body had also started to coarsen and become prickly. As her appetite grew, so too she became more unruly. In addition to taunting local villagers' dogs, she also developed an interest in the rather pathetic little corn cobs that these same villagers grew in the mountains, so much so that she was known to steal them from time to time. In such instances, it was invariably Old Sun who had to pay compensation. It served him right! That's what everyone thought, including the team leader: Old Sun had no one to blame but himself for not keeping close enough watch over the bear.

As for the bear, she appeared grateful to the members of the geological exploration team. She was friendly towards them. In fact, she would let anyone in a team work uniform pat and play with her, even allowing people to lift up her hind legs so that she could do handstands. If you were a shabbily dressed peasant, though, you couldn't get within thirty or forty yards before she would begin to growl, rear up, and look as if she were about to attack. Once, one of the peasants put on Old Sun's clothes. As he approached the bear, she still threatened to attack. Through this experiment, it became apparent that what mattered to the animal was not the clothes that a person was wearing but, rather, that person's scent. If you smelled of smoke and firewood—as the mountain peasants did—you were an enemy. This fact, according to Old Sun's reckoning, must have been related to the cub's earliest experiences; like humans, bears remember. Looking at the cub as she waved her front paws and bellowed in anger at the peasant, Old Sun said, "Once full grown, she'll be quite a fearsome creature!"

Putting no stock in what Old Sun said, the others decided in jest to give her a delicate, feminine name. They settled on Shujuan, which, not coincidently, was the name of their team leader's wife.[3] Shujuan—that is to say, the team leader's wife—was much admired by the other male geologists for her kindness and beauty. To them—especially those who had yet to overcome the difficulty of finding a life partner—she was the model of an ideal spouse. It was thus no small consolation to this group of lonely bachelors to have the little bear in their midst. When they were bored, they could play with her. When it was time to eat, they could just eat; there was no need to observe the niceties required of men in the company of women. They even let her burrow under their quilts. A night of dream-filled slumber with "Shujuan's" warm body in one's arms was almost the same as sharing a bed with the real Shujuan, only "Shujuan" breathed a bit more heavily and snored a bit more loudly.

In the autumn, when the exploration team moved back to the city from

---

3. Taken separately and together, the two Chinese characters of this name conjure ideal feminine qualities. *Shu* means gentle and virtuous; *juan* indicates grace and beauty.

the mountains, neither Shujuan nor the team members could bear to part, so interdependent had they all become. The team members, therefore, allowed Shujuan to return with them. Thus, she changed her residency status from "rural" to "urban" and began eating commercial grade grain (as it was most convenient to come by).[4] She didn't, however, have to pay any of the sundry fees and surcharges—such as the Urban Maintenance and Construction Tax—that were required of other city dwellers.

It was at this time—on the day when the entire field unit of the geological exploration team delivered the bear to the zoo as if they were seeing off a younger sister on her wedding day—that the zookeeper Lin Yao first encountered Shujuan. She entered the zoo riding on Old Sun's shoulders, looking first left and then right, with the air of a triumphant hero. Had her mouth not been stuffed full of roasted sweet potato, she most certainly would have roared with excitement. At the same time that the geological exploration team handed Shujuan over to the custody of the bear house, they also made a present to the zoo of some leftover tinned meat, sausage, and white flour. Lin Yao not only thought these gifts unnecessary, but he also considered refusing them outright. The geological exploration team had spoiled Shujuan, he knew. Now, given the decline in her standard of living that would follow upon her loss of freedom and conversion to the standard zoo diet, she was faced with a period of great mental suffering. If she were human, she would be able to understand, adjust, and exercise some self-control. Could a bear do that? Lin Yao was acutely aware that the geological exploration team members, despite their great self-satisfaction, had handled everything with shocking—one might even say the most unconscionable—stupidity.

As soon as the bear cub was locked in its cage, everyone on both sides of the enclosure reacted with predictable outrage. Unused to such a small, restricted space, Shujuan threw her body, repeatedly and with ferocious force, against its walls. Afterwards, she turned to gnawing and pawing at the bars, causing blood to flow in small rivulets from around her teeth and the corners of her mouth. A fleshy lump that grew on her left front paw also began to bleed. Shujuan's human "family" was indignant. Why, they demanded of Lin Yao, did he have to put such a cute thing in a cage and take away her freedom? They explained to him that, when they were at their mountain camp, they had treated her just like a little dog; they hadn't even had to chain her up. She was used to life with people. Why not let her roam freely around the grassy areas of the zoo? She wasn't that different from a little child, after all. That would certainly be an innovative attraction! Lin Yao had to explain to

---

4. All Chinese citizens have an official residency status—the so-called *hukou* system (household registration)—that determines where they may live. Certain residency statuses—e.g., urban, as opposed to rural—are considered more desirable than others.

them, in that case, the zoo would go out of business; people would be afraid to come.

*   *   *

All of these events happened twenty years ago. Lin Yao had just returned to the city after having spent time working in the countryside.[5] He had a new bride, Lu Xiaoyu, who had worked in the same rural production unit as himself. Later she would go abroad to study in Japan, but, at that time, she was just an ordinary factory worker. She—like the newly caged Shujuan—was about to start a whole new life.

Now, twenty years later, Shujuan was already old. Lying motionless in a corner of her enclosure, she had had nothing to eat or drink for four days. She wasn't hibernating; she was sick. Having lived for such a long time under human care, she had lost the instinct to hibernate; her various offspring never had it, either. Since the day Lin Yao first put her in that cage, the members of the geological exploration team, her saviors, had never come to visit her. Maybe they simply forgot about her. Maybe, when they returned to their exploration in the field, they never again encountered a cat-like bear. Or, maybe they did and just never wanted to think about sending it to meet its fate in such a cruel, "animalistic" cage.

On his bicycle ride home from work, all Lin Yao could think of was the black bear Shujuan. Although over forty years old, he still had the vigor of a much younger man, a fact that was especially evident at Shujuan's feeding time. Then, dressed in his work uniform—a cream-colored jacket—he would lead Shujuan in a performance that was just as good as any you might see at the circus. Shujuan really knew how to please the crowd: she'd stand up straight to eat; then, moving in a circle, she'd give a military salute to the men and women at the railing around her enclosure, the fleshy lump on her outstretched front paw glistening in the sun as if she held a black pebble in it. With ample rump and thick waist, how much she resembled a middle-aged peasant woman, a mother of many sons! The crowd would erupt into peals of laughter as they watched her waddle clumsily around on her stocky hind legs.

---

5. The events described in this and certain other parts of the story refer to the Cultural Revolution (1966–1976) and its immediate aftermath. Initiated by Chairman Mao Zedong (1893–1976) as a means of wresting control of the Communist Party from the perceived corrupting influences of party bureaucrats and elites, the Cultural Revolution was a period of great political and social disruption, during which large numbers of urban youth were "sent down to the countryside" for reeducation. This resettlement movement reached its peak in the late 1960s when schools across China were closed and young people were encouraged to learn from "poor and lower-middle peasants." At the conclusion of the Cultural Revolution in the mid to late 1970s, many of these so-called educated youths returned to the cities in large numbers.

The problem now was that Shujuan had had nothing to eat or drink for four days. Her gums were a bloodless color, indicating severe anemia. That afternoon Lin Yao had sought out the director of the zoo to let him know of Shujuan's condition. The director had referred the problem to the head of the department of animal husbandry, who said to Lin Yao, "This is just the way things are when an old bear reaches the end of its life. Who's to say you or I will be any better off than she when we reach that point?"

"But you can't just throw your hands up in the air," responded Lin Yao. "When she was healthy, Shujuan was a great asset to the zoo. It would be unconscionable if we did nothing to help her now!"

The department head said, "The zoo's finances are strained. We have a hard-enough time just keeping up with the cost of providing the animals with water every day. Income from ticket sales is extremely limited. Everyone is busy nowadays. Who has time to spend a day at the zoo? If you really want to do the best for Shujuan, you can get her put down as painlessly as possible. But, keep a good eye on her. It will be a blessing enough to keep the bear traffickers from dismembering her and cutting off her paws."

*   *   *

When Lin Yao smelled the delicate scent of the wintersweet blossoms, he realized he was home.

The wintersweet that filled the courtyard of the Lu family home had all been planted there by Lin Yao's father-in-law, Lu Junqing. The ubiquitous yellow of the flowers—pure and austere—in a courtyard of such size couldn't help but cause one to shudder with the realization that it looked rather like a cemetery. The Lu family home, a solid edifice with a large front gate, maintained its dignified air, despite the fact that its bricks were now broken and worn and its paint was peeling. The roof tiles, from which sprouted grass that swayed in the breeze, and the rounded corners of the old stone steps all clearly bore the impress of time's passage. Nevertheless, whether from the seamlessly laid bricks of both the front portico and the rear hall, or from the exquisitely carved stone drums that stood on either side of the entryway, one could still detect hints of the family's former glory. The people in the neighborhood referred to it as the "Lu family mansion."

During the Cultural Revolution, the mansion had been occupied by some organization of the city's revolutionary committee.[6] Afterwards, however, with the implementation of the new policies, it was returned to its orig-

---

6. For the Cultural Revolution, see note 5. During the Cultural Revolution, the first revolutionary committee was established in Shanghai in 1967 in emulation of the Paris Commune of 1871. Soon afterwards, revolutionary committees became common throughout the rest of China.

inal owners.[7] In this way, unlike many other similar large mansions, which were occupied by ordinary citizens, its interior sustained relatively little damage, retaining, more or less, its original appearance. There were no small kitchens here and there; nor had there appeared temporary emergency shelters in the courtyard. Instead, the new drainage system and plumbing—including a flush toilet—were a welcome addition. One might even say that, through this marriage of old-world charm with modern convenience, the Lu family mansion had been somewhat improved.

The mansion consisted of three courtyards and a rear flower garden, all of which were linked together by covered walkways. To the east and west of the main living quarters, round moon doors allowed passage from one courtyard to the next. The courtyards themselves were covered with square bricks, while the winding garden paths—designed with such care—were paved with stones. In the northeast corner of the rear garden, hidden amongst the wintersweet bushes, was a three-bay belvedere. It was the quietest and most secluded spot in the mansion. Back in the day, it was where grandfather Lu, a senator in the early Republican period,[8] had held court, attending to his various responsibilities, such as hearing the petitions of local people, advising the government on legal and other matters, composing inquires to the various ministers of state, and so on. The belvedere served him as a sort of praetorium, from which he pulled the levers of power. It was then that the Lu family was at the height of its glory, when visitors thronged the gates of the mansion, and when confidants of the patriarch and close friends with important matters to discuss were ushered to the rear garden for consultations. Despite its seclusion, then, the belvedere was actually the center of action.

Currently, the belvedere was where Lin Yao lived with Lu Xiaoyu, his wife. It had been their home for twenty years. At first, Lin Yao had found it hard to get used to living in three rooms separated only by lattice partitions. Once you stepped inside, a single glance was all that was required to take it all in. Even the double bed, which by rights ought to be in a more private location, was there for all to see, pushed up against the western wall. The overall effect, he felt, was like living in the set of a stage play. He suggested to his father-in-law that the partitions might be taken down and replaced with wooden walls. But, his father-in-law refused, saying the belvedere must remain a belvedere; it wasn't something that could be changed just because people were living there now; were the finely carved hardwood partitions

---

7. Beginning in 1978, the government of China, in a reversal of past practices, promulgated new policies conducive to political reform and economic development. These policies are regularly credited with spurring China's incredible economic growth during the final decades of the twentieth century. During this same period, many people previously accused of political crimes had their convictions overturned and their reputations rehabilitated.

8. The Republic of China existed on mainland China from 1912 to 1949.

removed, the entire structure would lose its aesthetic value; what's more, a garden without a belvedere could hardly be called a garden! Of course, if Lin Yao couldn't accustom himself to living in the belvedere, he could move to rooms in the eastern wing of the front courtyard. They were, in any event, empty. If he relocated there, in fact, he might find it more convenient to come and go as he pleased.

After giving the matter some consideration, however, Lin Yao decided not to move. First, the belvedere was peaceful and quiet. Second, if he did move to the rooms in the eastern wing, he risked being referred to by others as a "carefree son-in-law," as in the old story of Wang Xizhi.[9] But, as he well knew, from the perspective of the Lu family, he was more a member of the hired help than a "carefree son-in-law."

Under the moonlight and through the shadows created by the canopy of trees above, Lin Yao pushed his bicycle towards the back of the mansion. Walking first through each of the three courtyards and next through the eastern moon gate, he then passed by the flowering bushes before finally reaching his rooms. He knew the way well; were it anyone else, he thought, they would certainly get lost in the vastness of the place. Ever since the government had returned the mansion to the family, large parts of it had remained unoccupied. His father-in-law, Lu Junqing, and his wife, Lin Yao's mother-in-law, lived in rooms off the first courtyard. The next courtyard was home to Lu Junqing's widowed sister-in-law, a woman everyone referred to as the Second Lady. The third courtyard, now empty, belonged to Lu Xiaolei, Lu Junqing's son, who had moved to American three years ago. At this same time, the municipal government, under pressure from the city's residents, was exhausting all possible means just to increase, on a yearly basis, average living space allotments by a fraction of a square meter per person. In the Lu family mansion, however, there was more than room to spare. The slightest sound echoed throughout the empty spaces, and grass had begun to overgrow the courtyards, despite the fact that Lin Yao's father-in-law devoted an inordinate amount of his time to upkeep. Simply put, there was a limit to what one man could do: as soon as he had cleared the weeds from the eastern courtyard, he discovered that they had taken hold with abandon in the western one. The wintersweet bushes required pruning; the vines on their trellises, watering; fallen leaves, sweeping; and drainage pipes, cleaning….

---

9. Wang Xizhi (303–361) was a famous calligrapher. In the anecdote referred to here, a powerful official, a man named Xi Jian, desired to make a match for his daughter. He was told that the young men of the Wang family were all good looking. The minister, therefore, sent a servant to the Wang household to make an appropriate selection. When the servant arrived, he was taken to a room on the eastern side of the family home to meet the potential bridegrooms. All except Wang Xizhi were anxious to make a good impression. As for Wang Xizhi, he lay on a bed, stomach exposed, reading a book. Xi Jian chose Wang Xizhi as his son-in-law on account of his carefree spirit.

And still the mansion looked deserted. The feeling it conveyed of being cut off from the outside world was enhanced in no small measure because its great front doors remained permanently closed. Believing the building to be an as-yet unopened historic site, tourists would often loiter about outside, compelled by curiosity to peer through the crack where the doors met. Location scouts for a television series that was to be based on Pu Songling's *Tales of the Strange*, a seventeenth-century collection of ghost stories,[10] even sought to rent the mansion for their shoot. Lu Junqing, however, refused the request, saying the mansion was desolate enough without dragging in a bunch of ghosts to add further to the sense of disorder. The producers were quite disappointed; it wasn't every day that one found such an ideal location. Having been refused by the Lu family, they had no option but to shoot their show on a studio set, all the while regretting their missed opportunity.

As Lin Yao passed by the wintersweet bushes, he saw the glow of a light coming from his rooms, causing a tingle in his scalp. He thought of one of Pu Songling's stories, in which a female ghost removes her head to comb her hair. Then, he recalled the fox spirits, such as those described in the ghost stories by Ji Xiaolan—strange creatures that, through the practice of magical and alchemical arts, may live for more than four hundred years.[11] He shuddered. The belvedere was all there was in the rear garden. If something untoward should happen, who would answer his cry for help? Maybe he could rouse two or three useless old fogeys, but that would be it. Resolving to get to the bottom of things on his own, he concealed himself in the shadow of the bushes. Pushing aside some branches, he peered into his room, where he saw his father-in-law spreading an electric blanket out onto his bed. Filled with emotion, he burst into the room. "Dad!" he said.

Straightening his body, Lu Junqing replied, "You ought to have a fire in here. The garden's too damp. There used to be a pond behind the belvedere. The water has long since dried up, but it's still very dank. I don't want you getting sick from it."

"I only use the room to sleep in. With Xiaoyu gone, there's really no reason to have a fire," replied Lin Yao.

Lu Junqing said, "I knew that's what you'd say, so I brought you this electric blanket." Then Lu Junqing asked Lin Yao about the bear. He said she was still not doing well. "How about you feeding her some honey mixed with rice flour."

---

10. Pu Songling (1640–1715) was a famous Qing dynasty author. His *Tales of the Strange* (*Liaozhai zhi yi*) is the most famous collections of ghost stories in the Chinese language.

11. Ji Xiaolan (1724–1805), also known as Ji Yun, was a famous Qing dynasty scholar and writer of anecdotes. Influenced by, although also critical of, Pu Songling (see note 9), he wrote a collection of ghost stories entitled *Notes from the Thatched Abode of Close Observations* (*Yuewei caotang biji*, 1789–1798).

"Where am I going to get the flour now?" Lin Yao replied.

"You can grind up some rice and make it yourself. The Second Lady taught me how to make it just today. She told me to show you," said Lu Junqing.

Lin Yao said, "The Second Lady knows everything there is to know about cooking, doesn't she? She's an expert not only on what people eat but also on what animals like."

"When grandfather was alive," Lu Junqing said, "the Lu family had dinner guests every day, but there was no chef. Rather, it was tradition for the women of the family to do all of the cooking themselves. Naturally, what they cooked was quite special, unlike anything you could get at any restaurant. Among the women, the Second Lady was the best. She's slowed down quite a bit in the past couple of years and doesn't cook much anymore, but she was quite an accomplished woman in her prime."

Lin Yao said, "I know that her duck with bamboo shoots is a legend in the family; but since I married Xiaoyu, I've only had it three times."

Lu Junqing said, "I'm afraid that the recipe for this dish won't be passed down to the next generation. Xiaoyu doesn't have an interest in learning how to make it, nor, by any means, does her brother. So, in the end...." As he spoke, he walked outside. Then, turning around, he added, "Make sure to cover yourself well when you sleep tonight."

Just then the phone rang. It was Xiaoyu calling from Japan. She told Lin Yao that there was a typhoon raging in Tokyo. Lin Yao asked her what a typhoon was like. She said it was just a lot of wind and rain....

Lu Junqing shook his head. "She called all that way just to say it was windy and rainy. Well, that goes to show how easy it is to make a call nowadays. It's got to be more than a thousand miles from here to Tokyo, and she called just to say it's windy and rainy...."

2.

Everyone was concerned about money.

The financial situation of the zoo was not unlike that of so many other mid- to large-sized state enterprises: because they relied on money from the government, they were short of funds. In order to prevent the zoo from getting sucked under in the whirlpool of economic competition, the zoo leaders were constantly worrying about how to find new sources of revenue and diversify operations. Regardless of the difficulties of the situation, however, their thousand or more animals were as hungry as ever.

It was as if the zoo were trapped in a vicious cycle: whatever they did, their debt only increased. The head keeper in charge of large animals was the first to report a crisis. The per-diem expense of feeding their adolescent female tiger—

who daily consumed eight kilograms of grade-A beef, five hundred grams of milk, forty vitamin C tablets, twenty vitamin E tablets, six raw chicken eggs, and a chicken—was more than one hundred *yuan*; and, still, she was losing weight. Tigers were a nationally designated class-one protected species, and, as such, their preservation was one of the nation's paramount priorities. More to the point, however, if a city's zoo didn't have a tiger to keep up appearances, it could hardly be considered a zoo at all. They held a meeting at which it was decided to tighten the belt in other areas in order to protect priorities.

Of course, nothing could shake the aristocratic stature of the pandas. You might say they were the first to get rich under the new system! Every three days they received a new delivery of fresh bamboo shoots from the mountains, and there always seemed to be supplemental funds for their up-keep available through national foundations. Foreigners also took a special interest in them; whenever they visited, the pandas would be called out to greet them. In recent years, preferential treatment had caused the natural disposition of the pandas to change; while, outwardly, they seemed like simple creatures, inwardly they had become capable of ever more clever manipulation. Thus, whenever there appeared blonde-haired, blue-eyed visitors, they became antic, engaging in all sorts of silly behavior just to provoke a smile. Of course, the foreigners reached for their wallets. Whatever donations they gave, a portion of the money went to the pandas. With these funds, their habitat could be refurbished and cleaned, so that next time—with even more donations—they could ascend even higher up the ladder of the zoo hierarchy.

Alas, poor Shujuan, the black bear! She was only a nationally designated class-two protected species. In fact, in the mountains, black bears weren't that rare at all. What's more, they were often the victims of poachers. China Central Television once did an exposé on the criminals who poached Manchurian tigers, but no one said a word about those who killed black bears for their gallbladders.[12] If it hadn't been for the interference of the exploration team, Shujuan would have remained free and wild in the mountains.... There it might have been her fate to be killed and dismembered. Instead, she found herself in completely different circumstances.

Thinking of these things made Lin Yao angry at Old Sun, on whose shoulders Shujuan had ridden into the zoo without a care in the world. Lin Yao wondered: How would Old Sun feel if he could see Shujuan now? Today, since the start of Lin Yao's shift, Shujuan had lain in the corner of the habitat next to a wall, her neck bent, her paws tucked against her body, just as she had

---

12. According to certain practitioners of traditional Chinese medicine, the bile extracted from the gallbladders of bears is reputed to have medicinal properties. Medicines containing this bile are used to cure a number of ailments ranging from gallstones, to muscle aches, to the effects of the overconsumption of alcohol. In recent years, the Chinese government has placed various legal restrictions on the harvesting of bear gallbladder bile.

been all those years ago when she was first tied up next to that sack of flour by the members of the geological exploration team. Lin Yao opened a little door that allowed the winter sun to shine a ray of dusty light in the shape of a small circle onto Shujuan's unkempt fur. Looking out the door, Lin Yao saw a couple leaning against the railing just beyond the little mountain in the bear habitat. They were certainly more interested in each other than seeing any bear. Lin Yao hoped that Shujuan would take advantage of this rare moment of quiet to go out and lie in the sun and perhaps move around some. At this point, her body was thoroughly infested with mites and fleas. Had she been healthy, they could have hosed her down with disinfectant. But that wasn't an option now. Shujuan had become so weak she seemed even more fragile than a sixteen-year-old maiden.

Li Yu used a basin to bring Shujuan her lunch—several steamed bran buns mixed with greens. Lin Yao said, "Aren't those the same buns that she didn't eat yesterday? Why are you trying to feed them to her again today?"

Li Yu replied, "That's what they gave me. What can I do? The higher-ups said that all the money allocated to us by the national government, as well as what we make from daily admissions, must be directed to top priorities. Shujuan is an omnivore. Her meals are prepared together with those of the monkeys. They don't eat meat, so neither does she."

"Bullshit!" said Lin Yao. "Monkeys and bears are two different species. By feeding them the same food, we're sure to make Shujuan anemic, if she isn't already."

"Well, be that as it may, that's what they gave me. She'll have to take it or leave it," replied Li Yu.

Lin Yao took the basin to his department head's office and threw the buns onto the table where he sat, filling out a form. "You don't mean to say that a zoo of our size can't even care for a single black bear?"

The department head said, "You mean that old bear? Granny bear? The one that's only got a few days left to live?"

Lin Yao said, "She's not old. She still has life in her, if only we fed her properly."

The department head said, "Give it a rest! Why do you have to get so worked up about an old bear? If she were still in the mountains, she wouldn't be able to eat any buns at all. As it is, she's enjoying the communist lifestyle!"

Lin Yao argued that Shujuan ought to receive different food from the monkeys.

The department head said, "It's not going to happen. Our expenses can't all go to feed the bear, can they? What about the giraffe? The orangutan? And the Malaysian Elephant? They're all gifts from foreigners. What if, by chance, they send someone to check up on them? We can't allow them all to look like hungry wolves."

"Shujuan is the only one who's a native, then," said Lin Yao.

The department head said, "Of course, under certain circumstances the natives have to get sacrificed."

Lin Yao left the office fuming. Off in the distance he could see Chen Hongqi feeding his monkeys on the monkey mountain. The lackadaisical Chen and his lackadaisical Guangxi monkeys seemed well matched. Chen Hongqi got along quite well with Lin Yao. When he had nothing better to do, he'd often stop by bear mountain for a visit and maybe a game of Chinese chess. Then, just as he was leaving, he would snatch a few buns to give to his monkeys. The buns were of little use to Shujuan, but, for the monkeys, they made quite a nice midnight snack.

Lin Yao didn't want to return to the bear house. He didn't want to see Shujuan continue to suffer. Instead, thinking of the Second Lady and his father-in-law's idea, he left the zoo and went to the store to buy some rice flour. Of course, when he got there, there was none. Children nowadays had become spoiled; they didn't eat that stuff anymore. Feeling anxious, Lin Yao approached the front counter, behind which, keeping the store, stood a matronly woman. Looking at Lin Yao, she said, "So your child's getting bigger. Needs to try something new, right?" Lin Yao nodded perfunctorily, although he had no experience whatsoever raising a child. His wife, Lu Xiaoyu, because she had wanted to go abroad, had refused to have any.

The shopkeeper took out a bag of Star Brand nutritional powder. "Try this," she said. "It's made of rice and egg. It's more nutritious than rice flour."

Looking at the price, Lin Yao said, "It's too expensive."

"What kind of father considers cost when it comes to what his child eats?" replied the shopkeeper. "A package of imported infant formula costs more than one hundred *yuan*. This is only eight. You call that expensive?"

Lin Yao was too embarrassed now to make her take it back. What could he say but "I'll take it."

Putting the nutritional powder into a plastic bag, the shopkeeper was preparing to take Lin Yao's money, when he added, "I want ten bags."

"What!" The shopkeeper stared at him with opened eyes.

"Ten bags," Lin Yao slowly repeated himself, using hand gestures to confirm the number.

The shopkeeper said, "You must be a new father. That's no way to buy food for a child. Buy one bag first and see if he or she likes it. Then you can buy more."

"My kid's got a big appetite. Four or five packages should be about right for one sitting," was his retort.

"A boy or a girl?" asked the shopkeeper.

"A girl," said Lin Yao.

"No girl can eat that much!" the shopkeeper replied. "You must want to do some sort of experiment with it. But, honestly, the more you buy, the happier I am, even if you're going to turn this all into paste to post big character posters!"[13]

Lin Yao picked up his ten bags of nutritional powder, went to another counter and bought a bottle of honey, and then, under the puzzled gaze of the shopkeeper, left the store.

When Lin Yao tried to feed the nutritional powder to Shujuan, it was the first time in several days that she opened her eyes and lifted up her head. Perhaps it was the smell of the honey, redolent of her mountain home, that enticed her to eat. In any event, with much effort, Shujuan lapped at the porridge in her basin, before finally, once her strength gave out, resting her head back down in exhaustion on the icy-cold cement floor and closing her eyes. At least she's eaten something, Lin Yao thought to himself. The nutritional powder and honey have some calories. This food will last for about a week. Maybe that will be long enough to save her life.

At the end of his shift, Lin Yao passed by the monkey mountain, where he saw Chen Hongqi throwing tangerines into the monkeys' cage. Prompted by Chen Hongqi's greeting, Lin Yao realized it had been a number of days since his friend had stopped by the bear house, so he said, "Why haven't you come by to steal any buns lately?"

Chen Hongqi laughed and said, "Our standard of living over here has jumped ahead of yours." As he spoke, he took a few of the bigger tangerines from his basket and gave them to Lin Yao.

Looking into the basket, Lin Yao saw that, expect for a few damaged ones, none of the tangerines were terribly rotten. In fact, they were good enough for people, let alone monkeys. He peeled one and put it in his mouth. "Is it some kind of monkey holiday?"

"A holiday, my ass!" Chen Hongqi said. "The monkeys have new masters."

"They've been sold?"

"No, they've been adopted," said Chen Hongqi, gesturing with his chin towards the monkey cage.

That's when Lin Yao saw it, a shiny brass plate, under the monkey cage sign, that read:

ADOPTED BY THE YOUBANG TRADE CO.

"I've never seen anything like that before," said Lin Yao. "They're not children. How can they be adopted? Certainly, the company won't take them away, right?"

Chen Hongqi said, "There's no need for that. Two or three of these creatures would be enough to turn their offices upside down."

---

13. Big character posters were a common feature of life during the Cultural Revolution. Mounted in public places and written in bold handwriting, they contained political slogans and, just as often, denunciations of individuals who were deemed enemies of the revolution.

Lin Yao asked, "So how have they been adopted?"

"They give us money," said Chen Hongqi. "And we hang up a sign for them."

"Why did the Youbang Company want to adopt monkeys?" asked Lin Yao.

Chen Hongqi said, "I hear that the company made its money exporting tree bark and tree leaves. On account of all those trees, the general manager is said to have felt bad for the monkeys. On top of that, his mother was born in the year of the monkey. So, that's why they adopted them."

Lin Yao wondered, "Why wasn't the general manager's mother born in the year of the black bear? In that case, my Shujuan would have a reliable source of funds."

"Well, it's one solution," said Chen Hongqi. "Nowadays everyone's talking about sponsoring things as a way of expressing their concerns and interests. If you think it's only happening here at our zoo, you must be living under a rock. It's a nation-wide phenomenon."

"But if we go around hanging up signs all over the zoo, won't it look tacky?" asked Lin Yao.

"You're out of step with the times, don't you think?" said Chen Hongqi. "Who's concerned about appearances! That our animals have a way to go on living is all that matters. So what if the monkey cage has a sign on it with Hitler's name, so long as the monkeys have tangerines to eat!"

Lin Yao and Chen Hongqi sat outside the enclosure, eating tangerines and chatting.

The Guangxi monkeys sat inside the enclosure, gnawing at their tangerines and raising a racket.

"I hear that the tiger Mingming is going to be adopted too by some American Chinese. I'm not sure what the family connection is to tigers," said Chen Hongqi.

Lin Yao was feeling a bit impatient. It seemed like getting adopted was like being selected as a model worker. But, where was the justice in all of this for Shujuan? Sensing what was on Lin Yao's mind, Chen Hongqi said, "Bears just aren't that popular, especially old bears that have lost their teeth."

"Says who?" Lin Yao's voice raised in pitch. "You just haven't spent enough time with her."

"Nonsense!" said Chen Hongqi. "If you spent enough time with a rat, you'd start to have feelings for it, too."

Lin Yao said, "Now you're just arguing for the sake of it."

Having been inspired by Chen Hongqi, Lin Yao decided to find a sponsor. The first thing he thought of was the Star Brand nutritional powder, so he went back to the bear house to get the address of the factory off the bag. Li Yu's shift had already started, and he was just getting ready to feed Shujuan dinner. Looking at the nutritional powder, he said, "One bag for eight *yuan.*

That's eighty *yuan* for ten bags. In no time at all you'll be out your whole salary. You can't do that."

Lin Yao told Li Yu about his idea of finding a sponsor at the Star Brand factory. As luck would have it, Li Yu's sister-in-law was the factory's bathhouse attendant. Tomorrow, if he went to see her, she might be able to help him find a contact there.

It was settled, then. Tomorrow they would go to the Star Brand factory.

*   *   *

As soon as he arrived home, Lin Yao ran into his mother-in-law. "We made dumplings today," she said. "The Second Lady made the filling herself. Eat with us tonight. Don't make something on your own."

Lin Yao agreed. First, however, he went back to the belvedere to fetch a bottle of Ozeki *sake*, which Xiaoyu had brought back from Japan.

When he entered the main room of his father-in-law's apartments, he felt everything grow a shade darker, due in large part to his father-in-law's suite of mahogany furniture. Along the room's western wall was a dressing mirror made of several panes of glass, which, due to great age, were streaked with a variety of colors in such a way as to resemble the oily rainbows that appear in puddles on rainy days. The weak tick-tock of an ancient clock kept a steady pace, although the instrument could only be consulted for general reference, not the actual time. A piece of white felt covered the large desk in front of the window, upon which were spread brushes, ink, paper, and an inkstone. A sprig of wintersweet, with as yet unopened buds, stood in a flower vase. Just at that moment, bent over the desk with great attention, Lin Yao's father-in-law, Lu Junqing, was painting a picture of plum blossoms. Lin Yao knew nothing about painting, but he knew his father-in-law was good at it and that he had a decent reputation in artistic circles. In truth, however, there was very little connection between Lin Yao's work taking care of black bears and his father-in-law's painting. They were two separate things, and, although the two men had a decent relationship, they did not share a common language.

Lin Yao put the *sake* down on the table, while his mother-in-law set out the bowls and saucers. The Second Lady, pushing open the door, entered. Diminutive but not wizened, she maintained her strength and her mental faculties despite her near eighty years of age.

Lin Yao's mother-in-law said, "I was just about to send Lin Yao to fetch you. There's moss on the bricks in the courtyard. They're slippery."

The Second Lady replied, "I've walked that way so many times! I know exactly where it's slippery and where it's not!"

Seeing that the Second Lady had arrived, Lin Yao's father-in-law put down his brush and walked over to the table. The *sake* caused him to furrow his brow. "Why don't we drink *baijiu* instead,"[14] he said. "Pairing Chinese dumplings with Japanese *sake* makes me feel like we're traitors to the nation."

"The *sake* is only twelve proof. It's easy to drink," said Lin Yao.

"Like water for washing your feet," said his father-in-law, replacing it with *baijiu*.

The dumplings were served, but there were just three plates—only enough for each person to have about a dozen or so. Lin Yao's father-in-law asked why there were so few. His mother-in-law replied, "With such special filling, you don't suppose we'd eat them by the bushel?"

Lin Yao asked, "What kind of filling?"

"Taste one, and see if you can tell," said the Second Lady.

When he bit into one of them, he discovered the meat was finely minced and tender. There was a slightly bitter taste accompanied by a delicate fragrance. Looking more closely at one on his plate, he still couldn't determine what was in them.

His mother-in-law said, "It's chicken, pigeon, and chrysanthemum blossoms."

So chrysanthemum blossoms are edible, and you can put them in dumpling filling, Lin Yao thought to himself. No wonder the potted chrysanthemum bush that was usually in his father-in-law's room had gone missing.

The Second Lady said, "The Empress Dowager loved to eat white chrysanthemum blossoms with fleshy petals. In the palace, they used to make a special kind of hotpot just for Her Majesty. They added chrysanthemum flowers and called it chrysanthemum hotpot. Later, when Zhang Lande, chamberlain and chief eunuch, left the imperial service, he transmitted his knowledge of this dish to Grandfather Lu, and so it became one of the Lu family specialties. The last thing they would add to the hotpot was these little pigeon and chrysanthemum filled dumplings."[15]

Lin Yao's father-in-law said, "How appropriate to the season! How refined! Food, just like painting, has its own mysteries. It would take more than a single life to penetrate them all!"

"Of course, what the imperial family ate was refined!" said Lin Yao's mother-in-law. "But such cuisine is not meant for the common man. Imagine if those stout fellows who tore up all the railroads back in '01 had feasted on these dumplings[16]; they'd have eaten all the chrysanthemums in the city, to be sure!"

Lin Yao knew that his mother-in-law had a rather common background,

---

14. *Baijiu* is a clear, strong, grain-based alcohol, often referred to as China's national drink.

15. The Empress Dowager Cixi (1835–1908) served as regent for most of the period from 1861 to 1908. The eunuch Zhang Lande (1876–1957) entered the imperial service in 1888.

16. The reference is to the Boxer Rebellion that raged over northern China from 1899 to 1901. The predominantly peasant supporters of the rebellion tore up railroads as a sign of their opposition to foreigners.

and, as the daughter of the proprietor of a pharmacy, there was no way that she could compare in cultural refinement with the Second Lady—a Manchu princess by birth. It was no wonder, then, that she expressed herself rather crudely in comparison. That said, she was far more familiar with the ways of the world than the Second Lady.

3.

It was morning. Remembering that he had planned to go to the Star Brand factory, Lin Yao first gave a call over to the bear house to ask after Shujuan.

Li Yu, his voice still groggy with sleep, responded, "She's good enough."

"What do you mean 'good enough'?"

"She ate a whole basin of nutritional powder porridge."

"What's she doing now?"

"No change. She's lying on the floor."

The two men determined to meet up at the southern pedestrian overpass at 9:00 a.m. Before hanging up, Lin Yao instructed Li Yu, "Don't let anyone know what we are up to, especially Chen Hongqi. We might be going begging, but we don't want to lose face."

"Don't worry so much about appearances," replied Li Yu. "Even in the old days, beggars weren't the most disreputable members of society. And, of course, nowadays things are completely different. Just think about all those people in marketing and promotion jobs. Imagine what they have to go through! If other people don't have a problem with begging, why should you! Now that capitalism is all the rage, it's time to shove your fine compunctions down your trousers...."

As Li Yu was still dispensing this remarkable advice, Lin Yao hung up.

* * *

When Lin Yao and Li Yu arrived at the nutritional powder factory, they met with the director. Like Lin Yao, he had graduated high school at the very beginning of the Cultural Revolution. Both he and Lin Yao had also been sent to work in the same provincial town.[17] So, although they weren't personally acquainted, that had heard of each other before. They found it easy to strike up conversation.

"I have no interest in adopting a black bear," the director said. "If our

---

17. From 1966 to 1968 most urban middle- and high-school graduates were "sent down" to work in the countryside (see note 4). The strong bonds forged among the so-called "sent-down youth" during this time often endured into later life, allowing individuals from this generation to make social connections on the basis of their shared life experience.

product were Black Bear brand, whose parents would buy it? Whose kids would eat it?"

Li Yu, sparing none of the details, told of Shujuan's critical condition, adding that perhaps they could, at least in the short term, count on the director's material support.

"Impossible," said the director. "The bear, you say, eats eight packages of nutritional powder a day. Over ten days, that's eighty packages. The prices of grain, eggs, and oil are rising by the day. It costs me 0.16 *yuan* to produce a bag of powder. I just can't afford it."

So that was that. Lin Yao never imagined that, in just three sentences, there'd be nothing left to say. He supposed it was time to say "see you later." But, he knew—damn it!—once he said it, neither of them would actually "see each other later." Shujuan's everything—her life!—would be over. Then, somehow, Lin Yao managed to say, "I ... I ... I'd like to see the shop floor. I've never been to a food manufactory. I wonder.…"

"You're most welcome!" replied the director. "I'll give you a tour."

Lin Yao got the impression by talking with the director that he was, in both manner and speech, straightforward and to the point. This man, with his crew cut and love of hand gestures, was the same age as Lin Yao, and yet Lin Yao felt intimidated by him.

Once on the shop floor, the director launched into a jargon-filled explanation of the production process, while Lin Yao nodded his head repeatedly up and down, doing his best to look like he was listening attentively. To himself, however, Lin Yao couldn't stop thinking about how to turn the conversation back to Shujuan. Pointing to a worker who was operating a machine in a cloud of powder, he said, "You ought to bring in some foreign machines and production techniques. What you have here seems rather antiquated."

The director said: "I'd love to. But, I don't have the capital. Also, I haven't been able to find a suitable business partner."

"Perhaps I could help," said Lin Yao. "But you'd really have to want to do it."

Li Yu added, "His wife is a researcher in Japan, studying economics. She knows quite a number of entrepreneurs."

"You don't say!" the director stopped in his tracks, eyeing Lin Yao with a serious look.

Lin Yao nodded.

"I'll make you a conditional promise," said the director. "If we succeed in setting up a joint venture with a foreign company, and if we make some money out of the deal, the first thing I'll do is adopt Shujuan. On top of that, no matter what we produce, the brand name will have something to do with a bear, since it was a bear, after all, that brought us together in the first place."

"That settles it, then!" said Lin Yao. "I guarantee you'll make some money!"

The three of them continued into another part of the factory, where Lin Yao noticed nutritional powder piled up under the machines and in the corners. "Is that edible?" he asked.

The director said, "That's what's left over from the cleaning machine. You can't eat it."

"How about you give it to me?" The discussion they had just had served to give Lin Yao a bit more confidence. "The bear can eat it."

"Maybe so," said the director. "But, you'd still have to sift it out some. Otherwise, there might be some rocks or bits of metal in it."

Lin Yao was delighted when he heard this, as was Li Yu. He thanked the director so profusely that the director began to feel a bit embarrassed. "It's just the waste product of our process. What's there to thank me for. If you had started off by mentioning the bear could eat something like this, we could have solved your problem a lot faster!"

The director had some of his workers bring over a broom, with which Li Yu proceeded to gather up the powder, ever so thoroughly, from all the nooks and crannies around the room. Seeing Li Yu stretched out under one of the machines, Lin Yao couldn't help but be touched by a sense of the poignancy of the scene, causing his eyes to water just a bit. The director, noticing how emotional Lin Yao had become, patted him on the shoulder. "Brother!—I hope you don't mind me calling you that!—You're a good man! A tender soul, who, despite all that's happened over the years, has retained an un-callused heart!"

"That's because I've spent my life in the company of animals," said Lin Yao.

Li Yu had, by this time, gathered up the nutritional powder into a single pile and was now, measure by measure, transferring it into a bag. When finished, he lifted the bag up and, with great excitement, addressed Lin Yao, "Thirty *jin* in all!"[18]

"We'll be back to sweep up some more in several days," said Lin Yao.

"You don't need to come yourselves," said the director. "I'll have the workers take care of it. Once they've collected a specific amount, they can deliver it over to you." As he was saying this, he grabbed a few bags of nutritional powder from the production line and gave them to Lin Yao and Li Yu. "These are for your kids, not the bear."

The director helped Lin Yao secure the bags of nutritional powder to the back of his bicycle. Then, he accompanied them to the factory gate to say goodbye.

Lin Yao said, "We've been talking together half a day, but I don't think I caught your name."

---

18. See note 2.

"Ding Yi," said the director. "Ding, as in the common surname; Yi, as in the number 'one.'"

"Well," said Lin Yao, "if you ever become a representative on some committee, you're in luck! Your name will appear at the top of every list."[19]

The director said, "First I've got to get things in hand with the production at this factory. Otherwise, I won't even be a factory director anymore, let alone a 'representative.'"

"That's not necessarily so," replied Lin Yao.

"You're too pessimistic," interjected Li Yu. "The road might be full of twists and turns, but our prospects are bright!"[20]

Everyone shook hands and said their goodbyes. The factory was already far behind them, but Lin Yao continued to turn the name Ding Yi over and over again in his mind.

* * *

The two men returned to the front gate of the zoo, where they saw a noisy crowd had formed. The ticket window was closed, and Xiaomi, the ticket seller, had sat herself down, crying, in the security guard's office. Li Yu, who was Xiaomi's boyfriend, set his bicycle up on its kickstand and hurried over to her to see what the problem was. Xiaomi said, "Why are they blaming me? It's the zoo leadership that brought in this outside group to put on an exhibition of famous cats. Admission to the zoo plus the exhibition now costs five *yuan*. I don't get a penny of it, so what's the point of yelling at me?"

One of the tourists shouted from beyond the door, "We came to see the zoo animals, not cats! We have four cats of our own at home. There's nothing special about them!"

A peasant, with her grandson in tow, added, "Everyone says that we peasants are rolling in it nowadays. But, I had to sell four quarts of corn in order to bring my grandson into the city to see the tiger. We didn't come to see cats. There are cats everywhere. You trip over them walking down the street. There's no way to get free of them. But no one cared when I said I didn't want to see the cats. They said the tickets are sold together. But the cost of two cat exhibition tickets is the equivalent of a single quart of corn. When I tell people back in the village, they'll all laugh at me for being a fool!"

---

19. Chinese names may be ordered into lists based on the number of brushstrokes needed to write them. The fewer brushstrokes a character has, the earlier it appears. The characters in Ding Yi's name—Ding 丁 (requiring two brushstrokes) and Yi 一 (requiring only one)—are two of the simplest characters in the language, making his name likely to appear at the top of most lists.

20. Here Li Yu quotes from one of Mao Zedong's speeches, namely "On the Chonqing Negotiations" ("Guanyu Chongqing tanpan") delivered on October 17, 1945. During the Cultural Revolution and for quite a number of years after, quotations of this kind were common in everyday life, as people were required to study and memorize the chairman's works. Some famous lines are still quoted today.

Speaking up for Xiaomi, Li Yu countered, "The tiger belongs to the cat family, although, of course, it is a great cat. See the cats first, then go look at the tiger. You can make a comparison."

"What the hell!" contributed another tourist. "The zoo might as well also exhibit ducks, pigs, and rabbits. During school holidays, people can bring their kids here and teach them the difference between roosters and hens!"

Someone who looked like a party cadre said, "We ought to report this to the authorities. This is price gouging. It's unethical!"

Li Yu wanted to continue arguing, but Lin Yao dragged him away. He understood the predicament the zoo leadership was in. The cat exhibition was rather ridiculous, to be sure. But was there another way? How was what they were doing all that different from what, just moments ago, he had been doing—begging for Shujuan, scruples be damned! Everyone's back was up against the wall.

"I feel really bad for Xiaomi, attacked like that by the crowd and forced to hide in the security guard's office," said Li Yu. "I'm sure that tickets sales will suffer this quarter, all the same."

"It's all about the money. What else is there to say," replied Lin Yao.

*   *   *

Just as Lin Yao was heating up Shujuan's porridge, Li Yu came in from the kitchen carrying a big bowl of bone-marrow broth. Pouring the whole thing into the porridge, he said, "This is just what the doctor ordered. It will do Shujuan a lot of good."

What it did do was cause Shujuan to get the runs by that afternoon. Already too weak to raise her head, Shujuan now had to struggle in her enclosure with serious diarrhea, which Lin Yao knew was brought about by stomach pain. The pain was so great, in fact, that Shujuan began to emit human-like moans. But Lin Yao could offer no help. Normally, he was able to enter Shujuan's cage without concern for his safety, but he couldn't today, because bears in pain were irascible and capable of turning on those who cared for them.

Lin Yao called the veterinary department. When Dr. Du arrived, he said, based on her symptoms, Shujuan would be dead in two days.

Li Yu lost all the color in his face, when he heard this. After all, he was the one who had brought Shujuan the bone-marrow broth. Strictly speaking, therefore, he was the "prime culprit."

Dr. Du said, "Did you really expect a black bear with an already weak digestive system to be able to handle such oily food? You wanted to help her live, but, instead, you've just about killed her. As the saying goes: 'More haste, less speed.'"

Li Yu tried to reason with Dr. Du, and Lin Yao implored him, saying that Shujuan was really such a lovable bear.

Dr. Du said nothing. He merely took out his metal syringe, grabbed hold of Shujuan's scruff, and gave a thrust. In a rage, Shujuan tried to resist, flailing her two front paws this way and that, refusing to submit. In the end, however, the clever "Mongolian doctor" demonstrated his skill, taking advantage of Shujuan's twisting and turning to push all of the medicine into her body.[21]

Lin Yao asked, "What was that?"

"An anesthetic," replied Dr. Du, as he packed up his medicine bag and prepared to leave.

"Just an anesthetic?"

"Wait for it to take effect," said Dr. Du. "Then, put her in a cart and take her to the infirmary. She needs to be treated there."

Li Yu said, "You're not going to help us?"

"I have to go to monkey mountain," replied Dr. Du.

"What's the matter with the monkeys?"

"They also have the runs."

"Chen Hongqi probably saw me with the bone-marrow broth, went and got some himself, and gave it to his monkeys," said Li Yu.

Lin Yao replied, "Don't worry about the monkeys. Let's instead figure out how to move this great big creature."

"I think that we'll have to get help from Chen Hongqi and his men."

"Didn't you just hear that the monkeys have the runs?"

"They owe us, though. Don't you remember when we had to catch a monkey for a zoo from the south. We all pitched in, but they never even took us out for a meal afterwards."

As the two men talked, Shujuan gradually slumped down, her pupils grew small, her eyes closed, and her breathing became more rapid.

"Quick! Go and round some people up!" Lin Yao ordered. "Otherwise, if the effect of the medicine wears off and we are only halfway there, she'll wake up and we won't be able to control her."

"Who should I go get?"

"The director."

Li Yu ran off as fast as he could.

Lin Yao entered the cage and stroked Shujuan's back. Opening his hand, he was shocked to see he had a handful of bear fur. When people are very ill, he thought, their hair also falls out clump by clump. Looking now

---

21. As commonly used, the term "Mongolian doctor" may refer to someone who practices medicine without formal professional training. Its connotations are often negative. One theory of the term's origin, however, connects it to the positive reputation enjoyed by Mongolian soldiers in the Qing dynasty (1644–1912) military, as these men were said to be expert at keeping their horses healthy and healing them after they had been wounded in battle. Based on this reputation, and in the absence of a regular doctors, people became willing to allow so-called "Mongolian doctors" to cure them of their ailments. The mixed results of this practice led to the less-than-positive associations that the expression has today.

at the fur in his hand, he wondered just how long Shujuan would last. His spirits sank.

The director of the zoo arrived with a group of workmen. They, however, were afraid and stubbornly refused to enter the cage. Their contract, they said, contained no clause pertaining to the direct handling dangerous animals. If they were going to do this kind of very risky work, they would need extra pay.

"Don't worry," said Lin Yao. "She's been anesthetized."

"But what if you didn't give her enough medicine?" the works asked. "She might wake up. And, when she does, she won't attack you; you're her keeper. She'll attack us."

"Shujuan's a good bear," said Lin Yao.

"Good bears, just like good dogs, may still bite people," the workers replied.

The director had the final say, "Everyone will get an extra ten *yuan*. If something untoward should occur, the zoo will make full compensation for all damages."

"Get to it, then!" said Li Yu. "If she wakes up, it will be too late then to decide to run."

Hearing what Li Yu said, the workers, who had already entered the cage, rushed back out. Lin Yao said: "She'll still be out for a while. Quick! Bring the cart!"

So, in came the cart. With everyone lending a hand, they managed to hoist Shujuan up onto the cart and into a cage which sat atop it. This small cage—just big enough for a single bear—became Shujuan's "sickbed."

As the workers pushed her towards the infirmary, they were surrounded by zoo guests. Someone said, "Hey! A bear's died!" "She wasn't much to see when she was alive; now she's a big dead heap!"

One of the workers grabbed the bear's paw and waved it at the guests: "She's alive!"

To the workers' great satisfaction, the guests then fled in all directions.

*   *   *

Now that she was in the infirmary, Shujuan lay, under the effects of the anesthetic, in the corner of her cage and received her treatment. Both Lin Yao and Li Yu, when they were not taking care of necessary tasks at the bear house, took turns performing "bedside duties." Over the course of several days, they became quite exhausted. In addition to Shujuan, there were two Guangxi monkeys in the infirmary. Since these were fertile animals, they were entitled to treatment, too. Whatever medicine they had been given caused the monkeys to lie quietly, almost human-like, in their cages, from which they watched the coming and going of all the people. Their eyes, just like Shujuan's eyes, frightened Lin Yao. They were beautiful eyes: naïve and pure, and filled with mournful pleading. Chen Hongqi would also come by to see his monkeys. Lin Yao asked him if he had given them any bone-marrow broth. Chen Hongqi said, "If they had eaten the bone-marrow broth, everything would be just fine. It was the tangerines that caused the problem."

Lin Yao asked how the tangerines had caused the monkeys to get diarrhea.

Chen Hongqi responded, indignantly, "They were treated with pesticide. We humans peel tangerines, but monkeys don't. Some just eat the whole thing, peel and all. We're lucky that they only got the runs; they could have been poisoned to death. In the future, when I feed them apples and such, I'm going to have to sit outside the cage and peel them for them, just as if I were serving my ancestors."

Lin Yao said, "Indeed, in a manner of speaking, aren't they our ancestors? We evolved from them. It's fitting, then, that we serve them." While he said this, he thought to himself: adoption may indeed lead to some negative consequences, as it had for the monkeys. Everything needed to be considered from all sides.

As he sat by Shujuan's metal cage, Lin Yao wrote a letter to his wife, Xiaoyu, asking her to help the Star Brand Food Manufactory find an international business partner. He mentioned to her that the factory director was an old comrade in arms from the days when he worked in the countryside[22]; that the director had made a promise to support Shujuan; and that Shujuan's life very much depended on her help. Just as he finished writing, he was struck by a strange inspiration: he picked up a tuft of Shujuan's fur and put it in the envelope. Then, he added a few lines to the end of the letter: "Shujuan's condition is critical. All I have to do is pat her, and a clump of fur, such as this, falls out. Isn't it enough to chill your heart?" Once he finished the letter, he looked over at Chen Hongqi. The monkeys were in a bad way. One of them had died, and a worker was removing it from its cage. Its lifeless arms swayed back and forth and its small round head, like that of a deeply sleeping child, drooped down.

Lin Yao walked over to Chen Hongqi, who sat facing away from him.

Chen Hongqi said, "She was pregnant."

Lin Yao knew that Chen Hongqi's eyes were filled with tears.

4.

With the fall of snow came the New Year.

As usual, the Second Lady was in charge of preparing the New Year's Eve banquet; and, as usual, whenever the Second Lady cooked Lu family recipes, she oversaw the purchase of the ingredients in person. In her youth,

---

22. See note 17.

when the Lu family had been at the height of its wealth and power, she had never had to consider cost when doing her shopping. Whatever delicacy she needed, whether from land or sea, all that mattered was that it was of the highest quality. Indeed, she was able to tell with ease which shark fin had sand in it and which swallow's nest had too many feathers. In those days, whether at the fishmonger's or at the game seller's, she was on intimate terms with all the shopkeepers, each of whom recognized her expertise and none of whom dared try to cheat her. With the passage of time, and under the direction of the Second Lady, the feasts that the Lu family provided to their guests assumed a regular order: six appetizers and eighteen main dishes, as well as soup and dessert. But now, try as she might, the Second Lady was simply not up to the task. It was fortunate, therefore, that this year her niece Jinjing had come to visit her. Taking advantage of this fact, the Second Lady determined to teach Jinjing how to make some of the Lu family recipes.

Jinjing was now unemployed. She had once trained as a Peking Opera singer, specializing in *ingénue* roles; later, she had been assigned to work in a pottery factory. When the factory fell on hard times, however, they changed what they produced and let her go. Now, completely at loose ends, she idled away her time at home.

The atmosphere at the New Year's banquet table was considerably enlivened by Jinjing's presence. A former actress, her cleverness and unreserved nature very much pleased Lin Yao's in-laws. After a lengthy speech in praise of the Lu family cuisine, she said, "Why don't you take advantage of your courtyard mansion and this beautiful food to open up a Lu family restaurant?"

Everyone at the table was astounded by the suggestion.

Jinjing continued, "You should share my auntie's skills with the world. Otherwise, they'll be lost, and won't that be a pity!"

Lu Junqing said, "But, the Second Lady can barely look after herself now. How can she be expected to cook all that food?"

Jinjing replied that she could help: Auntie would instruct; she, Jinjing, would cook.

"I think we ought to give serious consideration to Jinjing's idea," said Lin Yao's mother-in-law. "If we do it right, who wouldn't want a taste of how a noble family, such as the Lus, once ate under the old regime? What's more, the dishes that the Second Lady cooks are so unusual; most people have not only never seen them before, they've never even heard of them! If there's anything we Chinese are known for, it's our discerning palates! This is just the sort of thing people will embrace with gusto! Opportunity presents itself; maybe we should take advantage of it."

Lin Yao's father-in-law added, "Chinese people all know the eight major regional cuisines: Sichuanese, Cantonese, Shandong style, Jiangsu cuisine, and so on. But Chinese food can be categorized otherwise: palace cuisine, the cuisine of the nobility, folk cuisine, foreign-influenced cuisine, ethnic cuisine, etc. At present, people know very little about the cuisine of the nobility. But, the Lu family lacks....."

Jinjing said, "Auntie will direct me. I'll take care of the rest, from buying the ingredients to the cooking. I'd rather have something to do than sit idle at home all day. We'll hire two other girls from the labor market to help. That should be sufficient."

Lin Yao didn't say anything, but he was nevertheless impressed.

For the rest of the day, everyone in the Lu family continued to discuss the matter with Jinjing. Jinjing came up with a general plan. The Second Lady drew up a banquet menu. Every night there would be a single sitting for a table of no more than twelve. Customers would be treated as if they were guests of the family. There would be two kinds of banquets: formal, to be held in the main hall, and informal, to be held in the belvedere.

After a period of intense preparation, there were some major changes in the Lu mansion.

First, Jinjing moved in. Second, Lu Junqing and his wife moved out of the main hall and into the apartments on the eastern side of the compound. Finally, Lin Yao moved out of the belvedere and into a small room at the southern side of the outer courtyard.

Under the supervision of Lin Yao's mother-in-law, a crew of workmen with experience in restoring traditional buildings undertook renovations of the main hall, transforming its three rooms into a single larger one. Two smaller rooms—one to the east, the other to the west—were converted into reception rooms. Summoned forth from the storeroom, where it had sat covered in dust and cobwebs for several decades, was the Lu family's large round dining table. Polished and shined, it was covered with a white tablecloth. Next, the small room to the west was furnished with wooden chairs and tea tables. Directly across from the door was set up an alter table, upon which was arrayed fresh fruit, and over which now hung a portrait of grandfather Lu, wearing the hat and robes of a court official of the second rank. Upon entering this room, one was prompted by its atmosphere of power and opulence to a sense of reverence and awe.

As for the belvedere, it was restored with restrained elegance. On its main wall now hung a painting, from the hand of Lin Yao's father-in-law himself, entitled *Fishing on a River in Winter*. Framing this painting, to the left and right, was a calligraphic couplet. On one side, the couplet began: "Neither favor nor blame arouse passion: at leisure, I but watch the flowers outside the pavilion as they blossom and fade." On the other side, it concluded: "Neither coming nor going excite attention: free of care, I merely observe the clouds in the sky as they form and disperse."[23] There was a large dining table to the east with eight chairs made of rosewood. To the west was a desk, on top of which sat the scholar's tools: brushes, ink, paper, and an inkstone. Behind it was a hardwood flower stand with a potted asparagus fern; full of vitality, its branches—more than four feet in length—hung down in sweeping cascades. Overall, the room gave the impression that its owner was a man of the highest taste and refinement; welcomed inside, guests themselves could not help but abandon some of their own vulgar tendencies.

Under the careful supervision of the Second Lady and Jinjing, the Lu family cuisine was given the opportunity to shine, providing fine examples of the original tastes and flavors that would have been characteristic of the food of an old noble family. In particular, it featured dried delicacies from both the sea and land. There were in the past, of course, no refrigerators, so fresh ingredients were seldom used. Thus, in noble households—and even in the palace—if you wanted to eat a rare treat, it usually had to be dried, whether it be shark's fin, abalone, sea urchin, fish maw, shark's lips, bear's paw, or camel hump. The flavors were mild and redolent of the painstaking processes that produced them. What one savored was not just the food itself, but, rather, a kind of spiritual nourishment based in quiet appreciation of and identity with the cuisine itself—an experience that provoked one to believe that one had penetrated into one of the profoundest mysteries of five thousand years of Chinese cultural history.

The funds to buy the ingredients and make the renovations came from money Lin Yao's father-in-law earned by selling his paintings. Additional funds came from the "filial remittances" that Xiaoyu and Xiaolei provided from abroad. Although they had no money themselves, Lin Yao and Jinjing were not reluctant to contribute their efforts. Profits, therefore, were to be divided equally amongst them all. From the start, however, Lin Yao's mother-in-law made it clear that there would be no profit taking in the first year. Everything would be reinvested in the business. In the second year, half of all profits would be reinvested. Thus, it was according to this business model—which resembled, to an extent, how one might roll a snowball—that the Lu family launched its cuisine into the market.

Thanks to her upbringing as the daughter of a proprietor of a pharmacy, Lin Yao's mother-in-law was widely reputed to be a good manager. The bourgeoisie, after all, had bourgeois skills. When, deep into the night, the Lu family mansion still echoed with the crisp click-clack of mother-in-law's abacus, everyone knew that this sound would be the basis for the family's

---

23. This elegantly composed expression of Daoist detachment appears in two Ming dynasty (1368–1644) collections of aphorisms: *Clandestine Jotting from My Little Window* (*Xiaochuang youji*), a work traditionally attributed to Chen Jiru (1558–1630); and the *Vegetable Root Discourses* (*Caigen tan*) by Hong Zicheng (fl. 1572–1620).

business success. Second Lady's skill in the kitchen and mother-in-law's business acumen—these combined would make possible the marketability of the Lu family cuisine. Placing an abacus next to an old-style account book with red-ruled yellow paper, Lin Yao's mother-in-law set up a small room in which guests could settle their bill. Its antique feeling was in perfect keeping with the overall flavor of the Lu family cuisine.

With everything ready, the day of the grand opening arrived. Both Lin Yao and Jinjing wanted to hang out a sign and set off firecrackers, but father-in-law was adamant in his refusal of this plan. "We're not opening a restaurant," he said.

"If it's not a restaurant, then what is it?" Lin Yao countered.

"Even if it is a restaurant, we can't call it that," father-in-law persisted with a shake of his head.

Mother-in-law smiled and said nothing. Then, after a while she added, slowly and deliberately, "Of course, it's not a restaurant. The Lu family would never open a restaurant."

Lin Yao and Jinjing had no idea what they were talking about.

Mother-in-law said, "In any event, let's not lose sight of our main objective! When talking to others, we won't say we are running a restaurant. We'll simply say that we're having guests over to sample how the Lu family used to eat in the old days. If anyone wants to come, they should make reservations three days in advance. A member of the Lu family will be there personally to greet them, otherwise how could we possibly receive them?"

Everyone thought this suggestion was most original, although they wondered if it would work.

Not unexpectedly, after several days, despite all the people who passed by the Lu family mansion, no one knew that you could make reservations to eat there. The two hired girls had nothing to do, so Lin Yao's mother-in-law put them to work trimming trees and sweeping the courtyards. The Lu family mansion became absolutely spotless.

*   *   *

One day, Ding Yi came looking for Lin Yao. He said that, thanks to the recommendation of Lin Yao's wife, a delegation from a Japanese company—Nichimori Foods, Ltd.—would be visiting his factory the day after tomorrow. Lin Yao, he said, must be there to greet them, too.

"Don't be blindly optimistic about this," said Lin Yao. "Nine times out of ten these visits amount to nothing. Of course, in some cases the Chinese side will make use of this situation to set up a fake joint venture. They'll register the business, return the funds to their partner, but still get to benefit from their preferential status."

Ding Yi responded, "That's not what I'm interested in. I want to improve the Star Brand factory. If I can't make better products, I have no use for preferential status."

Lin Yao said, "Ding Yi, you're a good fellow. I knew it from the moment I met you."

It happened to be the fifteenth day of the first lunar month—the Lantern Festival—when the Japanese delegation arrived. Lin Yao had already instructed Li Yu to have Shujuan remain in the infirmary for few more days. There was no need to get her out too soon; at least in the infirmary she could get better food. As that was the case, Lin Yao set off for the Star Brand factory early in the morning.

It was snowing, and Ding Yi and all of the Star Brand factory workers were dispirited: everywhere the Japanese delegation walked—through the shop floor and offices that the workers had spent days diligently cleaning—they left a slushy mess. The leader of the Japanese was a little old man named Yokomichi Tatsuzou, who paced about, with a displeased look on his face, peering critically at the windows and the ceiling, but hardly casting a glance at the machines. This annoyed Ding Yi, because he had paid no attention to dusting the ceilings, having rather spent all his time making sure everything at eye level looked up to snuff. So, he tried to guide Yokomichi's attention elsewhere, with talk of the city's investment environment and preferential policies. He also pointed out that here in the north they were in grain producing territory, an especially favorable location for those in the business of processing wheat. On top of that, the city had a national reputation for its beautiful scenery and cultural and historic sites.

Yokomichi said something in Japanese. The translator translated, "The roof will have to be removed and rebuilt. Such a shoddy old structure is simply not suited to our production needs."

Ding Yi said he had been planning to do that.

Yokomichi then inspected some other parts of the factory. Hurrying behind him, Ding Yi instructed a tall and leggy girl to hold an umbrella over Yokomichi's head, as the snowfall intensified. Covered in a layer of white flakes, everyone scrunched their necks into their overcoats, except for Yokomichi, who, thanks to the protection afforded him by the young beauty and her umbrella, kept on gesturing here and there as he spoke. The poor umbrella-holding girl! Her teeth chattered, and her slight, close-fitting Chinese style dress was soon drenched by the wet snow. For the future of the factory, however, she withstood the freezing cold with equanimity. Lin Yao wanted to walk over and smack the arrogant Yokomichi right in the face; thinking of Shujuan, however, he closed his eyes and pretended he didn't see the scene before him.

*　*　*

On Lin Yao's suggestion, it was decided to hold the evening banquet for the Japanese delegation at the Lu family mansion. They told the Japanese that Lin Yao, the vice-director of the factory and descendant of a noble family, was honored to invite them, as guests from a friendly nation, to experience how the upper classes once ate. It was a private invitation, not a business meeting. Hearing this, Yokomichi seemed rather intrigued.

That evening, a number of small sedan cars parked in front of the Lu family mansion, bringing with them a measure of excitement to the long desolate residence. Accompanied by Ding Yi and Lin Yao, Yokomichi paused in astonishment at the top of the flight of stone steps that led to the mansion. With doors opening inward, the great crimson archway, motionless and stately, gave those who stood in its imposing presence a feeling of their own insignificance. Two cold, round stone drums stood silently on either side of the doors, adding to the mansion's overall atmosphere of icy aloofness. No one dared speak above a whisper, and, at that moment, as if caught by an ineffable sensation, Yokomichi straightened his tie and adopted a reverential attitude.

To the right of the main gate, was a square stone, the use of which Yokomichi inquired after. Lin Yao said it was a mounting stone, but the foreigner still did not understand.

"People used the stone to help them mount their horses," Lin Yao said. "It was a mark of distinction to have such a stone in front of your house in the old days. Only officials of the second rank, first class, or higher were allowed to have such stones."

Yokomichi asked what it meant to be an official of the second rank.

"A provincial official of the second rank, first class, was the equivalent of what we would nowadays call a provincial governor," said Lin Yao.

Immediately, Lin Yao rose in Yokomichi's estimation. Whereas Yokomichi had previously addressed him as Lin *kun*, he now referred to him, more respectfully, as Lin *san*.[24]

And, so, a single mounting stone had the remarkable effect of improving the possibility of a joint venture between the Star Brand factory and their Japanese investors, brightened the business prospects of the Lu family "restaurant," and made Shujuan's future that much sunnier.

Everyone entered the front doors, walked around the screen wall, passed through the secondary gate, and approached the main hall. The courtyard was gleaming, without a trace of snow. The following couplet was carved into two wooden boards that hung from pillars on the veranda:

> *Irises and orchids embody the character of the noble man;*
> *The pine tree and cedar reflect the spirit of the ancients.*

---

24. In Japanese, *san* is a politer form of address than *kun*, which is usually used to refer to a person younger than oneself.

Two red lanterns, bright and large, added a festive—and seasonally appropriate touch—to the scene; the full moon was just visible above the ceramic animals on the tiled roof; and, from the distance, one could faintly hear the sound of someone playing the flute—all of which contributed, among the Japanese guests, to the sense that they had been transported to another time.

Lu Junqing was on the veranda awaiting their arrival. His ruddy, child-like face framed by silvery hair and a wispy white beard that seemed to flutter in the breeze, he had the appearance of a fairytale immortal. Cupping one hand in the other before his breast and bowing slightly, he greeted Yokomichi. Yokomichi made haste to return the gesture, straightening his feet and bowing deeply at the waist in Lu Junqing's direction. The old man, guiding Yoko-michi inside with a smile, responded, "There's no need for such ceremony!"

There, when Yokomichi caught sight of the portrait of grandfather Lu, he made another bow with a reverence that one might have expected if he were offering his respects to his own ancestors or, perhaps, the emperor of Japan himself. Lin Yao thought it was all a bit ridiculous.

Next, the two men—Lu Junqing and Yokomichi—arranged themselves appropriately, as host and guest, around one of the tea tables. For conversation, Mr. Lu, quoting generously from the Chinese classics, offered a series of lofty moral sentiments—"A true gentlemen, even when alone, must be ever vigilant of his conduct," etc., etc.[25]—none of which were all that familiar anymore to the younger generation of Chinese and must have been largely impenetrable to the Japanese. Nevertheless, they succeeded in creating for Yokomichi the impression that he was in the presence of a man worthy of his respect—a man, who, although affable and courteous, was, all the same, possessed of profound intelligence and strength of character.

Wearing a small jacket with decorative trim, a young girl came forward carrying tea and six small plates, each with its own delicacy: amber colored walnuts, roasted cashews, crispy nut cake, peanut balls, candied kumquats, and sugar-coated dried melon strips. The tea was green from Mengding mountain in Sichuan, and it was served in covered porcelain cups from the famous kiln in Dehua County, Fujian.

Yokomichi removed the cover from his cup, took a sip, and exclaimed, "What wonderful tea! What a beautiful cup!"

Twirling his beard with his fingertips, Lu Junqing smiled slightly.

Lin Yao and Ding Yi tried to restrain themselves from showing any emotion.

---

25. This quotation appears in various classical texts, including the *Classic of Rites* (*Li ji*), the *Great Learning* (*Da xue*) and the *Doctrine of the Mean* (*Zhong yong*); of course, before becoming independent works, the *Great Learning* and the *Doctrine of the Mean* were themselves originally constituent chapters of the *Classic of Rites*.

Jinjing then appeared to announce that dinner was served, whereupon everyone walked over towards the dining table.

Although it is often said that all are equal at a round table, nevertheless, as everyone exchanged pleasantries, Lu Junqing positioned himself in the host's chair just to the right of Yokomichi. Ding Yi sat on Yokomichi's other side, so as to converse with him more easily.

The first dish consisted of various fruits and vegetables arranged in such a way as to create a tableau of a phoenix soaring towards the sun. The Japanese guests vied with each other to take photographs, saying that they hardly dared to eat it, lest their chopsticks disturb its beauty!

Soon the two serving girls began carrying other dishes, one after another, to the table. Each remarkable creation presented the possibility of a new culinary experience to the expectant diners. A sealed jug of the finest alcohol was then opened, filling the room with its sweet fragrance. After the alcohol was heated, the girls poured some for everyone. Lu Junqing raised his cup and said, "Help yourselves!"

No sooner had Yokomichi downed his drink than he aimed his chopsticks for a platter of pork braised in cherry sauce. As cooked in the Lu family, this dish consisted of cherry-sized slices of lean pork marinated in cherry juice, put in a pot, and cooked over a low flame for seven hours so that the flavor of the marinade fully suffused the meat. Only once the color of the meat was itself as shiny and red as a cherry was it ready to be ladled out, put on a platter, and served. Sweet and tender, its fruity flavor was the perfect accompaniment to the alcohol. The other dishes—cinnamon smoked fish, garlic scallops, etc.—were equally unique and delicious. Under the influence of the alcohol, the faces of the Japanese soon began to resemble cherries themselves. The alcohol also made it impossible for Yokomichi to maintain his superior attitude. Growing intimate with Mr. Lu, he asked him his age. Upon learning Mr. Lu was twenty-four years his senior, Yokomichi practically fell over himself addressing the older man, in Japanese, as *otōsan*.[26]

The first of the main dishes was shark's fin braised in brown sauce.

The second was deep-fried king prawns.

After the abalone in red sauce, the serving girls offered small pure white teacups, each filled with nothing but clear water, to everyone. None of the guests understood their purpose. So, not wishing to look foolish, they all turned to watch Mr. Lu, who swished the water around in his mouth and then spit it into a basin especially prepared for that purpose, after which one of the girls gave him a towel, with which he wiped his mouth. The warm water was a palate cleanser, everyone now realized. Thereupon, following the example of Mr. Lu, they too used the water to clean their mouths.

---

26. Japanese for "grandfather"; a polite form of address.

Ding Yi said, "Everything tastes delicious. What's the purpose of a palate cleanser?"

"The next dish," said Mr. Lu, "is steamed bird's nest. You need a clean mouth to be able to savor its delicate taste. The strong flavors of everything we've just eaten would interfere."

Just as he was saying this, there arrived at the table a covered tureen, decorated with gold filigree. One of the girls lifted the top to reveal, floating in a bath of chicken broth and pink ribbons of ham, the bird's nest, its translucent, crystalline structure enticing the diners to discover its flavor. Once the serving girl had given everyone a portion, Lin Yao took a taste. Indeed, it was delightful; but, alas, the bowl was so small: two spoonfuls and its contents were gone. The tureen, too, was empty. One couldn't help but admire the chef's talent!

The banquet concluded with dessert: walnut paste and cakes stuffed with red bean paste and sweet potato filling.

Having experienced this feast for both the eyes and the palate, the Japanese were overcome with admiration for the way the Chinese nobility had once eaten.

Before leaving, Yokomichi wanted to meet the chef.

Mr. Lu said, "The cooking was done by my sister-in-law herself. She married into our family at sixteen years of age; she's now seventy-six. In her time, she's cooked for a great number of exalted personages, many of whom were most desirous to try her cooking for themselves."

Hearing this made Yokomichi all the more eager to meet her. One of the serving girls was sent back to fetch the Second Lady. When she returned, however, the girl said, "The Second Lady is tired. She's already retired for the evening."

Yokomichi expressed his regret.

Mr. Lu then saw the Japanese delegation out to the secondary gate, where he stopped. Lin Yao explained to Yokomichi that, in noble families, it was considered quite an honor for the host to walk this far out of the house with his guests. Normally, the host would just say farewell on the veranda. Grandfather Lu had not even ventured as far as the secondary gate when, all those years ago, he bade farewell to the president of the Republic Li Yuanhong[27]; at that time, he only walked out to the courtyard.

Hearing this, Yokomichi bowed to Mr. Lu to express his gratitude. Then he said to Ding Yi, "I've been to China many times before, but this is the first time that I feel like I've actually arrived in China! Ding *kun*, I truly appreciate your sincerity. I'm certain that the future holds for us a very happy partnership!"

---

27. Li Yuanhong (1864–1928) was president of the Republic of China three times during the period from 1916 to 1923.

Ding Yi was secretly delighted at the tone of Yokomichi's remarks.

Once the Japanese were gone, Lin Yao and his father-in-law turned back towards the main hall. On the dining table was an envelope, which, when they opened it, was found to contain three hundred thousand Japanese *yen*. Yokomichi must have left it as an expression of his appreciation, but, knowing that the Lu family mansion was not a restaurant, he hadn't wanted to offer the money as if he were paying a bill. Instead, it was intended as a slight token of appreciation for the trouble a noble family of the "second rank" had gone through to host him.

That evening mother-in-law recorded the three hundred thousand Japanese *yen* in her account book—its very first entry.

5.

Shujuan's diarrhea having stopped, she returned from the infirmary to the bear house. Nevertheless, her condition was not otherwise improved: her teeth were gradually falling out one by one, and she continued to lose large clumps of fur.

Lin Yao, full of hope, waited for news from Ding Yi. Li Yu received word from his sister-in-law that Ding Yi had already signed a joint venture agreement with Nichimori Foods; that the Japanese had already sent over their machines; and that with them had come four Japanese workers.

Not long thereafter, Lin Yao received an invitation from Nichi-Star Foods, Inc.; it was to a ceremony celebrating the commencement of production of a new brand of biscuit. On the day of the ceremony, however, because he was busy removing the mites and fleas that infested Shujuan's body, Lin Yao couldn't go. He sent Li Yu in his stead.

Li Yu came back from the Star Brand factory with two tins of biscuits under his arms. They were from Ding Yi, he said. Lin Yao asked how the ceremony went. "Ding Yi sure knows how to do things right," said Li Yu. "Not only did he invite a lot of bigwigs, but he also hired a bunch of musicians. What with all the drums and trumpets, it was quite exciting! The factory floor is also now completely different; it's divided into many different sections. The machines are white, as are the workers' uniforms. They were wearing disposable face masks and hats, all of them imported from Japan. They throw them out after just one use. Once the bigwigs cut the red ribbon, the production line started up, and it didn't make a sound. After a while, on the conveyor belt, you could see little black and white things, which the workers packed into little tins...."

"Did Ding Yi mention anything about adopting Shujuan?" Lin Yao asked.

"How could he?" said Li Yu. "He had a full plate as it was!"

Looking at the two tins of biscuits in Li Yu's hands, Lin Yao said, "Don't you remember? Ding Yi promised, if he could start up a joint venture, then the first item he'd produce would have something to do with a bear."

Li Yu said, "These biscuits…. How could they have anything to do with a bear? Don't take things so literally, Lin Yao!"

"Fine, I won't," said Lin Yao. "But, Ding Yi should. Your word is your bond: That's the first rule among us old comrades in arms. I told him I'd help him find a business partner, so I did. He told me he'd adopt Shujuan. But what's he done?" As he said this, he tore open the transparent plastic wrapper around one of the tins that Li Yu had brought back. "Let's take a look at what exactly Ding Yi has produced."

Li Yu said, "They're called *qu-qi*. Ding Yi said they're called *qu-qi*. What a strange name!"

"*Qu-qi*: that's a transliteration of the English word 'cookie.' It's a kind of sweet," said Lin Yao. "That Ding Yi, he's trying to be too clever, like a foolish dog who thinks he's a wolf."[28]

When they took the lid off the tin, both Lin Yao and Li Yu were, momentarily, at a loss for words.

The boxes were filled with cookies—a kind of milk biscuit—all in the shape of fat-bellied bears. The white ones had out-stretched arms and stuck-together legs; the black ones—so colored because they had chocolate in them—had separated legs and arms held close to their bodies. Their eyes were made of small shiny pieces of rock sugar. They were delightful! Lin Yao and Li Yu took the little bear cookies out of their box and lined them up— first a black one, then a white one—in a row, along the edge of the table. If you looked quickly at them, you could almost imagine they were performing jumping jacks, as in a cartoon.

Li Yu scratched his head and said, "I'll be damned! Ding Yi really came through! To think, he came up with this!"

Lin Yao said, "They really do have something to do with bears!"

"Say what you will," said Li Yu. "He's kept his promise!"

Lin Yao said, "Well, let's see what comes next."

Dancing along the table, the little bears were too pretty for anyone to eat. That is, except for Shujuan, who ate two of her fellows—one back, one white.

* * *

With the passing of the wintersweet season, the winter jasmine began to bloom, brightening the courtyards of the Lu family mansion with their brilliant yellow petals.

---

28. While *qu-qi* is a translation of the English word cookie, when taken literally, it also means "strange" or "unusual." The implication is that, with its double meaning, it is a clever name for a product. The Mandarin word *qu-qi* (cookie) entered the language in the 1980s under the influence of Cantonese. The Cantonese pronunciation (kuk-kei) shows its relation to the English much more closely.

Similarly, the Lu family's business venture began to flower, mainly due to Lin Yao's mother-in-law, who had made a connection with the city's main tourist office. A feast at the Lu family mansion had now become a special tourist attraction: Eat like the nobility in an old mansion! It was not only foreign guests who were attracted; Chinese people themselves wanted to try. The price was phenomenally expensive, to be sure. Nevertheless, everyone said it was worth it. In fact, there were no small number of repeat customers.

During the day, Lu Junqing painted, while, at night, he kept company with guests. When they were men with literary pretensions, he'd be sure to impress them with all manner of refined entertainment: writing verse, painting, singing, admiring flowers, and drinking. Every evening at the Lu family mansion guests filled the halls for what seemed to be a never-ending feast. Every day there was a single sitting, sometimes in the main hall, sometimes in the belvedere. They also came up with a clever new idea: on nights when the moon was full, guests could eat in the garden amongst the rockery and flowers. With the Lu family's ink and paper at the ready, those who were so inspired might take brush in hand and compose some calligraphy. If the result was worthy, it could be mounted and hung; if not, it could be sent with the used wine bottles to the recycling station. In either case, there was a place for it. As the reputation of the Lu family's banquets grew, a TV crew came to produce a report entitled "Laid-Off Female Worker Re-Creates Magic in the Kitchen." Even if Jinjing hadn't been featured, they would have had enough material with the shark's fin soup and footage of the play of tree shadows on the ornate mansion walls.

With the further increase in the fame of the Lu family banquets, people had to wait for days to get a reservation. Each banquet cost, on average, more than several thousand *yuan*; some even cost over ten thousand. At that time, it was becoming more and more common for people to use public funds to pay for entertainment. Following this trend, the Chinese restaurant business experienced a boom. There were all sorts of options: street-side cafés, place to eat steamed bread, restaurants that served food of the Dai ethnic group, Korean barbecue restaurants, etc. Still, if one were to recommend somewhere where the food lived up to the fastidious standards of Confucius, then a banquet at the Lu family mansion would have to be at the top of the list.[29] It was commonly known that private restaurants were better than state-owned ones. Furthermore, once people became aware that they could eat like the nobility once ate, it became a matter of status for them to say that they had tried the real thing. Naturally, then, there were those willing to plunk down large sums for Lin Yao's mother-in-law to enter into her account book.

---

29. The reference here is to a passage in the *Analects* (*Lun yu*, 10.8), in which are discussed the various rules Confucius observed for the preparation and consumption of food.

For her part, Jinjing called upon her experience as a Peking Opera actress, getting in touch with old acquaintances from her former company. She invited these handsome lads and winsome lasses—none of whom wanted to give up their artistic ambitions, but all of whom had to earn a living—to sing, out of costume and wearing no stage makeup, at the Lu family mansion in the evening; dinner was on the house, and they'd be paid by the hour. Among this lot, not a small number of talented individuals were getting by on reduced wages from the opera company—down to sixty percent of what they once had been—by performing at funerals and the like. For them, Jinjing's offer was too good to refuse. Some, of course, because they were actors, had a hard time lowering themselves in this way. But insisting on one's status was no way to fill one's belly in hard times. So, after some consideration, they cheered themselves with the thought that people had done similar things in the old days. With their addition, the Lu family banquets could truly be said to resemble the elegant scene depicted in *Han Xizia's Evening Feast*.[30] Guests were delighted.

As time passed, Jinjing became more and more of an expert chef. Relying on her inspiration, she added her own modern innovations to the strict traditional style of cooking that she learned from the Second Lady. Soon it was necessary to hire another cook, who took care of the standard dishes, while Jinjing herself cooked the Lu family specialties. The Second Lady, at first, supervised. After a while, however, viewing such oversight as unnecessary, she retired to her own quarters and came no more to the kitchen.

Lu Junqing was himself getting on in years, and it became impossible for him to attend the banquets every night. All the same, an empty place with a small bowl and a pair of chopsticks was always set for him as the host. In this way, he continued to maintain the polite fiction that he wasn't running a restaurant. When special guests came, however, he'd make a symbolic appearance and drink a few glasses with them. He might also recite some verse—"Alone in my secluded mansion, I lock the doors on a courtyard scattered with fallen flower petals,"[31] or the like. Platitudinous though these sentiments were, they nevertheless elicited the knowing nods of his guests, putting them in a suitably poetic, if maudlin, mood.

And, thus, the money continued to pour in. One sitting a night could hardly meet the ever-increasing demand. People had to make a reservation two weeks in advance. Lin Yao wondered if they might be able to add another sitting. At the same time, he suggested opening during the day.

His mother-in-law said, "In that case, we'd become a real restaurant."

---

30. A masterpiece by the artist Gu Hongzhong (937–975); the original is lost, but a 12th-century copy survives in the collection of the Palace Museum in Beijing. It depicts a lavish evening feast at the home of the official Han Xizai (902–970).

31. Paraphrased verse from a well-known poem by Liu Yong (987–1053), a famous poet in the Northern Song dynasty (960–1127).

She then added, "Before liberation, I remember Old Wang ran a place just to the west of the Fire God's temple, where he sold tripe and dumpling stew. It was no bigger than a single room, but he never wanted for customers. In fact, the place was always crowded; everyone was envious of how much money he made. If you wanted to eat some of his stew, you'd have to wait by his stove for what seemed link half the day, almost till you couldn't wait any longer. After a while, someone suggested to Old Wang that he buy the adjacent Fire God's temple—a three room structure—and make it part of his restaurant. So, he did. After renovating the space and hiring new help, what should happen? Business got worse by the day. No one came anymore. Do you know why?"

"He offended the Fire God?" said Lin Yao.

"No, that's just superstition," said mother-in-law. "The reason why Old Wang had a thriving business was precisely because his place was small and people had to wait. As customers stood there watching others eat, they themselves could hardly wait to try some of the stew. Precisely because of the unusual amount of effort required to get to eat it, it was considered to be a real treat! You have to play to your strengths and avoid your weaknesses! In that way, the businessman is not so different from a painter, such as your father-in-law. Now, our banquets are successful because they capitalize on the reputation of our noble family. What our guests want is a certain kind of experience. The more difficult it is to obtain, the more valuable it is. If we served all comers, we'd be no different from that dumpling shop on the west corner of the street."

After this discussion, regretting that he was in no way a match for his mother-in-law when it came to business matters, Lin Yao very seldom concerned himself with the business of the Lu family banquets. Instead, he directed all of his attention towards his sick bear Shujuan.

It's perhaps worth mentioning that Shujuan's diet improved considerably during this time, because Lin Yao would gather up the majority of the food left over from the previous night's banquet and bring it to work each day in a big plastic bag, which he attached to the back of his bicycle. In this way, as the fat duck and tender chicken found their way from the Lu family banquet table to the zoo's bear house, Shujuan's strength improved considerably. Li Yu said, "With things as they are, whether Ding Yi adopts Shujuan or not doesn't seem that urgent anymore."

Lin Yao said, "Holding true to your word should have nothing to do with the urgency of a situation."

Li Yu said, "I hear that Ding Yi is doing really well now. The city government is set to name him as one of its ten top entrepreneurs."

"And with his name—Ding 'Number One'—he's sure to appear first on the list!"[32]

---

32. See note 19.

Li Yu laughed.

Just then Jinjing came in, carrying a bag. She said she had been cleaning out the refrigerator. There was quite a bit of old food that, if it wasn't used up, would go bad soon. So, she had brought it over for Shujuan to eat.

Shujuan, seeming uneasy at Jinjing's arrival, let out a low growl, stood up, and extended her paws out from the bars of her enclosure. Seeing this, Jinjing let out a scream and tried to run away. She was stopped, however, by Li Yu. He said, "She's just playing with you." Hearing this, Jinjing regained her composure and took a look at Shujuan. "At home, Lin Yao is always carrying on: Shujuan this, Shujuan that. I imagined her to be like a little dog. I had no idea she was so big! When she stands up, she's like a tower. If she were to catch hold of you, that would be it!"

Lin Yao said, "That's not true." As he spoke, he reached out his hand and grabbed hold of Shujuan's head. Seeing that Lin Yao wanted to play, Shujuan poked her snout out of her cage and grunted lightly. "She has a good nature," Lin Yao said. "Look at her eyes. See how bright they are."

Plucking up her courage, Jinjing approached the cage, hoping to get a closer look at Shujuan. Just as she moved her head closer to the bear, however, Shujuan made a sudden swiping motion with one of her paws, causing Jinjing to retreat a fair distance in fear.

Li Yu said, "What's the matter with her today? Usually, she doesn't behave this way. Just a while back, Chen Hongqi brought his daughter by to see her, and Shujuan played so nicely with her."

"You smell of firewood," said Lin Yao.

Jinjing sniffed her jacket and said that she had been wearing it that morning when gathering fruit-tree branches, which she later used to roast a duck.

"No wonder," said Lin Yao. "She's hated the smell of wood fire since a cub. Quick! Go and change your clothes and wash your face."

After she washed her face and took off her jacket, Jinjing approached the bear enclosure again. Shujuan was much more relaxed now. Patting the bear's head and pointing to Jinjing, Lin Yao said, "This is Jinjing. She's a friend."

Jinjing said, "Since you treat her as a child, she must know what a friend is."

"Of course, she knows what a friend is," said Lin Yao. "Her intelligence is about the same as that of a three-year-old child. She just can't speak."

"Really!" Jinjing came closer to the bars of the enclosure.

Lin Yao took a section of a sausage from Jinjing's bag. He gave it to her to give to Shujuan.

Jinjing was still a bit afraid. "Will she eat my hand, too?"

"No," said Lin Yao. "She already knows you're a friend. If you don't believe me, just try."

Taking the sausage in her hand, Jinjing got even closer to Shujuan, who ingratiatingly opened her mouth.

Jinjing hesitated.

"Feed her quickly," said Lin Yao. "She's waiting!"

"She really won't bite?"

"No, she won't!"

Finally, making brave, Jinjing dropped the sausage into Shujuan's open mouth, from which she was now only a few inches distant. Shujuan smacked her lips and let out a contented grunt; her small eyes—which reminded Jinjing of those made of black buttons on the flannel teddy bears she saw on sale in the shops—glistened more than ever with happiness. As she hadn't before, Jinjing now felt a connection with the bear: it seemed possible to have a dialogue with an animal of such intelligence. As she reached out to touch Shujuan's downy paw, which was still stretched out beyond the bars of the enclosure, she noticed its pigeon-egg-sized fleshy lump, black and shiny from constant licking. Jinjing fed Shujuan some more food, causing the bear, out of happiness, to wander in a circle around her enclosure before returning to sit close to the bars. From this position, the bear made a begging gesture, thereby exposing, yet again, the fleshy lump on her paw. Did she think Jinjing liked it? Jinjing gave her still more food; and, attracted by its brightness, took the opportunity to rub the lump. Sensing that she had found a friend in Jinjing, Shujuan made another happy circle around her enclosure.

"She likes you," said Lin Yao.

"And I like her," replied Jinjing.

Lin Yao then entered the enclosure, dunked a metal brush into some disinfectant, and used it to brush Shujuan's coat. Shujuan gave a contented snort. She rocked her head back and forth, sometimes intentionally either prodding Lin Yao with one of her paws or butting him with her head. She behaved just like an impish child playing with an adult. Captivated by this delightful scene of harmony between human and bear, Jinjing asked if she could come inside.

"No!" said Lin Yao.

"But you're inside," Jinjing said tartly.

"I'm allowed; you're not," said Lin Yao. "I've raised her since she was a cub. She knows me." As he said this, he opened up Shujuan's mouth and stuck his hand inside. Sure enough, Shujuan merely held it gently between her jaws but did not bite.

6.

As the Lu family business prospered, so did production increase at a phenomenal rate at Nichi-Star Foods. Ding Yi, spending money hand over fist, seemed always to be entertaining guests at the Lu family mansion. Gone were the days when he would fret about the cost of a couple of bags of nutritional powder. He now wore, rather stiffly, a western suit and an expensive name-brand tie (both, naturally, imported); and his pot belly, which he stuffed generously with delicacies from the Lu family kitchen, seemed to increase in size by the day. His bear-shaped cookies were a hit with a broad base of customers; and, once they were nationally recognized for their quality, supply could not keep up with demand. As for the Star Brand factory, it was completely transformed; as part of an economic development zone, it now had a spacious and bright shop floor. … Once he was named a top entrepreneur, Ding Yi became even busier than he had previously been; he also became an even more frequent guest at the Lu family mansion. He no longer rode a bicycle. Instead, he upgraded to a simple Volkswagen Santana sedan. This relatively unpretentious choice of car earned him a reputation for modesty, hard work, and fiscal responsibility. There was even talk that he might be a candidate to serve as a deputy to the next meeting of the National People's Congress. In sum, there seemed to be no obstacles in his path, whether as a businessman or as a government official.

One night, as Lin Yao was helping his mother-in-law add up receipts in the accounting office, Ding Yi came in to settle his tab. He had spent seven thousand four hundred *yuan*. With a toothpick dangling from his mouth, he said, "I'd like to reserve an abalone banquet for next week."

"We won't be able to do that for anything less than fifteen thousand *yuan*," said Lin Yao's mother-in-law. "Top-grade dried abalone from Hong Kong is currently running several hundred *yuan* a piece."

Ding Yi responded, "If it's over ten thousand *yuan*, then it's over ten thousand *yuan*. Sometimes you've just got to pay up. If you don't, you might undermine your own bigger plans."

"Sometimes you've just got to pay up.…" Lin Yao butted in.

Ding Yi looked up and said with feigned surprise, "Oh! Lin Yao, it's you! I thought you were.…"

"Ding Yi," said Lin Yao, not mincing his words. "Do you include Shujuan's adoption among those things that you've just got to pay up on?"

Ding Yi said, "Of course, I do! It's at the top of my mind. Once we turn a profit, I'll absolutely adopt Shujuan."

Pointing brusquely at the check Ding Yi had just signed, Lin Yao asked, "So, you're not turning a profit now, are you?"

With a spray of saliva, Ding Yi said, "This is all just a brave show! We're really still struggling to get by. As they say: 'The big tree gets buffeted by the wind.' With a big reputation comes additional expenses. Everyone wants a piece of you." Then, leaning in towards Lin Yao, he added, "To be honest, if you were to ask me now to sweep up a few bags of nutritional powder, I couldn't even do that for you. Those Japanese machines produce no waste at all!"

Lin Yao said, "So, you're telling me you can't afford to consider Shujuan?"

"That's not what I mean. Shujuan's situation is constantly on my mind. One of these days...." Ding Yi's voice trailed off, as even he felt that his excuses had become, after having been repeated so often, rather weak. Lin Yao wasn't a child, after all; there was no need to try to deceive him with empty words.

Lin Yao's mother-in-law peered at Ding Yi from behind her reading glasses, causing him to become even more uneasy.

Lin Yao persisted, "So when will you turn a profit, then?"

Ding Yi said, "You were there for the discussions. We agreed with the Japanese to a thirty-seventy split of the profits. Believe me, there is no end to the difficulties of putting yourself out there as the Chinese partner in a joint enterprise, when all you have to work with is thirty percent of the profits. Representatives of Project Hope ask for support: how can you say no?[33] The city wants to repair the roads: everyone's got to pitch in. They want to build a cultural plaza downtown: when the powers-that-be make a request, you'd better hop to. It's for the common good, after all. Then, there's the electric company. They say that, because of increased electricity usage at the factory, they've got to upgrade to high tension lines. That's not something that you can cover with a mere thirty or forty thousand *yuan*...."

As he listened to Ding Yi, Lin Yao's heart went cold, causing him to shudder. He knew there was simply no hope for Shujuan.

When he saw the look of distress on Lin Yao's face, Ding Yi grabbed Lin Yao's arm and said, "I know that you helped me find a partner for my joint venture because of Shujuan. I'll never forget how good you've been to me. Your concerns are like my own. Next month, I plan to have negotiations with our foreign partners about producing black rice vinegar at our factory. If the talks are successful, I'll adopt Shujuan right away." He patted Lin Yao on the shoulder. "Cut your brother some slack this once. I'm not my own master at the moment." As he spoke, Ding Yi got rather emotional, and a tear glistened in his eye.

Lin Yao took absolutely no notice of how Ding Yi departed. His mother-in-law, sliding the beads of her abacus back and forth, said, "Don't pin your hopes on that rascal Ding. He's a businessman, and there's often not much substance to what they say. I've just done some calculating: Since the first time him came here to eat till now, he's spent three hundred thousand *yuan*. Just think of the fortune he must have to squander such money. As I see

---

33. Project Hope is a large public charity run by the central committee of the Communist Youth League and the China Youth Development Foundation.

things, you ought to come up with another plan for your bear. Don't, as they say, hang yourself from this tree!"

"Right now," Lin Yao replied, "I can't even find a tree to hang myself from, even if I wanted to!"

"In that case, your bear is really in dire straits!"

It seemed to Lin Yao that some large object had become lodged in the back of his throat making it difficult for him to breathe. Having lost all of his strength, as if someone had simply plucked all the muscles from his body, he walked with feeble step back to his rooms.

7.

Lin Yao fell ill.

His diagnosis was terrifying: hemorrhagic fever. As he struggled for his life, his wife, Lu Xiaoyu, called home from Japan twice a day to see how he was doing. There was, however, no one from the Lu family to watch over Lin Yao in the hospital. This job, therefore, fell to Jinjing, who, in addition to cooking banquets in the evenings, spent her days by Lin Yao's hospital bedside. In a coma, Lin Yao suffered through high fever and hypouresis before finally surviving. Like a snake that has shed its old skin, Lin Yao now lay on his sickbed. Listlessly, he turned his head towards the window. Outside a light rain was falling. He could smell the scent of the mud in the hospital courtyard, and he could see the snow-white petals of the magnolia flowers tremble as they were pelted by the fine droplets of water. He thought: it's a spring rain; spring's arrived. He made two calls to the bear house, but no one answered. Li Yu came to visit him several times. When Lin Yao asked him about Shujuan, Li Yu responded, "She's the same." One of the young doctors, a young specialist in infectious diseases, was very concerned about Lin Yao and saw in his illness an opportunity to investigate the hypothesis that hemorrhagic fever, a disease that was normally spread through contact with the striped field mouse, might also be transmitted by the fleas or mites that infested Shujuan's coat.

After leaving the hospital, Lin Yao had to rest at home for more than half a month before he could finally get out of bed and walk around. One bright clear spring morning, he left his room, supporting himself by holding his hand against a wall. The crabapple tree in the courtyard was in full bloom. A delicate butterfly, as if it sensed it may have emerged too early in the season, alighted almost bashfully on one of the flowers. The sun shone on Lin Yao's bloodless face; nearly unable to support himself after such a severe illness, he swayed from side to side. With one hand he held on to the doorframe, while, with the other one, he shielded his eyes from the brilliant sun and stared dumbfoundedly at the courtyard for a while: there was newly planted grass; the garden paths had been restored by replacing the old broken bricks, from which they were made, with new ones; and, along their sides, had been planted a plethora of new flowering plants; the main hall and those to the east and west had also been refreshed with a new coat of paint; finally, the characters on the decorative signs had been re-gilded. The Lu family mansion looked now as grand as any princely palace!

Slowly, Lin Yao walked towards the front courtyard. As he passed through one of the moon gates, he caught sight of Jinjing and Li, the new chef, butchering a snake. The sinewy snake thrashed and struggled in Chef Li's hands before he callously nailed it to one of the walkway posts. As soon as he let go of the snake, its body curled up from the pain into a ball. Its tail smacked against the post, producing a series of crisp, clear thumps. The more it struggled, the more the snake seemed to suffer; it seemed as if it would go mad from the pain. Turning to Chef Li, Jinjing said, "Why don't you just have done with it? What's the point of letting it bang around like that?"

"It's too strong. I can't get hold of it properly," said Li.

Jinjing ordered one of the hired girls to go over and help, but the girl let out a cry of horror and ran in the other direction. So, Jinjing went over herself and grabbed hold of the snake. With a sharp knife, Chef Li skinned it. Even once it had been skinned and gutted, the shiny, white body of the snake continued to writhe about for a while. Observing this scene from a distance, Lin Yao became dizzy; hearing a bee-like buzz in his ears, he wanted to vomit.

Although still unsteady on his feet, Lin Yao made himself go to work.

As it was springtime, the zoo was filled with student groups on school trips. Their happy laughter brought the place new life after the dreary winter season. As usual, the children flocked to the monkey mountain. Lin Yao knew that this was the busiest time of year for Chen Hongqi; it was also an extended holiday for the Guangxi monkeys. Thrown by the children, bread and candy fell like rain into the monkey enclosure, causing about seventy percent of the monkeys to develop digestive problems. Not only did Chen Hongqi have to quarantine the monkeys sick with the runs, he also had to clean out seven to eight loads of garbage a day from the monkey enclosure. Lin Yao noticed that the Youbang Trade Co. sign still hung from the monkeys' cage. As the children read aloud to each other information about the special characteristics of the Guangxi monkeys, they naturally also read out the name of the company.

In contrast to this activity, bear mountain, although quite close to monkey mountain, was quiet—indeed, deserted. When Lin Yao walked over to take a look, he didn't see any bear there, only two or three piles of dried-up bear feces. Going around to the back door of the bear house, he found it locked. He pressed his face up to a crack in the door and shouted Shujuan's name. Startled by his call, two house sparrows, which had been scavenging for food in the empty building, fluttered up to the rafters.

Lin Yao sought out the director of the zoo, who told him that Shujuan had been sold to a traveling folk circus.

When he heard this, Lin Yao was speechless.

Seeing Lin Yao's expression, the director explained: "Black bears can expect to live for no more than twenty-five years. Shujuan had already been with us for more than twenty; her time was up. Simply put, she was just too sluggish to attract the attention of visitors to the zoo anymore. What's more, she was so sickly; in fact, she was the source of your hemorrhagic fever. No one wanted to get anywhere near her. It was the collective decision of the zoo leadership to sell her to the circus. It was best for Shujuan, too: the director of the circus said that he wasn't expecting Shujuan to perform any tricks; he just intended to put her in a cage and use her as a sort of advertisement to attract more customers."

"Why didn't you inform me first," Lin Yao asked.

The director said, "You were sick—struggling for your life, in fact. How were we supposed to talk to you? Li Yu handled everything related to Shujuan."

"When she was younger," Lin Yao said, "Shujuan was one of the zoo's star attractions. People crowded around bear mountain in rows—three inside, three outside—to see her. Now, however, you couldn't even find the heart to let her die here in peace?"

The director said, "Calm down a bit. As long as we held on to Shujuan, she was our one allotted bear. With her gone, we can apply to get a new bear— one that's young and lively. Of course, as your boss, I can completely understand what you're going through. It's natural to feel sad for a few days when we lose even something as small as a cat. Of course, it's even harder to lose something as big as a bear!"

"You simply don't understand animals!" said Lin Yao.

"You could learn a thing or two from Li Yu," said the director. "He's already happily transferred to the groundskeeping division."

Lin Yao looked around the zoo for Li Yu, whom he found, pruning shears in hand, trimming a holly bush. "Li Yu—" said Lin Yao.

Li Yu, lowering his head and continuing to work, didn't respond.

"Li Yu, I'm talking to you," said Lin Yao.

After a while, Li Yu replied, "I'm listening."

Lin Yao said, "Were you personally involved in the sale of Shujuan?"

"Yes," said Li Yu. "I put her into the cage myself."

Lin Yao said, "You were able to do that?"

Ignoring Lin Yao, Li Yu ground his teeth together and continued to prune the holly bush, as the clipping of his shears increased in speed and ferocity.

Lin Yao grabbed the pruning shears and threw them to the ground.

Without even looking at Lin Yao, however, Li Yu turned his body, picked them up again, and resumed trimming.

There was something wrong with Li Yu, Lin Yao decided, as he himself turned to go.

Just then, Li Yu called to Lin Yao, saying, ". ... While you were sick, there was no one to feed Shujuan. When they took her away, she didn't even have the energy to grunt. ... She looked at me; she wanted me to rescue her. Then, she looked at those men from Henan who were taking here out of the zoo. ... When they got to the gate, Shujuan was still looking at me, but I did nothing but stand there. ... I'm more worthless than a brutish beast."

Losing all strength, Lin Yao sank to the ground.

Li Yu squatted down and put his arm around Lin Yao's shoulder. "I like to think of myself a moral person, someone with human feeling," he said. "I promise you, Lin Yao: I'll never care for another bear. I can't take this kind of torment!"

For some time, Lin Yao just sat on the ground, staring straight ahead. It wasn't clear what he was thinking.

Li Yu said, "Why don't you transfer to the groundskeeping division. It's hard work; you're out in the sun all day; no one likes to do it, but it's peaceful. You won't have to deal with animals ever again. It's just the right kind of job for people like us."

"I want to find Shujuan and bring her back," said Lin Yao.

"That's impossible," said Li Yu. "How will you be able to find that circus?"

"First, I'll go to Henan, track down some old circus hands, and follow whatever clues I can find. It shouldn't be too hard to find an old bear."

"You'll be looking for a needle in a haystack."

"We'll see when I get there."

No sooner had Lin Yao said this than he was gone. He said goodbye to no one; he didn't even ask for time off from work. After several weeks, for the sake of keeping good order, the director of the zoo instructed the those who worked in the department of animal husbandry to mark Lin Yao as absent without leave; should he be gone for more than three months, he'd be considered to have resigned voluntarily. Afterwards, the director thought that maybe his approach was less than ideal, so he posted a missing persons ad in the newspaper. It instructed Lin Yao—should he read it—to report to work immediately.

Still there was no news from Lin Yao. He seemed simply to have disappeared. It was almost as if he had never even existed. Each time his wife called for news, she received the same reply: they were still looking for him.

The Lu family business didn't suffer at all from Lin Yao's absence. With one banquet per night, everything proceeded as usual.

Ding Yi and Nichi-Star Foods were now not just making little bear cookies; they were also producing, among other things, Chinese black rice vinegar, Japanese-style rice crackers, peanut-flavored milk powder, and refreshing instant milk tea. Business was booming. It was now rumored that the monthly salary for a worker at the factory was double that of the city's mayor. As for what Ding Yi earned, it had already reached the mark of what one might expect under the utopian first stages of True Communism. In the poor, mountainous communities around the city, there appeared over ten "Ding Yi Elementary Schools"; and, in the eastern part of the city proper, there was now a "Ding Yi Retirement Home." All of these projects were, of course, funded by money from Nichi-Star Foods. When the residents of the retirement home gathered to chat after dinner, they often spoke of Ding Yi, their benefactor in old age. As the initial surprise at their good fortune waned, they naturally thought to express their gratitude to the man who now provided them with everything from the clothes on their backs to the food that they ate. One among them, being good with a fine turn of phrase and with time on his hands, wrote a composition in praise of Mr. Ding Yi; others copied it out and sent it to whomever they could think of. It was better than having nothing to do, after all. There was even one old woman, who had once been a music teacher, who wrote a song: "Greetings, Ding Yi!" Once she taught everyone the lyrics, they sang it with the sincerest of passion. Oh, Ding Yi, that man among men!

It was not long before word of Ding Yi's philanthropy reached the ears of Li Yu. He didn't have any intention of digging up old grudges. In fact, mingled with his feelings of regret, he actually felt some admiration for Ding Yi. Before he could even forget his promise to adopt Shujuan, he was already going ahead with plans to build schools and retirement homes. Certainly, this was a mark of the man's intelligence. After all, if you adopt a bear, it can't write any compositions in praise of your support; nor can it sing "Greetings, Ding Yi!" All you get for your money is a little brass plaque hung in an out-of-the-way spot where people will hardly take notice of it. Why would Ding Yi do a thing like that? Li Yu finally realized: while he might be your friend, Ding Yi was, first and foremost, a businessman.

That day, Ding Yi drove his car over to the Lu family mansion. He said that Yokomichi was coming back to town to sign another agreement and that he specifically mentioned wanting to attend another one of the Lu family banquets. Was there a dish in the Lu family repertoire that he, Ding Yi, hadn't yet tried, he wanted to know.

Looking over the menu, Lin Yao's mother-in-law said, "You've had just about everything before."

Ding Yi took a look: it was true; everything seemed familiar.

"But," said Lin Yao's mother-in-law. "It can't hurt to ask the Second Lady."

The two of them walked over to the Second Lady's apartments. As they went, Ding Yi asked what Lin Yao had been up to recently. Not wishing to divulge Lin Yao's disappearance, Lin Yao's mother-in-law was evasive: "Like always, he's busy with that old bear."

Ding Yi said, "Next time I'm here to eat, I'll bring a check. I've never made good on my promise to adopt Shujuan. I'm sure Lin Yao thinks I'm pretty horrible, but it's time now to follow through and help that bear out a bit."

Lin Yao's mother-in-law smiled slightly but didn't say anything.

When the Second Lady heard Ding Yi's request, she thought for some time. Then she said, "The cuisine of the Lu family is really quite exceptional. In the old days, the amount we spent on a single banquet was easily the equivalent of what a well-off peasant family might earn in a single year. That's not the kind of thing just anyone can afford nowadays."

"Second Lady," said Ding Yi. "Help me out a bit: Is there something I haven't had yet?"

"Of course, there are things you haven't had," the Second Lady said. "I just don't think we can get the ingredients now."

Ding Yi replied, "I think you're underestimating me. Sure, I might not be able to buy the moon and the stars, but let's suppose someone were selling a nuclear bomb. I could afford it."

"There are two dishes," said the Second Lady, "that I made with my mother-in-law a few times just after I was married. Afterwards, I never made them again."

Ding Yi asked how rare they were.

"I assure you, no one has ever tried their likes," said the Second Lady.

"Well, tell me! What are they?" said Ding Yi.

"Stewed bear's paw and deep-fried camel's hump."

Ding Yi clapped his hands. "You're remarkable, Second Lady! Truly amazing!"

The Second Lady continued, "The paw must be the bear's left front paw. That's the paw that the bear usually licks. It's the most prized. As for the hump, it must come from a white dromedary. They are the most tender and most nutritious."

Ding Yi said, "You just wait, Second Lady. I'll get these two ingredients within one week and give them to you."

8.

Both heaven and earth were bathed in numinous light, as the long rays of the sun, on its westward descent, struggled to cast their fading brilliance onto the rooftops of the houses in the village of Zhaojiaji. One of the villagers, as he first looked up at the quickly setting sun and then looked at the village, rendered almost foreign by the astonishing colors of the setting sun, said, "The sky's so strange now. Perhaps we should expect an earthquake."

Another old villager said, "It's called a demon's twilight. It means God's going to vent his anger. I've only ever seen the likes of this once or twice before. Whenever there's a demon's twilight, something untoward is bound to happen...."

From out of this strange light emerged an emaciated figure, clad in rags: it was Lin Yao. On his feet, he wore what had once been walking shoes; now they were nearly sole-less. His heavy footfall on the dirt road kicked up a trail of dust. Cracks in his parched lips revealed white skin marked with shining rivulets of blood. Due to exhaustion, his eyes appeared unfocused and detached, while the disheveled hair on his head, as well as that of his beard, was covered in a layer of grime. Under the watchful eyes of the villagers, he walked down their main street, stopping in front of a shop that sold hand-pulled noodles.

"Do you have any noodles with broth?" Lin Yao asked.

The shopkeeper said, "Yes, we do. It's 1.50 *yuan* a bowl."

Lin Yao entered the little shop and sat down at one of the plain tables. "I'll take two bowls."

"Your money first," said the shopkeeper.

Lin Yao didn't understand the shopkeeper's distrustful glance. Nevertheless, he reached into his pocket, pulled out his wallet, fished out some money, and put it on the table.

Seeing that Lin Yao wasn't there to beg, the shopkeeper relaxed. He became friendly and talkative. "Do you want your noodles thick or thin, sir?" he asked.

Lin Yao, hearing himself called "sir," laughed. "Have you ever met a 'sir' that looks as shabby as me and smells of firewood and corn cobs like he's just off the farm?"

"Of course, I have!" replied the shopkeeper. "We've seen all sorts of 'sirs' come through our village since the implementation of the new economic policies. The richer they are, the poorer they look. It's fashionable to look poor. People will tear holes in the knees of a nice pair of pants just to look a little bit like you!"

Resting against the wall, Lin Yao felt too tired to go on talking.

The shopkeeper, however, wasn't finished. "I can tell you're exhausted," he said. "That's fine. Rest here. Although you've got a long beard, I suspect you're not any older than me. Anyway, about two month ago, another fellow stopped by my shop. He was walking along the Yellow River doing research of some kind. He looked worse off than you. He was so tired he couldn't even put his words together right."

Soon, he brought the steaming noodles over to Lin Yao. Two bowls. Little pools of oil floated on top of the broth in each. Picking up his chopsticks, Lin Yao dug in.

A drum sounded in the distance.

"Is there a circus in town?" Lin Yao stopped chewing.

The shopkeeper replied, "It's already been here for four or five days. There are only so many people in our village. Everyone's already seen it. They should really pack up and move on, but instead they're still out there banging the drum and beating the gong. Who wants to see it twice?"

"Is there a bear?"

"Sure. A big one, locked in a cage. It lies there all day."

That's all Lin Yao needed to hear. Without saying another word, he threw down his bowl and raced towards the sound of the drum and gong. The shopkeeper followed after him, saying, "You forgot your bag!"

"Hold on to it for me," said Lin Yao.

"Wow, that guy!" said the shopkeeper. "He looked half dead a moment ago. Now look at him, full of energy. He must really like the circus!"

The "World's Big Circus" from Fuyang had stopped in Zhaojiaji.

Just outside a cloth fence, inside a cage, lay a large black bear; it was barely breathing. Several children surrounded its cage and poked it with sticks, but the bear, its eyes closed, didn't move.

Someone said, "It's dead. They're trying to rip people off with a dead bear! What a joke!"

The children, in turn, shouted, "It's dead! It's dead!"

"Who says it's dead?" The director of the circus walked towards them with a cigarette hanging from his mouth. "I'll show you it's not dead." As he said this, he walked over to a nearby food stall, grabbed a red-hot poker, and, with it, savagely stabbed at the bear.

The black bear convulsed, raised its body with a roar, and, with a gaping red mouth, surged ferociously forward, rattling its metal cage. The children, in fear, ran off in all directions. None of them dared get close to the cage again. Satisfied, the circus director said, "Now who says it's dead? It was just too lazy to acknowledge you. There's much more to see inside: 'Zhang Fei Sells Pork,' 'Li Cuilian Commits Suicide,' 'The Cuckold's Great Transformation,' 'Man Battles Snake.' … four *yuan* per person, continuous performances. The stage is never empty!…"[34]

By the time Lin Yao reached the cage, the black bear had lain back down, but the smell of burning flesh lingered, and a trace of black smoke still

---

34. All of these are various circus acts: "Zhang Fei Sells Pork" refers to a theatrical representation of the story of the meeting of the two Three Kingdoms–period heroes Zhang Fei and Guan Yu; "Li Cuilian Commits Suicide," another theatrical piece based on folkloric sources, tells how, after her suicide, Li Cuilian is visited in the underworld by her husband.

curled up from a spot on the bear's body. Lin Yao headed straight for the cage, crouched down, and looked carefully at the bear. Covered with wounds and emaciated, the bear struggled for breath. It had lost much of its fur, exposing its bright red flesh, on which numerous flies feasted. From its appearance, Lin Yao couldn't readily make out whether it was Shujuan or not. "Shujuan! Shujuan!" he quietly called to the bear, which showed no indication that it would respond to any stimulus from the external world.

All the while, the circus director, his head cocked sideways, stood watching Lin Yao. Based both on how Lin Yao was dressed and how he behaved, he assumed Lin Yao was crazy, so he walked over to him, rudely pushed him away, and told him to keep his distance.

Caught off guard by this shove, Lin Yao fell into a puddle next to the cage. Covered now head to toe with mud, ash, garlic skins, onion peels, and other garbage, he elicited a burst of laughter from the assembled bystanders.

The circus director, arms crossed in front of his chest, looked down at Lin Yao and said, "Calling a black bear Shujuan! You seem to miss your wife so much that you've gone crazy!"[35]

The crowd laughed again.

By this time, the noodle shop shopkeeper had arrived. He helped Lin Yao out of the mud. To the circus director he said, "What right do you have to treat others so high-handedly?"

"He's crazy," said the circus directory.

"No, he's not," said the shopkeeper. "He was just eating noodles in my shop. He didn't seem a bit crazy."

Lin Yao said to the circus director, "I'm looking for a bear—my black bear. She's called Shujuan. Did you buy this bear from a zoo?"

The circus director said, "I bought this bear from a circus in Heyang. Before me, it had already changed hands a number of times. I regret the purchase. It's so sick, it can't even stand up."

"I think she's Shujuan," said Lin Yao.

"Shujuan?" Hearing this, the circus director pointed to the bear with his lips. "Call her and see."

As everyone watched, Lin Yao crawled once again over to the cage and called Shujuan.

He called several times, but there was no response from the bear in the cage. The circus director said, "There are lots of black bears. Why should this one be yours?"

Lin Yao said, "I just have a feeling she is. I can't be wrong."

"But she shows no sign of recognizing you," said the circus director.

Lin Yao reached his hand into the cage and lightly combed through the

---

35. See note 3.

bear's matted fur with his fingers. "Shujuan," he murmured. "Shujuan, I know that you think that my smell is all wrong. But you must recognize my voice...."

The shopkeeper said, "You smell like firewood and sweat, just like a peasant. As it is, your own dog wouldn't recognize your scent, let alone a bear."

Slowly, the black bear opened its eyes and peered at Lin Yao. For a moment, it seemed to recall something. Then, nothing. It closed its eyes again.

Calling Shujuan, Lin Yao gently picked up and massaged the bear's paw, which lay pushed against the cage. Then, suddenly, the bear stood up, thrust its paw beyond the bars, and, in a ferocious rage, swiped at Lin Yao, as he crouched by the side of the cage. Lin Yao had no time to take cover. In an instant, the bear's paw had clawed off a chunk of flesh from the side of Lin Yao's face. Immediately thereafter, the bear swiped down, clobbering Lin Yao again. ...

A flow of blood covered Lin Yao's eyes, but he felt no pain. Everything happened with dreamlike swiftness. There was no time to think. But, just before darkness overcame him, Lin Yao clearly saw, as the bear's paw raced towards him, a glistening, fleshy lump.

A glistening, fleshy lump....

* * *

Ding Yi wasn't joking when he said he could afford a nuclear bomb. In just a few days he was able to supply the Lu family with a fresh bear paw and a camel hump. With them also arrived two items that Ding Yi wanted Lin Yao's mother-in-law to pass on to Lin Yao: a check and a letter of agreement addressed to the zoo authorities, explaining his intent to adopt Shujuan.

"When it comes to Shujuan, you should deal directly with Lin Yao," said Lin Yao's mother-in-law. "I don't want to get involved."

Ding Yi asked when Lin Yao would be at home.

Lin Yao's mother-in-law said she didn't know.

Jinjing didn't have the slightest idea of what to do with the downy and bloody bear's paw, so she sought out the Second Lady. Lifting the paw up, she examined it with care. Then she said, "Excellent. It's the left front paw. That Ding Yi is really quite something to be able to get a fresh bear paw. Back in the day, not only the Lu family, but also princes of the royal blood, could only manage to get dried bear's paw. We had to rehydrate them before cooking."

Hearing this, Ding Yi acted as if it was nothing. "Hey! It's just a bear's paw. A simple dish...."

The Second Lady said, "Bear's paw should be cooked on a low heat. There must be plenty of water." Then she gave careful instruction to Jinjing: "It's sufficient for the water to begin to simmer. There should only be little ripples on the surface. Don't let it come to a rolling boil. That'll destroy the skin. If the skin is destroyed, when it comes time to serve, it will be just like presenting a chicken that's had its skin boiled off—Repulsive! Worthless!" Before leaving, the Second Lady said, "After it's simmered for three or four hours and the fur is ready to come off, come get me. With a dish like this, I need to be in charge."

When the bear's paw had simmered for about half the day, Jinjing called for the Second Lady. Once she had put on her apron, the Second Lady fished the paw out of the water and cleaned it with warm water. Holding it close to her breast, she used tweezers to remove the fur, one hair at a time, as if she were plucking her eyebrows. Jinjing stood to the side and watched.

The Second Lady said, "When you remove the fur, you absolutely must not rush. Simmered bear's paw has skin that's as delicate as paper...." The Second Lady finished removing the coarse fur, but then she handed the bear's paw over to Jinjing, saying that her eyesight wasn't good enough to remove the finer hair. She then explained to Jinjing that once the fine hair was removed, she must carefully peel off the paw's black membrane. It should then be simmered again, to soften it even further. Finally, the bones were to be removed. When placed on the table, it must be in its original shape and unblemished. The broth must be clear; the meat, tender....

Jinjing sat on a stool beside the door to remove the fine hair. Next, she peeled off the black membrane. The hairless bear's paw was as shiny as a human being's. Jinjing thought to herself what odd creatures humans are: they'll eat just about any living thing. The stranger something is—the more unreasonable it is to eat—the more prized it is. Confucius had once said that he would eat nothing but that which was clean and finely prepared; nowadays, however, people said they'd eat only what was new and unusual.[36] As long as they could put it in their mouths, between a bear's foot and a human's, there seemed to be no difference.

Unexpectedly, she felt a round fleshy lump on the inner side of the bear's paw. It was about the size of a pigeon's egg. Something jogged her memory. She looked more closely at the bear's paw. First, her hands began to tremble; then, her heart—"Shujuan!" She called out in horror, as she threw the paw back into the basin, causing a flood of water to scatter on the floor.

From its resting place, the white claws on the half-cooked paw pointed shockingly skyward; its palm seemed curled into the shape of an astonished question mark. This paw had once been linked to a life that had seemed almost human. How many times had Shujuan reached out with it to the people on the other side of her cage to communicate her tender feelings of happiness, dependence, and love? ... How could she have known that her paw would one day be transformed into something simmered in a pot of broth, stripped of its fur, and served as a delicacy to those whom she loved.

Those who had adopted her were now about to eat her.

---

36. See note 29.

Jinjing couldn't bring herself to pick the paw back up. Instead, she removed her apron and walked quietly to Lin Yao's small room, where she sat in silence on his small bed. His bedding was bunched into ball, but, she discovered, it no longer smelled of him. All it smelled of now was mildew. Lin Yao was long gone.

The Second Lady finished preparing the bear's paw.

The stewed bear's paw she served that night was in a class of its own—its consistency, tender; its flavor, rich; the broth, clear and refreshing. It made quite a deep impression on those who ate it. For a long time afterwards, those who were present at that night's banquet would affect a jaded attitude whenever they tasted any other rare delicacy, saying, "Well, it certainly can't compare with that bear's paw I once had."

Having paid with her life for these words of praise, Shujuan ought to be able to rest in peace.

19

In Love with the Gen River

YE MEI

In June, the Gen River flows alongside the Greater Khingan Range high-way, keeping the range in close company like a lover. It bends and rushes with mighty force; it disappears into the verdant, luxuriant woods only to reappear bold, open, straightforward, and bashful.

What surprises me is that the river water looks dark and gleams much like the darkened lustrous skin color of a young man. What gives the river this color? Local friends smile at me and say the dense grass and trees on the banks give the river its color. Trees and grass nestle intimately together along the river; they cast their reflections onto its bosom, becoming part of it. Cloud reflections undulate with the river's current. The clouds float high above in the blue sky. The river is their mirror. The clouds' lightwaves and soaring atmosphere flow through its flowing water. Is the sky in the river, or the river in the sky?

Then I found myself wishing to be a tree, or a cloud, so as to forever nestle against the river, or keep close to it, this River of Roots.[1]

In spring, the river's enormous life force will burst out, shedding its thick frozen layers of ice, stretching its body with joy, and rushing on. During this ice-breaking season, the pristine river runs ice-cold, crystal clear, and pure. Along its banks, birches and shrubs stripped by the winter cold begin to show new green. The days of their leaf shadow intimacy with the river are yet to come. With its source in the Greater Khingan Range, the Gen River was originally named *Gegen Gaole* in the Evenki language, meaning crystal clear. Every year, the river comes to life again in its purity and repeats in its journey the life-cycle from childhood innocence to motherhood, nourishing tens of thousands of lives along its banks.

---

1. The character "根" (*gen*) means "root" in Chinese.

Translated by Zhou Xiaojing

Without rivers, there would be no human beings on Earth. Wherever there are rivers, there are traces of human beings, and human beings see rivers—large and small—as sources of life. We love to compare a river's water to mother's milk and to call rivers that flow by our hometowns mother-river. More than fifteen hundred rivers and lakes feed the area of Genhe, named after the Gen River. They comprise the sources of the great rivers in northern China. Countless ethnic groups have followed the Gen River and settled on the grasslands or on other nearby waterways. Among them are the Evenki, who are reindeer herders. The Evenki live close to forests and rivers. Their range extends as far as the banks of Ergune River in the west to Enhe Hada Town and Xilinji in the north, to the mouth of the Kamalan River and the headwaters of the Huma River in the east, and to the Gen River in the south. The Evenki and the rivers have depended on one another for their mutual survival for thousands of years. From this ancient relationship there has come a song of communication between their shamans and the river spirits: *Blue Sky, Blue Sky, how are you? Are you well? We are birds soaring in the sky! River, River, how are you? Are you well? We are fish swimming in the water!*

The Evenki have been living on this land for generations. The Gen River bears witness to it all.

The Evenki treat their reindeer like family members; they always keep them by their side when hunting or doing chores. Their reindeer have the head of a horse, antlers of a deer, body of a donkey, and hoofs of an ox. Their fur is light grey or white; their manner is noble, gentle, and elegant. A Tang poet, Li Bai, once wrote in a poem: "When will I return after parting from you? Why don't I leave the white deer in the green mountains for now?" Emperor Qianlong wrote in amazement:

> I heard that in the middle of the Fanpeng Lake
> Immortals come and go riding on white deer
> I doubted that until today when I see
> This tame, gentle, tribe of musk deer
> So different than I had heard.

Nowadays, children are widely familiar with reindeer, the kind that prance and pull Santa's sleigh, holding high their beautiful antlers. Reindeer belong to the world of fairy tales; when they prance and jump, tales are born like magic beans.

*   *   *

Although reindeer once astonished the poet and the emperor with their great size and gentleness, at present, only a small number of them survive. In China, there are only a handful of reindeer herding sites along the Gen River in the Greater Khingan Range, and even the Greater Khingan Range is not nearly as fecund as it once was. The Evenki have stowed their hunting guns to protect the animals and their habitat, but they have to continue on with their lives. Almost everyone has reasons to leave the forests for the city or distant places. But ninety-four-year-old Maria Suo, a respected Evenki elder of the Aoluguya tribe, stays with her reindeer.

As soon as we reached Genhe, we heard someone talking about her, and our minds call up the paintings we have seen of her. In those paintings, she looks indomitable and calm, her mouth is closed, the wrinkles around her mouth are like the veining in birch bark. It is as if her face had become the forest where she spent her life. Without speaking her face tells stories of her life with reindeer.

Perhaps she is the embodiment of the Gen River: motherly, kind and loving, mellow and strong, legendary. When she was younger, she was beautiful and capable. She was a famous hunter in the Greater Khingan Range. She would go hunting with her husband in the deep forests. No matter how far they were from their tribe, it was Maria Suo who led her reindeer to return safely home with their kill. Unlike those who often got lost in the forests or met with accidents, Maria Suo would literally blaze the trail. She used a hatchet or a hunting knife to carve small blazes on the tree trunks. She would follow these marks when moving with the whole family or hunting far away from home, or she would make a cut on a big tree, tie a bar to it horizontally, and then hang a small wreath of willow twigs on the bar. The wreath indicated the direction in which the family was moving, and the length between the wreath and the trunk indicating the distance from their home to the new location. Thus, no matter how mysterious and vast the forests were, she could map out her routes.

Brave and intelligent, Maria Suo was also a mother of seven children. The Evenki highly value fertility because historically, severe cold weather, various diseases, and alcoholism slowed the growth of an already small population. All seven children of Maria Suo have grown up to be strong and healthy. She is truly a river of life. Her husband became alcoholic after the birth of their first child and neglected household chores. Yet Maria Suo brought up the children with her abundant milk. Her tribe is thriving. Their herds of reindeer are thriving. Her name has become the symbol of the forest guardian of Aoluguya.

The other day, I planned on visiting Maria Suo's community, but after some hesitation, ended up not going. In my heart, I feel I have already met her. Her face looks familiar; her breath seems to brush past my ears. Although I have never heard her speak—even if I did, I would not understand her Evenki language—her voice stays deep in my heart like the breeze of the forests and the waves of the Gen River. A photo of her taken by the writer, Wure Ertu, caught my eye more than once. In a birch forest, old Maria Suo wears a robe and headscarf, stands beside a reindeer with seven-point antlers. She is smiling, bending slightly to touch the reindeer's fine, soft fur with one of her wrinkled hands. As the reindeer nestles against old Maria's robe, it chews on a favorite moss. She must feel motherly toward it. Like a painting and a poem, this photo is imbued with a natural simplicity. This great mother lives with such tranquility among her herd of reindeer. How could a stranger such as I intrude upon this life?

Actually, I myself would love to take a photo of Maria Suo to reflect my perspective with my understanding. In recent years, crowds of tourists from around the world have frequented the preserve of Maria Suo's community and presented it from their varied perspectives. To me, everyone has their own Gen River and Maria Suo in their hearts. But we come and go so quickly. How could we see as deeply, as profoundly, as Wure Ertu sees?

Wure Ertu is a son of the Gen River. The year when this young man who had lived in the Greater Khingan Range all his life appeared in the literary arena with his book, *Amber-Colored Campfire*, a bright light seemed to shine immediately. People recognized in his novel a solitary, passionate people. What he brought to literature was unexpected, but it came as an even greater surprise when he left his leadership position in Beijing and returned to his hometown. Years after that, I couldn't help feeling a stir in my core as I walked on the Hulunbuir Grasslands—the hills forming a winding and rolling skyline at the horizon; seas of flowers in full bloom or a single flower blooming in solitude; herds of horses grazing or looking up as if meditating; rivers meandering through the grassland. These scenes still make me think that this Evenki writer returned home for many possible reasons, none of which were perhaps very important. Yet only one would have been sufficient: to be among these grasslands, these rivers, and these people once again. They are calling to him all the time; it is the blood of his mountain and forest ancestors stirring in his veins. I might be wrong but this is what I think. One time I asked him if I was right, he gazed at me like a deer and nodded. "Yes, it is so."

Wure Ertu and Maria Suo see with the same eyes. Since his return to his hometown in the Hulunbuir Grasslands, he has completed *Journals in Hulunbuir* and a series of other works and photographs, which are his ways of searching cultural roots and showing his deep attachment and gratitude to the grassland, as a son of the Evenki.

* * *

The first day when I was in Genhe, everything appeared new and fresh to me. After dinner, our hosts prepared our outfits for entering the forest the next day: knee-high canvas boots and beekeeping hoods for protecting us from ticks, called *caopazi* in the local language. Back in Beijing, a friend from the Cultural Association at Genhe messaged me a few times to caution me about being bitten by these insects and to remind me to bring enough clothing and other protective gear. This friend followed up with a friendly reminder after I got to Genhe, once more noting the dangers and offering tips for dealing with *caopazi* in case I get bitten. My friend said, a *caopazi* is like a leech. They are tenacious. They won't withdraw even if it means death. They will burrow half of their bodies into the flesh, yielding only to smoke. If one tries to pull them out, their bodies will break, leaving half of them in the skin, causing infection. This indeed has happened to someone and that person contracted tick-borne encephalitis, among other things.

Everyone took my friend's warning seriously, but as we walked through the forests, we didn't encounter any scary *caopazi*, only clouds of blind midges. Ai Ping, a native from Hailar in the Greater Khingan, accompanied us all the way. She said there were not as many insects in these forests when she was a child. As far as she could remember, she and other children often played in the forests for hours and no one ever had any serious insect bites. Have human beings devolved, or has the environment changed? One can't help making such associations. Perhaps in the beginning this world was truly a commons that belonged to all living things. Do insects attack humans because the latter have occupied and taken too much? No sooner had we gotten off our van than the midges began to swarm us. They followed us all the way back into the van, dancing madly inside, despite our frantic efforts to wave them away. Ai Ping told us not to worry, as they would disappear as soon as the van started. She was right. Even though the doors were closed and the midges didn't fly out, they strangely disappeared before long, hiding who knows where?

I have heard that there are so many butterflies in the Greater Khingan Range. Unfortunately, I was unable to join my travel group to go into the mountains to see them because I was obligated to go over some picture proofs for *Literature of Nationality* before they were sent to the printer. So I stayed behind to review the photos. Everyone who returned from the mountains expressed their amazement. They said butterflies were everywhere. Along the freeway, in front of the cars, behind peoples' backs, layer upon layer of butterflies danced, like flowers in bloom, forming long floating blankets! Although I didn't see them with my own eyes, the vivid testimony of Zhou Xiaofeng (a writer and an editor) and the others made me feel as if I were right there.

Those who live away from them, travel far to see the mountains, but those who have been living in the Greater Khingan Range are moving out.

In the twenty-first century human beings are beginning to realize more deeply than before that we must live with nature on equal terms. Most Evenki living along the Gen River have said goodbye with reluctance to the mountains and forests to make more room for the boundless vegetation and black bears, wolves, chinchilla squirrels, butterflies and other insects. They have built a fairytale-like village not far from cities.

When we visited the village, the Evenki who have moved down from the mountains were doing chores by twos and threes in front of their homes. Men were wearing fashionable T-shirts and jeans. Some young women sported perms. Some had blonde or crimson highlights in their hair, which was very eye-catching in the sunlight. These women still wore long traditional dresses, like the aging Maria Suo's, but the colors and floral patterns of the dresses were the same as those that can be found in the city, with wavy laces across the chest. Women penciled their eyebrows with meticulous care, making even more prominent their typical Evenki foreheads and deep-set eyes.

All the houses are built with government funding, and feature coffee-colored exterior walls with angular roofs. Every Evenki family who has moved in decorates its rooms according to its own preferences. As I walked slowly past the open doors, I saw drawn curtains with floral motifs on them, motorbikes parked in front of the doors, the strands of red chili peppers hung on the walls. Villagers leaned at the doors, nodding and smiling.

Evenki are a warm and hospitable people. Whenever guests arrive, the whole family will come out to welcome them with both hands clasped and raised according to their traditional etiquette. The young have inherited what the old have taught them. "When outsiders come, they cannot carry their houses on their backs; when you travel, you cannot take your home with you. No one will take care of you when you are on the road if you do not receive your guests with hospitality. People will enter a house only when it has a fire in its stove; birds will only land on a tree when it has branches." For generations, the Evenki have followed their established code of conduct, called "Au Au Er," developed out of their labor, traditions, and religious beliefs.

Under a spacious eave, a little girl with a round face and rosy cheeks, wearing a floral hat, sitting in a stroller, was giggling at me. I opened my arms. She raised up her chubby little hands with complete trust. I lifted her up and held her tight. Her mother walked over. She was a young, full-figured Evenki married to a Han man from Shandong Province. This family of three live in a fairy-tale-like lodge. At their door, a birch board reads, "Bulina's Speciality Store for Reindeer Products." Their house has two stories. On the first floor there are glass cases displaying deer-antler liquor, little birch-bark boxes and cups, and other goods. The young man from Shandong seems content with his life here. He hands me his wife's business card, saying the reindeer products here are the most authentic, transported directly from the Aoluguya tribe. His wife stands by his side, nodding and smiling. Her name is Bulina. Inter-ethnic marriage between Evenki and people of other ethnicities is common, especially in recent years. Their children all take Evenki names, becoming part of a new generation of the Evenki community.

This small town is called Genhe. It is located in an extremely cold region of China, the belly of the Greater Khingan Range. The sunlight of June lights up this lively small town of the Northern country, making it hard to imagine that the temperature can reach minus 50°C. Nine months out of twelve heating is a necessity in the town. The heating fuels that came from the forests in times past have disappeared. Nowadays, most people burn coal; some just give up and move away. Except for the Evenki, the majority of people living in Genhe have migrated from Shandong, Liaoning, Jilin, and other places just a few decades ago.

For many years, the lumber of the Greater Khingan Range was transported continuously from Genhe to the rest of China, and this place was booming. Lumber yards and sawmills were the town's key businesses. The Bureau of Forestry's Farm could be the town's nickname. Scenes of the past are left in photo albums and generations of memory. Now, former lumberjacks have become guardians of the forests. *Tianbaogongcheng*, Natural Forest Protection Project (NFPP), are bywords of the day. Since 1998, the rate of logging in the Greater Khingan Range has dropped and the reduction of logging has reached the desired goal. A large number of lumberjacks had to re-tool themselves and find new jobs. They are producing compression boards and planks, and small pre-fabricated wooden houses. They are making every effort to prepare themselves to say goodbye to the past and move into the future. People of Genhe have lived by the riches of the Greater Khingan Range, but they can no longer obtain them easily. What kind of self-discipline does it take to repress the desire of just taking these riches all at once?

Dawn arrives at Genhe very early. On my first day here, I woke up in the middle of the night to find full sunlight outside the window. I thought it was at least seven a.m., but my watch said three. This happened a few times, so I got up out of bed and walked over to the window to have a look outside. The Gen River was right there under my nose. On the other side of it, people were dancing in the public square, so many of them—men and women, old and young, as if the whole town were gathering there. The dancing masters in the front wore bright colors: red shirts, white pants, white gloves and hats. Like an honor guard, they moved in unison. The motley-colored crowd followed along, also demonstrating impressive style.

Early in the morning and late in the evening, I watched them at the window, as the Gen River ran along keeping time with the music and dance, inviting all to join. One evening, I could not help crossing the bridge to immerse myself in the joy of the dancers. No need to feel any sense of unease, no one minded newcomers of any kind. Everybody came and went smiling. The women around me were tall, plump, and fair. I could tell from their clothing and speech that some of them were Mongolian, Manchurian, Daur, Evenki, and Russian. I imitated the ways they raised their hands, lifted their feet, swayed side to side from the waist, and I allowed myself to imagine the various pleasures of living here. This was the most joyful day I spent at Genhe.

There was only one woman whose dance stood out from the rest. It was already sunset when she caught my attention—most of the dancers had left by this point, heading off in all directions—but a group of diehard dancers remained. A series of folk songs kicked off another round, and this woman stood apart by herself, with only the music holding her there as if by a thread. She moved her slim body like a bow, now arched, now straight, changing as she liked. She waved her arms without the slightest restraint. As dusk gave way to nightfall, her arm movements looked like the mysterious waves of the dark Gen River in June, sometimes gentle, sometimes forceful. I had never seen a solo dance with such intense concentration taking place outside the concert stage. Perhaps she was not just dancing, but rather releasing her feelings. I could not see her features clearly in the dark and wondered what she was trying to express.

The music moved from "Zhuoma from the Grassland," to "A Winding River in Front of the Lad's Door," to Tujia dragon-boat songs. In this northernmost town, I heard a folk song from the Three Gorges region "Lassie Wants to Cross the River, Who'll Push Her Boat?"

The woman danced to the music as if she were crossing the river. She lowered her shoulders, lifted up her head, stamped her feet with all her strength. Maybe she is a wife. Maybe she is a mother. The big river in her heart must hold countless joys, sorrows, and hope! This woman of the Gen River! She brought tears to my eyes.

I turned my back and left the dance. The Gen River rolled by my side. The lights from the big bridge transformed the dark surface of the river into a parade of glistening colors. Even though I had directly encountered the Gen River, I knew that I would never be able to reach its depths. All I could do was keep these people, these moments in my memory.

These moments, slow-flowing, indelible, dissolving....

20

From Huorili River, Huorili Mountain

YILAN

She stood on the hillside, singing one song after another. It seemed as if she were singing out all the songs she knew. I listened closely to the tunes and the lyrics, mesmerized by the feelings they invoked—the gentleness of Huorili River, the bitter green scent of wormwood, even the fragrance of lilies, and the caresses of breeze and grass. How I wished it were for me that she sang those songs and she would sing them for me, forever.

Before long, she was joined by many other singers.

* * *

Feast time. We sat on the grass in small circles. Before eating and drinking, men and women dipped their right ring fingers in wine, then flicked upward to venerate the sky and downward to honor the earth and mountain gods. We youngsters didn't know much about rituals. We tore large pieces of beef and lamb with our hands or knives; gulped down bowl after bowl of wine. Some of us drank straight from bottles. The feast didn't end until men were drunk and women's faces turned red. By then, the sun had already set in the west.

* * *

I am not leaving here. All my land is here. Huorili Mountain is here. Huorili River is here. I grew up, like all my ancestors, drinking water from Huorili River and listening to the rustling forests. Is there a blade of grass, a tree, a mountain, or a stone that does not have my footprints on it? Is there a place that is not filled with my presence? I grew up by the mountain, the river, and the land. I won't move to the new village.

Translated by Xiangyang Xiao, Dong Isbister, Xiumei Pu, Stephen D. Rachman

Since last year, families with school children have moved to the new village, one after another. My grandson Echangshan has relocated there with his mother, as well. They had to move. Because the school had moved, the students had to follow; their mothers, of course, followed their children to take care of them. My son, Erite, stays behind to tend the crops and herd the sheep. He lives by himself in the empty, dust-covered house. Farming tools are stacked up. It is a mess. Fortunately, his house is just to the west of mine, so he doesn't have to worry about meals. For the villagers, sending their children to school is an important thing. Many families have sent their first- or second-graders to schools in the *qi* a few hundred *li* away, not to mention those families with middle-school children.[1]

Kids from schools in the *qi* speak fluent Chinese when they come back. Even my three-and-half-year-old granddaughter, who has lived in the new village for only one year, no longer speaks our own language. I saw her running around with other kids in a grocery store next door. When she saw me, she called me "Grandpa" in Chinese and then ran off, still speaking Chinese. For a moment, I felt I was losing my granddaughter. Tears filled my eyes. I watched her running around, her little braid tossing from side to side like a rattle-drum. Well, when living in the new village, one has to speak Chinese. How can one get by if one doesn't?

My daughter-in-law made lunch for us. My son, Erite, was back home. He drove his tractor to buy us a sack of rice, a sack of flour, some salt and soybean oil. We used to buy those things in the village, but we can no longer do that after the demolition and relocation started.

My grandson, Changshan, also came back home for lunch. He walked in, greeting me, "*Yeye*" and his grandma, "*Taiti*" in the Daur language.

Good. He still speaks his mother tongue. It looks like he won't forget his native language.

Taiti patted him on the head and asked, "Is school over?"

"We are taking a break from school."

"It is not time for summer or winter vacation. How come you are taking a break?"

"The foundation of the classroom building is sinking. There are cracks in some walls. One wall collapsed. The school is making repairs."

"Wasn't the building just completed last year? How come it needs repairing? It has only been used for one semester."

With his mouth full, Changshan mumbled, "I don't know." He continued to wolf down his food.

Well, how could a kid know this sort of thing? Construction is a business

---

1. *Qi* is the administrative division of county level in some Chinese minority autonomous regions in the north and north eastern regions initially used in Qing Dynasty and affected multiple ethnic groups, including Mongolian and Daur. Now it is mainly used in Inner Mongolia.

kept to those who have money and power. Common folks wouldn't know it, let alone kids.

My daughter-in-law bought some vegetables from a market in town. Eggplants, tomatoes, and chili peppers. We are not used to those vegetables. They are not fresh; they also taste different. Waterlogged. Etewo said regretfully, "How come I forgot to pick some eggplants and green beans from our vegetable garden? Vegetables from the market are not the same as those grown in the garden." My daughter-in-law said, "Vegetables from the vegetable garden are green, unlike those bought...."

Before she finished, Etewo asked, her eyes wide open, "Aren't the vegetables from the market 'green'?"

"No, *Taiti*, 'green' means vegetables free of chemical fertilizers, like vegetables from our garden." Changshan chimed in.

Etewo said, "If my grandson eats vegetables grown with chemical fertilizers all the time, won't he be poisoned?"

Etewo began to worry about vegetables. On the way back home, she kept muttering to herself, "We need to grow more vegetables in the garden; we need to grow enough vegetables for our kids and grandkids."

Yet, she forgot she had to move. Was she thinking she would live in the old village forever?

Walking in the new village, I find it is not like a village anymore. It looks more like a town. Tall office buildings, stores, hotels, restaurants, internet cafes, and dance halls. All the houses are brand-new with red walls and white tiles. When the sun shines on these buildings, the glare is like a blanket of white snow; people cannot open their eyes. The cement-paved roads are wide, straight, and clean. But the surfaces are hard. Our feet ache when walking on the hard surface.

We got back to the village. Walking on the soft dirt road, Etewo cleared her throat and said, "I can feel my legs again."

Like me, Etewo has lived here all her life. She knows very little about the outside world. It never crossed her mind that road surfaces could be so bare and hard. She feels their rock hardness with every step she takes. We don't have a television set. Our son Erite lives in the east room of our three-room house. When he got married, he had two more rooms built to the west and moved in to the extension. At this time, our son bought a TV set and this was the first one Etewo saw. She doesn't like the flamboyant and funky TV programs. She said she would rather smoke her tobacco pipe and watch the mountains, the grass, and the sun.

I enjoy watching her smoke. Her left hand rests on the edge of the *kang*. Her right hand holds the pipe and her right leg rests on the *kang*. She smacks her lips, inhaling and exhaling a puff of smoke after a long interval, producing a deep sound which flaps the wings of memory and floats with the light smoke, allowing me to see again the remote past. Etewo looked relaxed and graceful even when she was a maiden, with the pipe at the corner of her mouth. What a simple and easy life it was then!

We picked a full bag of eggplants and green beans and asked Erite to deliver them to the new village. We wouldn't want our grandchildren to eat too many chemically fertilized vegetables which will make them braindead.

But I am still worried. Houses in the new village stand side by side. Open space is limited, to say the least, and what little area remains is taken up with farming equipment. Planting a vegetable garden is absolutely out of the question. What choice do people have? They must buy vegetables. The old village has wide fields all around the houses where we can plant everything. Fresh vegetables are available for picking whenever you need them. Surplus vegetables such as eggplant, beans, and cucumbers are cut into long strips and hung in rows in all the houses. When dried, they are braided and put into bags for storage. We have vegetables to eat all through winter and spring. Daughter-in-law said that the new village is a place where everything costs money, and that without money one has no vegetables to eat.

Since the new village was established, local officials have been pressuring us to move. Those who have school children have already moved; those who don't have fields have already moved; and those whose houses are decrepit have already moved. Within one year, half of the village that once boasted over one hundred households has become desolate. Wormwood, head-high, grows in demolished buildings, untended gardens, and deserted lots. When people walk into these spaces, they disappear from sight. With rampant weeds everywhere, I feel dismayed.

I cannot bear to look at the scene, and yet I cannot look away. I wander around the village every day like a man under a spell visiting desolate homes and *sang-ge-le* (storehouses) that have seen many changes over the years.[2] The *sang-ge-le* really break my heart because they were built in the style of our ancestors. Now, they are so worn out, like feeble old men they totter in the wind. My heart aches. I feel like crying.

These *sang-ge-le* are decades old, some have stood for a hundred years and they all carry the weight of history. If you look carefully at the *sang-ge-le*, at its frame and skeleton, you will know why I care so much about them. It represents the Daur people's deep past. It symbolizes our abundant, ancestral tribal life, coexisting in harmony with nature. It embodies a world where trees and grass grow vibrantly, where people sow, harvest and hunt with complete freedom. The frame of every *sang-ge-le* represents the gift of heaven and earth, unstinting and selfless. Our ancestors were blessed to build their

---

2. The original Chinese text uses the transliteration of the Daur term *sang-ge-le* for storehouses, most of which are made of wooden planks, built three-foot off the ground to keep it dry.

homes and *sang-ge-le* with such "bones," using the best quality timber. The wooden city was once a symbol of the Daur, and its architecture has passed down to us through generations. Though today's lumber is inferior in size and quality, it remains essential to the house like the heart and bones to a human body, representing the spirit and soul of our ancestors. My emotional attachment to the house comes from a nostalgia for the vast range where our ancestors once lived, for the remote mythic times when,

> The mountains were filled with sable and deer
> And the fields spilled over with millet and oats
> Oh how we clubbed the musk deer and scooped up the fish
> And the pheasants flew right into our pots[3]

To tell you the truth, it is not merely a matter of nostalgia. When people get older, they rehash their childhood and adolescence, and find the old days more vivid than the present landscape before them. You might even find yourself missing and oohing and aahing over things that happened a decade ago. Although I feel I am still young, the color of the mountain and the river is not, in my eyes, as green as it once was. The mountain forests appear less majestic, and the hand of the wind that sweeps across my face feels less gentle. I feel uneasy as I look at the flat grassland. I really don't know if my eyesight has weakened or the color of the forests and grassland has faded.

I am not done yet. I have more to say about *sang-ge-le*. Be patient with me. It is the last time you would hear me rattle on about its structure.

Obviously, a *sang-ge-le* is used for storing grains and game. It must be dry and airy, it is built upon a wooden platform a little more than two-feet above ground and supported by four large columns. The walls and eaves are made of thick pieces of lumber. The door of *sang-ge-le* is just wide enough to allow one person to enter with one's back bent. In the front there is a small porch about a foot or so long for someone to sit and air-dry vegetables, or to stow small hand tools. My *sang-ge-le* is a larger one. It has three rooms in a long row. The south side of a *sang-ge-le* is unwalled and open for storing farming tools, ropes, and carts. Sadly, such an orderly life is going to completely disappear. The traces of the past that can be seen in the buildings are disappearing, too. There is no way to stop it.

* * *

I took my yellow cow to graze on top of the dam on the east side of the village. The dam was built for flood control of the Nen River. It has had maintenance every few years so the village has never been flooded.

---

3. These are words from a song titled "Beautiful Hometown" from a Chinese opera *Ao Lei Yi Lan* (1979) in memory of the eponymous Daur heroine of the opera who in 1643 led the villagers against the Russian invaders by the Jingqili River, which is on the left side of Heilong River Valley in north-east China.

The cow went down the dam to graze. I didn't need to worry a bit about her. The river running from north to south is the Nen River. It is famous throughout China and the Huorili River flows into it.

Not one of my ancestors has ever left the Nen River valley. In the past three hundred years, they left the north bank of Heilong River and migrated to the Enen River, the Jingqili River, and the Nen River basin. This long trail bears witness to the hardship of migration and the Daur people's history. The Nen River basin is lush, at times gentle, at other times, wild. It has been our beautiful home for generations. When you imagine how gently and gracefully the Nen River flows, then you will understand how beautiful, quiet, and nimble Etewo and other Daur women are.

We depend on the Nen River for our livelihood, and we have to put up with its rages. When flooded, it threatens the people living downstream. As early as the 1960s, the state had been making plans to build a reservoir on the river. Now there is a plan to build a reservoir at Nierji, the county seat, and over ten villages in the vicinity will be flooded.

We cannot live without the river, nor can we live without fishing. In summer we go to the river whenever we are free. Etewo is more outdoorsy than I am. She frequently goes fishing with Chuoluo's wife and her friend Kuihe and they hang out as a group. But more often, Etewo goes out alone after tending her garden even if the sun is setting. It is fun to see her silhouette. She carries all her fishing equipment—two dangling *tunzi* (creel), one in the front and the other in the back; a fishing pole on the right shoulder, and a small basket on her left arm. Rather than catch fish, she goes to the riverbank to listen to the water rippling, and to take in the green scent of flowers, grass, and trees.

She walks with her back straight and steps firm. Every time I watch her walking this way, I feel as if she were going on a date again. Maybe on one of these days, she will be spirited away by river sprites or mountain gods. It is our destiny to become part of the mountain, river and forest.

The cow stood grazing on the dam. If it were thirsty, it would go to drink by the river on its own, so I didn't need to worry about it. Atop the dam, I looked north and there sat the village—just a few scattered houses. In the distance, half-hidden by wild weeds and trees, I could just make out the roof of a solitary house. It made me feel lonely. Other houses remained standing but they were empty. Their owners had no time to tear them down before they moved out. Now weeds grew on the top of the houses; the outer walls had begun to peel away; and sheets of plastic flapped and fluttered in the windows like mourning streamers.

The mountain behind the village remains unchanged. It turns green or yellow as the season changes. Because of the reduced farming and grazing policies, the trees in recent years are making a comeback but the restoration cannot compete with what the forests looked like when I was young. In my childhood, the forests were so dense you could scarcely find trails to walk up the mountain. The weeds were as high as two people standing on shoulders. One had to hack away the weeds to get through. I knew the forest like the back of my hand, every branch and tree limb, the girth of every black birch, white birch, shrub lespedeza, and wild hazelnut. Women would easily lose their way or their companions when they went to the mountain to forage. Sometimes while they were pushing aside the thick brushwood, they would run into someone else and they were surprised to discover that their lost companion was right in front of them.

The mountain is a treasure trove. There are countless varieties of wild fruits and nuts. Siberian crabapples, plums, apricots, hazelnuts. ... All are very tasty. Monkey head mushrooms and black fungus can be gathered when the summer rainy season begins. Ferns and day lilies are local delicacies that are still permitted to be harvested, but wild animals are protected now. Today, none of us would kill roe deer, boars, rabbits, lynxes, grouse, pheasants, or black bears that we regularly hunted in the past. Animals and human beings live in peace now. Traditionally, we both hunted and farmed, but, with the changing times, we have to live by farming alone.

However, we still love our fish. We have inherited this fondness for fish from our ancestors, who lived on the north side of Heilong River with its natural abundance. Rivers large and small, like the Huorili River, Guo'en River, Yabuti River, Huarige River and the Nen River, have enough fish to meet our needs. When we were young, we would go in groups to the riverside or woods. Men went to catch fish while women went to pick artemisia sprouts. We used to set up an iron pot by the river, put in the freshly caught fish, and added some millet and wild vegetables. Even without a drop of cooking oil, the taste was unbelievably fresh. Even our hearts and lungs were filled with the green tastes and smells of the mountain and the water. My mouth waters with the thought of it. Nothing tastes that good today. I don't know if it is because my taste buds have become dull, or the fish and the wild vegetables have changed their flavor. I feel that the sun has grown old, and the sky and the earth have grown old, too. Everything I eat is less savory.

I don't want to move. It is hard to let go of the old house, the land, the days gone by. The land is my lifeblood; the mountain, the river, and the grassland are hard to leave behind. I can't leave them.

Watching the Nen River rolling towards the south, I think about what educated travelers who pass this way say about us: our dance movements are inspired by the ripples of Nen River, our songs are infused with the flavor of wild greens. They are correct. The young women are as beautiful as the Huorili River; the young men as strong as Huorili Mountain. Our lives have been shaped by the river and the mountain.

The sun was about to set. The yellow cow's belly was full. Before the relocation, my cow would graze together with other families' cattle. Now that so many families have moved out, I must herd the cow all by myself.

I walked the cow down the dam. The village was just a few steps away. It was so quiet, not even the sound of a dog barking. In the distance, a house was hidden among the trees and high weeds. It seemed abandoned. I occasionally saw smoke from the chimney of another house. Hazelnuts dried in the sun on its decayed thatched roof. This was how I knew that a family still resided there.

On both sides of the road, the weeds were taller and heartier than ever, obscuring nearly half of the doorways of some houses. If I didn't know who had moved and who had stayed, I would take it for granted that every house was abandoned, to judge by the broken-down storehouses and overgrown vegetation. Alas! A village with hundreds of years of history comes to its end in such a bleak way!

In order to soothe my heart, I spackled the walls of my home and storehouse. I could not bear to see the walls in such a state of disrepair with cracks both large and small. Even if I had to move, I didn't want my house looking like a ragged beggar. Etewo came out with a *weideluo* (wooden pail) to milk the cow. I tied the cow to a wooden stake, let go of the calf, waited a while for the calf to nuzzle its mother's teats, and then dragged the calf away. Etewo sat on a stool by the udder. She patted the cow's hind leg with her left hand. The cow moved her leg to let Etewo milk her. All the while, the calf tried in vain to get near its mother.

We had *sutiqie* (porridge cooked with milk) for dinner, as usual. It is in our Daur tradition to have it every day, and we have been doing that for generations. I wonder if life would be the same without it.

Etewo took out her long pipe again. Smoking is her routine after-dinner "treat." She was getting ready to smoke, but the moment she banged her pipe on the side of *kang*, Chuoluo showed up. He is a few years younger than me. He would come to my house whenever something happened in the village. Actually, I am neither the village head, nor the Party Secretary. I am just an elderly man. In our village a few older men like me make decisions on important matters. This is a tradition passed down from our *mokunda* (tribal chief). In this way, a tradition from the remote past still has an impact on our daily life.

Chuoluo is the father-in-law of my son, Erite. Emin and some other young men also stopped by. In the morning, they all got the news that we needed to move within ten days. They were calm and they always put on a brave face. To tell the truth, I know they feel the same way I do. They never show their emotions or act aggressively even if, in their hearts they are weighed down with troubles. They always keep their equilibrium, but our history of migration and hardship has shaped us and made us melancholy. Some things are in the bones and cannot be changed.

Several women came in and joined us. Men and women sat shoulder to shoulder on the edges of three sides of the *kang*. Like me, they still wanted to hold on to the land and did not want to leave. They remained in those houses that had not been torn down. The relocation has been dragging on for a couple of years. Everybody seemed to be tired. They spoke more calmly and softly than before, as if they were talking about other people's business. A plea to "move to higher ground" had finally been approved, but nobody looked excited. Everyone lowered their heads and stared at the floor, flicking cigarette ashes from time to time. Then Chuoluo broke the ice, "Our application of building harvest sheds on the higher ground has finally been approved after three years, but we still must relocate to the new village within ten days. They are coming to tear down the houses ten days from now."

"How can I move all my stuff within ten days? I have a large flock of sheep, a lot of pigs and chickens. If I could, I would have done it earlier. Why would I wait until now?"

"In ten days, the soybeans will be ready to harvest. A round trip from the new village to the field covers two hundred *li*. How can we travel and harvest? It doesn't seem possible, right? When men work in the field, women need to cook for them, don't they?" How can women cook for the men working in the fields if they are miles away in the new village?

"I get very worried these days. I can't eat or drink. I almost had a heart attack. Why didn't they approve our proposal earlier? Now that harvest is just around the corner, but we have to move, harvest, and build sheds all at the same time. How can we make it?"

"No. No way."

*   *   *

We raised many questions. The women delved into every aspect of the matter. Nobody was unreasonable. Nobody left until deep into the dark night. Although we had a lot of complaints, we somehow felt a bit relieved. We no longer have to worry about the daily commute of two hundred *li* and paying the No.111 National Road tolls. Allowing us to build harvest sheds on the high ground near the fields gives us hope of holding on to the land, and one day, to rebuild our own village.

Etewo began to make the bed. One by one she took the *derizhe* (sleeping pads) from the cabinet, and arranged them on the kang. Then she spread the *nenmensi* (quilts) over the pads and sat on hers. She rolled two cigarettes for me before taking up her beloved long pipe. We were quiet for a while. I liked nights like this. I enjoyed watching Etewo taking out sleeping pads and quilts one by one. I enjoyed watching her sitting on the pads with the pipe in her mouth, smacking her lips. After a busy day, at last some peace.

The next morning when I got up, I took a look at the backyard. I was somewhat stunned by what I saw. The fence on the east side had completely collapsed. I thought this was strange. The fence was old, but it was still in good shape. It was made of straight, thumb-thick willow twigs. The twigs were woven tightly and they looked like girls' braids. The wooden stakes of the fence were all logs of Mongolian oak, each the width of a small bowl, and they were not rotten. Why had the fence fallen down? As it happened, while I slept last night I heard my leg bones creaking. Did they sense the collapse of the fence? Or was I dreaming? I was not surprised because similar things had happened before. Many times, I have known beforehand or dreamt about what was going to happen in my family. It's nothing mysterious to me. It's simply because my house, my land, and I have depended on one another for a long, long time. We have developed some kind of mutual attachment or psychic connection. We can feel each other's happiness, anger or sadness.

I didn't care much for the fence now that it had collapsed, but I felt sorry that two plots of cabbages were under the debris. The other vegetables were fine. Green beans, eggplants, peppers, corn, tomatoes, and potatoes. We had more than enough vegetables to eat and dry. It was not the season for vegetables to stop growing yet. I did not want to leave them behind.

I don't like the label of "nail house." We will move, but we are not about to move two hundred *li* away from our land. We simply want to stay on our land. We cannot leave it; and it cannot leave us. The land is our lifeblood.

*   *   *

I pulled Emin away from the site. This kid is usually quiet but gets angry when agitated.

I began to tear down my *sang-ge-le* first. It was very old and we had weathered years of hardship together. I felt incredibly sad to destroy it with my own hands, as if I were dismantling a body bone by bone. I didn't know where to start. I seemed to be cutting into my own flesh no matter where I began. Finally, I set to it and removed the door. The big latch on the door had been passed down from my grandfather.

Our farmhand used to live in the room on the south side of the *sang-ge-le*. He moved out of there after he married our daughter and the room was converted into an open pigsty. In the past couple of years, we stopped raising pigs and used this open space to store farming tools.

The logs taken from the *sang-ge-le* were not rotten. They would be hauled to the north side of the mountain to build our harvest shed.

For ten days, the village was busy and noisy. Large and small vehicles were coming and going. Tractors rumbled and chugged. One after another, houses were hoisted by cranes and razed. They were torn down within a few days and the whole village was gone. It became a wasteland right before our eyes.

Just like that my beloved one-hundred-and-eight-year-old house fell down. Etewo stood by the house, stamping her feet in despair. She sighed, "*e-ruo-ruo; ba-ri-sen; ba-ri-sen*" ("Oy yoi yoi! Everything's gone! Everything's gone!")

Who knows how long the demolition took? The chaos and noise suddenly stopped and a stunned silence followed. My yard was a disaster. I had no clue how I got to my feet. I suddenly felt clumsy and stiff. I managed to take a few steps toward my ruined house. I stood there, tall, isolated, and insecure.

A couple of days ago, Erite took the remaining items to the new village. He came back after the demolition. The sheds up on the higher ground were almost completed. The harvest was about to begin.

* * *

Neither the potatoes, nor the napa cabbages in my yard have been tended to. My particular harvest shed was far from ready. Everyone was too busy with their own situation to lend a hand. I have no other choice but to hire some farmhands to work part-time in the field. I simply can't do all the field work by myself.

Etewo helped me put up a tar paper gable over our old *kang* so that Etewo and I might have a place to live while the shed was being finished.

The sun moves faster when we have a lot of work to do. It gets dark before we even know it. It had hardly rained this autumn, but it rained on the evening when our house was torn down. We slept miserably that night with the dampness. We got up and lit a candle, and then Etewo screamed, "My Goodness!" The sleeping pads were soaked! Rain ran down the sides of the gable and the pads absorbed it all. Our clothes were wet through, too. Everything was totally saturated except for the quilt covering us. We could not go back to sleep. Instead, we spent the night working as a team to wring the water out of our clothing and bedding.

Early in the morning, I stepped outside. The sky was so clear and clean. The red sun was shining from the southeast, gilding the land and the mountain range. As I looked around, my heart throbbed with pain. The houses were gone. The village was gone. All had vanished. Overnight, our noisy village had gone dead silent. Just weeds stretching out as far as the eye could see. I couldn't help but sigh, "Is this the village where we have lived for hundreds of years?"

With a last glimmer of hope, I went up to the dam. Looking down from a high spot, my bubble was totally burst: nothing but weeds and desolation. I was lost. The *tunzi* (village) has utterly vanished. Where is my home? Where can I go?

I was uprooted. The ground was moving beneath my feet, the grass and the trees were moving, and the mountains were drifting in the distance. I never used to feel like I was getting older, but now I know that I am old, and I began to lose heart. I have struggled in vain against becoming a homeless and helpless vagabond.

Look eastward at the Nen River. It runs slowly to the south as has for millennia. The river swells and contracts with the seasonal rains; this is the only change that can be seen. Look northward at the rolling Greater Khingan Mountains. The forest green lights up with fiery reds and yellows. What gifts these old mountains have given us! What a pity the mountain's village has vanished forever. My eyes blur and my heart goes cold. Autumn is really here.

Is this the homeland where we have lived and labored for generations? With the ancestral spirits' direction, our ancestors have cultivated it for three hundred years. Will it be lost by us? We have no idea where we are going. We don't know what is awaiting us, either. The Nen River has nurtured the Daur people for centuries, but now for the well-being of the people living downstream, we have to leave our homeland.

I shambled back to the gable. Etewo had cooked breakfast in an iron pot over a used oil drum cut in half. The filled steamed buns were left over from yesterday; the milk porridge was freshly made. Etewo said that the steamed buns should be fully cooked now. Yesterday, she explained, there was a big wind that blew the flames in all directions, and, as a result, the buns were underdone.

Dishes, pots, and bowls were stacked outside, covered in a layer of dust. I took a scoop of water from the big plastic bucket to wash them and I managed to get them passably clean. That's fine. The gable is just big enough for Etewo and me to sit in, one on the east, and the other on the west, with a pot in between. We can even sit comfortably without hunching over. It is fairly bright inside the gable when the sun shines in.

It's time to pick soybeans, but my harvest shed is not finished. This shed in fact resembles the Han people's storage with a *kang* and a kitchen stove installed just to make do till next spring.

Quite a few families are building their harvest sheds, too. Those whose houses have been torn down before the completion of their sheds now live in the blue relief tents. My younger girl came and told us that the relief tents are sweltering in the day and too chilly to sleep at night. Our son-in-law is going non-stop harvesting the crops and building the shed all by himself. Our daughter has a delicate constitution and can do little more than cook meals for her husband. She began to weep again as she spoke. She has been weeping ever since we learned the house was going to be demolished for the removal.

She continually murmurs, "Such a nice house is gone! What a pity! Where on earth can we find another house as good as this?" I have two sons and two daughters in my life. The elder daughter has gone to another world, and now this young girl has become the apple of my eye. My heart saddens whenever she cries. She has always been weak and has never done any heavy work. We worried about her and, in order to keep her around, we married her off to the hired hand. Though he is Han, he works hard. We don't discriminate against him.

This year, so many things are happening at the same time. It is rare to have such a good harvest after one natural disaster after the next for ten years straight. Although crop yields are only about seventy to eighty percent of what could usually be expected, it is a pretty good year compared with previous ones. Every family is spinning like a top with no time to lend anyone else a helping hand. Every day, those who have moved to the new village drive their tractors two hundred *li* back and forth, harvesting in the field from day to night. As for lunch, they make do by eating buns and pickles brought from home, and then go on with their work until the day is done. The other day, Erite didn't show up and I sensed that something was amiss. It is the busy season, and the crop harvest has only been half done. Why doesn't he come? I was stewing over this when Emin stopped by. He informed me that Erite was hit by a tractor on the way home the night before. It was dark. On the road there were so many people and vehicles traveling back and forth for the soybean harvest. There were motorcycles, too. The road was bumpy. Luckily, Erite reacted quickly and jumped off his motorcycle in the nick of time when he saw the tractor fully loaded with soybeans coming. Thank goodness, it could have been worse. He only broke his right leg and is now recovering in the local hospital.

I was very anxious. The harvest was far from finished, and we had no money to hire farm hands. If we wait until he recovered, the bean pods would burst in the fields. Erite must be as worried about the harvest as I was. I had no time to visit him in the hospital. The first priority was to get help with the harvest. The crops couldn't wait. Emin complained that Erite would not have been injured if he had not moved so far away and had to ride his motorcycle back and forth to the fields. What's the use of saying this? What's done is done. Life is nothing but trouble. One way or another we suffer and in the last few years we have had more than our fair share of bad luck.

A *kang* was finally built in my shed. Our two farm hands moved in, but we can't cook because there is no water. Everyone living in sheds and the relief tents have to fetch water from the old village. Each day tractors continually carry gallons of water to the upper fields. Water is needed not only for cooking but also for building sheds. This is no small undertaking. Three times a day, Etewo and I deliver meals cooked in the shed to the harvesters in the fields.

The nights are hard. The old village has become a wilderness in total darkness. The grass has turned yellow and so have the trees. When the autumn wind blows, it seems as if there are many people murmuring in a ghost language. In the open air, Etewo and I look at the sky, count the stars, and listen to the strange sounds. Neither of us can fall asleep, so we smoke. The coals from her long pipe and my cigarettes glow while we tell stories about small things from old times—sesame seeds is how we think of them—just to get through the endless night.

Actually, I have camped like this many times. When we were young, we logged these mountain forests, floated the logs downriver, hunted, and slept in the sheds. But, in those days, we all were young and strong, and there were ten or twenty of us in a group. The pursuit of game is nothing new to me. Hunting has come down to us from our ancestors. The elders tell us of its long history. During the Qing Dynasty young Daur men in the north of the Heilong River were ordered by the imperial court to serve in the army at the age of sixteen. Each man had to pay a tribute of sable fur to the Qing government each year. Consequently, the population of sable declined year by year due to the excessive killing. To fulfill the tribute, our ancestors pleaded to replace part of the quota of sable fur with grouse, boar, pheasant, and roe deer. At that time, they lived off the natural abundance of the mountains and enjoyed its gifts. After our people migrated to the Nen River region, they still lived off the mountains. Today, the mountains have become thin, and the wild animals are scarce. Everybody says that in the mountains there are still roe deer, wild boar, rabbit, lynx, fox, grouse, and other animals, but has anyone seen any of them? For my grandfather's generation, hunting meant not only food and fun, but also a pretty decent sideline. When I was a boy, in the long winter evenings, by the orange lamplight, and around the glowing fire, I listened to them swap hunting stories. Sometimes they got so excited that they would actually dance while boasting. Their simple lives—their joys and their satisfactions—are gone forever.

My generation only caught roe deer, wild boar, pheasant, and rabbit on rare occasions. Even so, we still felt proud. It was not until recent years that people stopped eating roe deer and wild boar, which used to be common meats served on every family's table. Today, when it comes to hunting, I can only choose to sing this song once sung by our ancestors:

> Once as straight as the ridge of the Khingan mountains,
> My back, now old, stoops and my spine bends.
> Still, I trudge over tall and nameless mountains.
> On my narrow shoulder still rests my gun.
> The paths are endless with twists and turns.
> In search of a precious bile, I prowl the black bear's den.
> I drink deeply from bowls and feel the spirits burn.
> I shout "Na Yi Ye!" like the ancients from whom I descend.
> Once as straight as the ridge of the Khingan mountains,

My back, now old, stoops and my spine bends.
Still, I ford wide rivers and nameless streams.
Beside me, my horse still comes along.
I taste the bitter salt of the wind and rain.
I come and go with the stars and sun.
In ice and snow I sleep beneath a roe deer's skin.
And the flame that is my soul still burns.
I am the mountain forests from which I descend.

Etewo lay down and then sat up again. Who could rest in the debris of the village on a night as black as the burnt bottom of a cast iron pot? In the dark, the living and the dead appear before my eyes, then those from the new houses, followed by those from the old village, followed by the young and the aged. They all wear different expressions. Some come with long faces and some come with knitted brows. They hurry by me quickly like ghosts, their heads lowered in deferential silence as if they were at work in the fields. I've never studied their faces so closely before. My cousin Morideng, who was murdered over a land issue, was the last to appear before me. With a bloody head and swollen eyes he asked me, "Big Brother, five or six years have passed since I was wrongly killed. Why haven't you avenged me? Will the murderer be at large forever?"

An eerie tension filled my body. Etewo said she saw Morideng, too, and she moved closer to me. I spit three times and said, "Morideng, don't worry. You'll have your day. The spirit in the sky will punish the bad guys in due time." I uttered an incantation three times and then his face disappeared.

The night is deathly silent and the night is unquiet. For over twenty nights in a row I have looked into the faces of the living and the dead and spoken to them. Most of them are long-dead old friends. They have returned to the village to haunt their houses. I even saw the coals glowing as they smoked, sitting in the ruins. Do souls also begrudge leaving their homeland?

It has become cool at dusk and at dawn, but it remains hot and dry at noon. Winter is cold and dry. Spring is dry. The rainy season comes in July and August. In autumn there are dramatic swings in temperature between day and night. One can wear a shirt at noon, but has to put on longjohns in the evening. Every day, Etewo and I shuttle more than ten *li* delivering meals to the shed. No one has any time for each other.

Chuoluo's shed was built first. Actually his "shed" will be a room or a wing in one part of a house. He says he will build a classical Daur house next year. So will I. He has seven sons and two daughters. Each of his children's families owns a different piece of farm equipment, so they actually have a full set. When it is time to work the farm, his seven sons and two sons-in-law all work as a team. They practically become a small-scale farming collective outfitted with the right machines for every season. This enables them to be more efficient in all respects than everyone else. His family is the richest here. In the eyes of the Daur people, Chuoluo has it all—sons and daughters, and all twelve animal signs of the zodiac. Since everyone is so consumed with their own work these days, no one has any time to see each other. One day I happened to see him and I was shocked. His black hair had gone totally gray. It is wild and wiry. His healthy face has turned pale and ashen. He stared at me in astonishment, too. We both laughed. He said, "Don't look at me. You're just as bad." Sure, I could see myself in his face. I might look even worse.

As we talked, Emin returned from the field. He said unhappily that the soil here is not compact enough to make good ground for threshing the soybean plants. If we thresh them here, the soybeans will mix with the soil and it will be impossible to pick them up one by one; but if we transport them unthreshed to the new village, it's a long distance away. It will cost a lot of extra time and work. What choice do we have? Either way, it makes no sense.

Erite has not recovered from his injuries. His wife has to take care of him and their child. She cannot spare any time for the fields. My son-in-law also works around the clock. They are old enough to think for themselves and yet, here I am an old man making suggestions and solving problems for them.

So much work to do all at once. We are all busy bees. And yet, busy as we are, we are happy for the huge piles of soybeans. We haven't seen a harvest as good as this one in years. Life is good for farmers when there is work to do. We have been idle for too long. There has been so little work that a few acres could be farmed in a couple of months. Most of the year, we stay home with nothing to do. The old didn't mind too much, but the young men were depressed. After finishing what little field work there was to do, they sat around the house every day twiddling their thumbs, without cash or any outlets for their surplus energy.

The construction site is booming. Many simple frame "houses" are going up. Although these houses cannot compete with the originals, they are "houses" after all, and can provide living space for the residents.

Napa cabbages are ready to be pulled up. Etewo cut the roots off all the cabbage heads. She boiled a big pot of water, put the cabbages in to blanche them for fermentation or pickling. Fermented vegetables are our major source of edible plants in winter. Since there is no water on the higher ground, and Etewo and I are too old to carry water back and forth, we had to prepare the cabbage here, and then move them over there. After ten days' work, a well has been dug, but there is no electricity, so it is impossible to have potable running water this year.

We were pulling up stakes tomorrow. Despite the shabby little shed for two, and the weeds that grow in every crack and spring up all around, this was once our beautiful home. It holds the traces of the progress of our pioneers, our happiness, our sadness, our sweat, our harvests, our life-stories. Leaving here means saying good-bye to the past and to all the memories. I know that Etewo and I have spent a full twenty-eight days in the wasteland of the old village. It has been so long that Etewo no longer even bothers to say, "How can I make it through?"

Our last night. Etewo and I spent it watching the stars and talking over all the old times. Our oldest memories were of jumping in the river every day, swimming, diving, doing the dog-paddle, backstroke, and treading water. We got punished for being late for school; we had gone to the mountains to bait pheasants and chase rabbits. We picked hazelnuts and black fungus. We cut green grass with a scythe. We would bring a birchbark basket filled with yo-gurt pudding to the riverside. We ate fish and drank wine while gazing at the river; we rolled down from high piles of grain. … On dark winter evenings, we listened to Uncle Yidemu's tales of rafting and hunting, or to Wuchun chanting a long heroic epic.…What a happy, innocent childhood! We didn't appreciate it when we were young. Does anyone really cherish those gold and silver days while they are young? No, only after they are gone do we realize how precious they are, and that they won't be found again. Those nights with black bears are gone; Uncle Yidemu and Wuchun are gone; those high piles of grain are gone, and so are the children who used to play hide-and-seek. The memory of a whole generation is gone with the village.

When I think of the villagers who have moved into the neat rows of brick houses in the new village, they are all the same to me. All of the houses are the same. All the yards look the same. There is no way to tell one house from another or one face from another because they have no individual character. This is how the memory of Huorili dies in the new village. I cannot find them.

That's why I insisted on not budging. I was unwilling to take even one step off my land. Life in the old village may be old-fashioned and basic but I know what I am. My grandfather's rusty shotgun hangs on the wall beside his hunting trophies; I can sense my father's solemn and kind presence in the room; and I can see the shadows of my grandma and my mother in their long plain robes walking around the yard. Gone are those days! But how sweet they are! They keep telling me something. My grandma has spoken to me the past few nights. She told me a story and she couldn't let it go. She kept asking me why I had lost what she left behind. What was that something? I tried several times to find out but failed. Each time I tried to ask her about it, her shadow faded out.

I must have lost a lot of things over the years, not just what my grandma kept asking me for. I have lost the power to keep these things and pass them on. The children don't care. I feel I am really too old and useless now.

The feeling of being old might have begun the day we moved out. One day, I noticed a piece of wood with a curved end from a pile. I took it out, and fashioned it into a walking stick. I got a real kick out of poking the ground with it. Etewo noticed it and grabbed the stick away from me, saying, "What are you doing? You are too young for such stuff!"

Sheepishly, I smiled back at her. I said that it looked nice and I kept it for fun. Then I saw the setting sun, the red, dazzling sun, though with less brightness. All of a sudden I realized that the greatest consolation for me is to follow the sun every day. I have followed the sun all my life. By following it, I can see my shadow, and then I will be centered.

*   *   *

It gets cold without warning. The first snow falls and the rivers freeze. Our dwelling is basically a small wing that faces west. It is really little more than a glorified storeroom but it meets our needs for shelter, serving as warm nest against the winter cold.

We still cannot access the well-water yet. We chisel ice from the Huorili River every day. We bring back blocks of ice to melt for drinking water. Taking ice from the river makes for chilly work, but sometimes we amuse ourselves catching the occasional fish that mistakenly thinks that spring has arrived. Anyhow, we see ice-chopping as a good workout for most of the time we have little to do.

I don't know when I began to lose my sense of smell. Maybe it was the day we moved into the new dwelling. I can no longer recall the scent of my father. I can no longer make out the long shadow of my mother. My grandmother no longer appears at all. Is she no longer interested in asking me about all that I have lost?

At night, I hear a different sound, a sad one. I tell Etewo about it, but she insists that she never hears it. This answer bugs me. How can she not hear it? Obviously, it is a dirge that drifts in and out of earshot, coming from the other side of the mountain.

I can hardly sleep at night because I hear that raspy song. It dawned on me that it sounds like my grandma's voice, or the voices of all the deceased old women of our village. The words get clearer and clearer:

> Wisps of smoke rise in the misty morn
> The days of my childhood are long, long gone
> I look back on the river and my hometown
> Ah! Jingqili River, cradle of the Daur.
> The frozen river thaws in the spring winds
> But I cannot see you cast your fishing nets
> The vast forests fill with the morning sun
> But I cannot see your arrows fly toward the marten
> I look back on my home, my old home
> I miss it. I dream of it.
> Morning has broken the endless night
> But I cannot hear your sweet morning song

Endless moons have risen full with the dawn
But I cannot see my kith and kin.
I look back on my home, my old home
I miss it. I dream of it.
Clouds drift across the sky
The river flows on year after year
I look back on my hometown and the river
Ah! Jingqili River, so far away....

Listening to the song, my eyes begin to well up. It's been a long time since I have shed a tear. Etewo says that she hears nothing. It makes me angry to see the skeptical way she eyes me. She looks at me as if she thinks I have a mental disorder. Is it not possible that, though she doesn't feel them, such things exist? I tell Chuoluo and the other villagers, who all stare at me in silence, saying nothing. It worries and exhausts me to go on explaining myself. But every morning when I open my eyes and see the red sun rising above the horizon again, I regain my strength. Whenever I see the sunrise, something in my heart rises, too. I am filled with the thought of building a proper house for us come spring, and of moving out of this glorified storeroom. It is a hope for me and all of us.

21

When Petals Fall Off Flowers

ZHAO YAN

Day after day, I walk through the city blocks, until one day, it occurs to me that more and more osmanthus trees are appearing in the city. They line the streets, neighborhoods, and green belts, releasing their sweet scent all day and night, and in all seasons, regardless. But I often feel that something is missing. I certainly miss a faraway osmanthus tree, and I certainly miss Xianghuashuxia. Xianghuashuxia, which literally means "Under the Fragrant Flowering Tree," is a village in the Gannan mountain region. Place names that stem from a landmark are not uncommon in the countryside. My guess is that the inspiration for Xianghuashuxia comes from a particular sweet osmanthus tree. Age-old. Richly-scented. Even today, a place name like this still holds a hint of poetic sentiment. Imagine it for a moment: a whole village enveloped by a tree, by an age-old powerful aroma that never dissipates, that leaves all the villagers with a long-lasting memory.

Even visitors like me are predestined to take on some of the village's "inheritance," and to be tightly bound to a tree called The Past. Twenty years ago, the tree was where I rushed by or stopped to rest numerous times when I was hungry and exhausted.

* * *

"Sticky rice balls, only five *jiao* a bowl! Good prices!" Sweet voices of women frequently called out from small rammed earth houses. What was I doing at that moment? My mouth watered furiously, but when no one was looking at me, I just gulped the saliva back down. It had to be that way. I didn't even bother to reach into my pocket because I knew money wouldn't pop out like a magic trick.

I saw many people go into the rows of little hole-in-the-wall restaurants,

Translated by Heidi Emerson

and many people come out belching with satisfaction. Like me, they came back from Tonggang Mountain where they chopped firewood, stopping in Xianghuashuxia to rest their shoulders. As the only way to go up the mountain to chop firewood, Xianghuashuxia became a paradise of food: milky white rice, shiny green grass jelly, golden fried cakes, and meatballs. ... All kinds of filling and tasty food presented themselves with steam and tempting color and luster, making people's stomachs growl and mouths water. I was often in awe of how industrious and clever the women of Xianghuashuxia were, and how they miraculously brought color and liveliness to this little mountain village.

As far as I can recall, the only time I ever sat at a small table was when my cousin, who earned a bit of money now and then, paid for me. I treated that bowl of sticky rice balls like a thing of unparalleled beauty. Light green celery leaves floated atop that huge wide-rimmed soup bowl. I savored it, one sip at a time, as if I wanted to inhale every last whiff of its freshness and sweetness into the deepest part of my lungs.

Most of the time, however, I just carefully removed my shoulder pole, and put it on the ground. I sat on the shoulder pole wrapping my arms around my knees, and telling myself that the liveliness and seduction had nothing to do with me. I was as hungry as all the other firewood gatherers, but I was even more prone to hunger because my body was going through growth spurts. So I longed for a hearty meal.

Even today, I'm still astounded by how cruel I was to myself: why didn't you buy something at least once? You didn't even buy a fried cake that cost only half *jiao*? I knew that, if I'd brought it up to my parents, they might have let me have that one little luxury now and then. But I just kept it to myself, and endured it in silence. I endured it while the blossoms on the osmanthus tree in Xianghuashuxia opened and withered, withered and opened. Somehow, I hated myself for growing up too fast, for being too sensible, and for understanding my family's hardships too well. Those things that shouldn't have been my burden at such a young age kept me from voicing my hunger for food from the time I was little. I missed out on the joys of reckless abandon, including the innocence of youth, sweet-talking my parents, and a lot of other things that spoiled children enjoy, such as the carefree notion that, even if the sky falls, someone will be there to hold it up for them.

But who is there to blame? No one forced me to behave this way. My parents were never big on conversation. They merely went about their lives with frugality and forbearance. Unknowingly, I floated along down the same stream.

A story goes like this: a psychologist brought together a group of children to conduct an experiment, giving each child a piece of candy and telling them that, if they waited twenty minutes before eating the candy, they could have even more candy. However, if they ate it immediately, they would only get that one piece. The psychologist followed the participants for a few decades, and found that the children who waited to eat the candy were more successful in life. When I read this story, I laughed. If I had been selected for this experiment, would anyone have surpassed my level of endurance? Unfortunately, success still seems far away from me twenty years later.

This kind of endurance also influenced my child. From a young age, she learned to distinguish between needs and wants. She managed her allowance wisely, and never threw fits at the supermarket. All advice on raising daughters say the same thing: raising girls in a rich way, but I don't think it is right. People who can control their desires are those who are at peace with themselves.

Starting off from the Maicai Mountain Ridge, the serpentine mountain roads lead up into the wilds of Tonggang Mountain, a place where we often gathered firewood. Xianghuashuxia is an unavoidable landmark along the way. Every time we arrived there, we felt we were approaching our destination. We travelled on foot. This was how we measured every gulley and crossed over every mountain ridge. We had long since lost count of how many kilometers we actually traversed, or how many hours it took.

In the countryside, the first of the seven necessities of life is firewood. It's the guarantee of food aroma and warmth from every home. Children over the age of ten all willingly take the responsibility of gathering firewood. Every weekend, as well as summer and winter breaks, the village youth would call out to one another and amass the younger children in a formidable army and head deep into the mountains.

Chopping firewood on nearby mountains was prohibited, so we had to rush back home from afar before the sun dipped behind the mountains. The call for work always started long before daybreak. We rolled out of bed, cutting short of our dreams. Mother cooked rice and steamed egg custard, a rare treat, to go with the rice. After breakfast, we waited for everyone to show up and then set off on the road. The journey was long but not at all lonely. Some people told jokes. Some sang songs. Those who told stories could really draw people in and make them forget their fatigue. My brother had read more *xiaorenshu* (illustrated storybooks) and martial arts novels, and was a good storyteller, so everyone happily gathered around him to listen to him tell tales.

I maintained a silly adoration of my brother, and was often completely unaware when he was tricking me. One time, on the road home, I was so tired I could barely move, and I kept asking for breaks. My brother said, I'll tell you a story. Why does the *zhong* in *zhongliang* and the *chong* in *chongfeng* sound the same in our dialect? Because in ancient times, *zhong* meant *chong*. What does that mean? When you feel like the burden on your shoulders is really *zhong* (heavy), you have to *chong* (press forward). If you press forward quickly, it won't feel heavy. I thought that seemed right, since they did sound the same. So, I believed it was true, and worked up the courage to press forward with him. To my surprise, it drastically shortened the amount of time needed to get home. Every kind of trickery that my brother invented was effortless and airtight, so even after I found out the truth, there was no point stamping my feet.

The journey to chop firewood provided food for thought. Besides the stories that filled the time, there were many beautiful vistas. In the mountains, the seasons were ever-shifting and alive. Every living thing thrived. The constant buzzing of insects and chirps of birds joined together to create a grand symphony. Wild mountain flowers of every color made us lost for words. Each flower had its own passion and ease. Mountain springs babbled everywhere alongside the path. When we were thirsty, we scooped up a handful to drink, and then another to wash our faces, all with so much pleasure. The most exuberant flowers were those hibiscuses along the mountain streams. I spent the entire autumn season bearing witness to their lives as they went from pale yellow to pale pink, then rose red, and finally withered. My heart was filled with a little sense of pride, but I had never mentioned it to anyone.

When the osmanthus bloomed in August, I loved sitting under Xianghuashu, the tree that gave the village its name. The wind blew tiny blossoms off and dropped them onto my head and shoulders. I could feel the smell of sweat dissipating into the distance, and a whiff of gentle fragrance sinking into my bones. I suddenly recalled a revolutionary song that my teacher taught me: "In August, the osmanthus flowers bloom everywhere, and bright red flags stand tall…." I wished I had never learned this song, so I could always enjoy this aroma, and this beauty, with the simplest and purest love.

*   *   *

Behind exceptional beauty, life-threatening danger usually lurks.

It was springtime. Flowers bloomed in profusion all around. Every kind of wildflowers in the mountain forests welcomed the revelry of a new season. Amid the wildflowers were azaleas. They were so red as if the color were about to come dripping out of them. They seemed as if they were staging a competition: the higher, steeper, and more dangerous the place, the more arrogantly and brazenly they bloomed. They were not just pretty to look at. When you picked one of those fresh and new flowers, all you had to do was pluck out the stamen, and put the petals straight into your mouth and eat them. In the midst of the sourness a sweet taste emerged, leaving a pleasant flavor in your mouth, one that lingered. During a time when food was not plentiful, this kind of flavor from the wild couldn't be passed up.

Only the mountains know the secrets of forests. Yet people always believe they can conquer everything, let alone Wei, who was only a mischievous teenager. Thus, an imminent tragedy inevitably loomed.

We were sitting under Xianghuashu. The azaleas, not far in the distance on the mountainside, seemed to be smiling broadly in the wind. Wei, never taking a moment to rest, was lured in by one bunch of bright red after another, and headed closer and closer to danger. After breaking off each stem, he realized that the flowers were not as dazzling as those at a farther distance. Flowers bloomed in the high places, on the cliffs, and in the crevices between rocks. As ardent as fire, they cast a red glow on Wei's little round face. He was like an alcoholic, climbing farther and farther away toward the most enchanting cluster of flowers. Upon a rock outcropping, an azalea bush beckoned to him with its red streamers: "Dearest, come here, come here. I will be the loveliest of all you hold in your hand." It was a spell hidden in brilliant color, chanting over and over in Wei's ear.

If it only takes a few seconds to jump, how many seconds does it take a soul to fly to heaven?

Wei flew toward that most beautiful bunch of azaleas, but the rock betrayed his trust in an instant. It crumbled. He fell to the bottom of the cliff.

When I heard Wei's scream, I was gazing into the distance quietly. "Ahhh!" His chilling cry of despair echoed through the forest. That was the most resounding cry he had made in his life. The older boys from the village quickly realized what was happening. They carefully crossed the mountain ridge. In the gulley, they picked up Wei, drenched in blood. They took him to Xianghuashuxia and laid him down in the open. Wei's chubby body looked soft and lifeless. An experienced elder came to see if he was breathing, then solemnly shook his head.

No one could believe that the active, boisterous, mischievous, indefatigable boy was simply gone. Was his death a random occurrence, or had the forest premeditated it as a form of punishment? The natural world always says no to the greedy, chasing them back to where they belong.

Yet the red azaleas on the cliff were still fluttering in the wind, as if they had nothing to do with Wei's death.

In Xianghuashuxia, I had witnessed blood-drenched scenes more than once. Alongside the stream, the sound of polishing axes was frequently heard, especially on the first day of group firewood chopping outings. Everyone diligently polished their axes, and then ran their thumbs along the edge of the cold gleaming blade. In the forest, experienced men seized this metallic gleam and brandished the axe with pleasure, but impulsive teenagers often hurt themselves with the blade. Qing was one of them.

Twenty years ago, one of the main jobs of middle and primary schools was to organize students to chop firewood in the mountains. Firewood for schools' kitchens relied entirely on students' labor. On the mountain road, teachers led the group and brought up the rear; students formed a long line, laughing and joking around, faces full of excitement.

In summer and autumn, the wild fruits of the forest competed with one another to be the first to ripen. For the children, chopping firewood was more of a gluttonous banquet than work. Wild raspberries grew by the roadside. You could just reach over, push aside the thorny branches, pick a few, and eat them as you walked. They were so sour they made your mouth water. Wild golden yellow lychees and soft persimmons looked lustrous. Some children climbed up the trees as agile as monkeys. They ate to their fill, and then threw some down to the open mouths below. There was no need to climb the trees for ripe chestnuts, because the ground was a carpet of burred balls. With a firm stomp, the chestnuts slid right out. You could bite open the shell and eat them raw, fragrant and sweet to the taste. If you were lucky, wild mountain pears, wild mangos, and wild pomelos would suddenly appear before your eyes. You could chop down whole branches, take your time to savor them, pack up what you couldn't eat, and take them with you. The teachers were lenient with joy like this.

Joy often makes people lose their sense of caution. When everyone was busy scavenging wild fruits, Qing was exerting all his energy to chop down what we called *sanliangchaizi* (Japanese cinnamon). This kind of tree was light to carry and burn longer. Qing was brave and strong. A few years earlier, he had already become skilled at chopping firewood. His father had equipped him with a powerful chopping ax. He wielded that ax with excellent posture and grace, striking and splitting with decisiveness and becoming the object of his classmates' jealousy. His grades at school usually weren't stellar, and he often hung his head about that. But at times like this, he became the rallying point for his classmates, and his spirits soared. There were many classmates who asked him for advice and help, including the students who were usually at the top of the class. Qing gained a tremendous amount of self-respect, and maybe even a hint of smugness. He was like a top that never stopped spinning as he showed off his prowess, whirling from tree to tree, felling them, removing the bark, and cutting them up. No one really knew how many trees he had cut down, or how much firewood he had chopped. They only knew that there was a constant stream of sweat running down his head and face.

In the midst of his elation, Qing felt a bit light-headed. The gleam of the blade slowly morphed into a hazy-edged flower scattering in every direction. In one distracted flash, that cold light struck the instep of his foot. At first, there was numbness, then blood, a large volume of blood, gushed out before his tired, blurry eyes.

The injury was certainly serious. After a month recuperating at home, Qing still hadn't returned to the classroom. After that, he simply never came back. That seat was empty for a whole semester. During a time when obtaining food and clothing was the top priority, school was only secondary. Every time I passed that empty seat in the last row of the classroom to collect homework, I was overwhelmed by sadness.

Many years later, I became a teacher. As teachers, we held our tongues out of concern for the safety of our students and remained humble when parents made reasonable or unreasonable complaints. I often thought of Qing and his parents. To thank the teachers for bringing their injured child home, his mother cooked a big pot of rice noodles with lean meat, and also had a large jug of homemade rice wine ready.

Time went by fast. Where did Qing go? Does he still remember the sky in Xianghuashuxia?

*   *   *

Memory is like a meandering river. You don't know in which direction it is going, but you forever remember from which direction it came. I was a person who would get tongue-tied. Not once had I ever called my brother endearingly, other than when I wrote him letters, or had to introduce him to people. Of course, he never called me sister, either.

My relationship with my brother is extremely difficult to describe. We got into one fight after another, almost since I was born. When my mother was going to punish me and asked him to grab a stick, he would run to get it. And I would do the same. But we couldn't deny the fact that we were bound together by something called a blood tie. Enemies and loved ones, mixed feelings of hate and love, like a tangled hemp ball. No matter what, we can't find the end of the thread.

It was as usual. We were walking and talking. How did the conflict suddenly occur? In a fit of anger, I left my brother and took a fork in the mountain road. He didn't come after me, and that was typical of my brother. In over ten years of discord caused by our love-hate tangle, he had never compromised with me.

Going separate ways like this was as puzzling as a riddle. The forest was so quiet except for the strange noises of birds and insects. I was alone, without a weapon. My feet took turns unknowingly and carried me forward. It was a valley that I had never been to before. Scare and regret suddenly struck me. I walked uphill and saw a burnt ridge. A lot of people liked to chop down burnt wood in a place like this. My only prayer was "May I run into someone."

In the news these days, I heard more and more stories about girls being robbed on the road. I'm still grateful that I met a stranger that day. He chopped down a tree that had all its leaves burned off, set it on my shoulders, and said, "go now and see if you can catch up with your brother in Xianghuashuxia."

Actually, I got to Xianghuashuxia before my brother showed up. My hands were completely black from holding that burnt trunk during the entire journey. I had been frequently wiping away tears, making my face look like a canvas stained with black ink. When I saw my brother, I could no longer hold my feelings, worries mixed with hate. But there was no way to release them. I stared unflinchingly at my shoes, a pair of *jiefangxie* (liberation shoes). There were holes in the caps of the shoes. One of my toes was peeking through the gap, just like my rage that was waiting to be lashed out.

My rage disappeared all of a sudden. The reason couldn't have been simpler. For a moment, I thought I was about to lose my brother.

The weather was not good that day. The sky pressed down gloomily, like a giant arc. My brother and I were on a mountain. One was on the top and the other was midway. "Damn the weather. Is it going to rain?" Some of us cursed.

Who could have known that the rain didn't fall from the sky in the end; it was my endless tears that fell.

The division of labor that day was actually quite reasonable: my cousin, the strongest, was responsible for finding tall and straight trees, felling them, and removing the branches. I was the intermediary. I stood on the top of the mountain, pushing bare logs down to the bottom of the mountain. My brother's job was to stack logs into piles once they rolled to the bottom. In keeping with our usual practice, every time I pushed a log down, I needed to yell to alert the people at the bottom.

But that day, why did I just blank out? I completely forgot to yell! At that moment, my brother was walking from the bottom of the mountain to the midpoint. I watched that log flipping over on its way down, unhindered, until it hit him on the head, maybe the temple, too. My brother didn't even have time to scream before he was knocked to the ground and rolled down the mountain, along with the log.

Absolute fear welled up, engulfing the gloomy sky, the trees all around us, the steep mountain road, and my stunned self.

It was practically by instinct that I ran to the bottom of the mountain as quickly as possible to look for my brother. He had stopped rolling. His body curled up as he lay on the ground. I moved closer, and then closer still, carefully calling out, "Brother, brother." How come I called him brother? Tears poured from my eyes like a torrential downpour. Was my brother going to die? In that instant, I wished, more than ever before, he could stand up and mercilessly bully me.

Suddenly, he opened his eyes, and forced a smile. "I'm okay." My sobs burst forth once more. My brother hadn't died, and I was willing, in my heart, to call him brother over and over.

After I went to attend a teacher's college, my brother wrote me letters, which opened warmly with, "Sister." It was the word that my brother had cried out countless times in his heart, a word that he would not use openly and affectionately.

Many years later, a group of writers and I went to Zetanxiang to gather source materials about the local culture. We happened upon a pile of firewood neatly stacked against an entire wall of a house, with just one window to let natural light in. My friends had their SLR cameras, and tried to get their pictures taken in front of the firewood. It was a perfect setting. In the photos, people looked like they were part of a painting.

In the painting, I'm wearing a flowing dress, and my skin is fair. There is no trace of me carrying logs in the old times. But I'm the only one who can see that my distant gaze is not one of merely simple happiness. Some people and some events are revived, like a chrysalis breaking through a cocoon and becoming a butterfly.

Nobody needs to chop firewood anymore. My parents and all those relatives in Maicai Mountain Ridge started using far more convenient fuel a while ago. Only the osmanthus tree is still in the same place. It hasn't changed its name, hasn't aged. It is standing there as a testament to the passage of time.

When firewood has become part of the scenery, who knows it can be stacked in many different ways: a cross, a square…; who knows, many years ago it was displayed in a much more beautiful way than this pile, decorating villagers' doorways; and who knows, the sweat and tears of an era hasn't dried up or been buried, but rather has been distilled into a jar of age-old wine.

Look, autumn's pace is slow and steady. With their delicate fragrance, osmanthus blossoms spread the news all around, but only one osmanthus tree truly belongs to me.

22

From Womanly Crops[1]

Zuo Zhongmei

Buckwheat

Crops are womanly.

The first crop that comes to mind is buckwheat.

Back in the day, buckwheat was a food of hard times. Deep in my memory, my family would eat corn *gedafan*, a kind of dumpling. Rice was typically for the Yi New Year's and the other festivals. Even when rice was cooked on festive occasions, it would simply be a thin layer covering the bottom of *luoguo*, our cooking pot. On top of the rice sat *gedafan*. Grandmother used the cooked rice to venerate our ancestors. By showing them we had rice to eat, she wanted them to feel happy. We had a sack of buckwheat flour in a cabinet upstairs. The flour looked green. We kept it for emergencies. If there was a shortage of corn flour, we would use buckwheat flour to feed the family.

Buckwheat *gedafan* needed to be cooked in a rice steamer. Even when cooked, it maintained its green color. It had a bitter taste. Our next-door neighbor had sweet buckwheat flour that looked light gray and tasted better. Food made with this flour had a hint of sweetness and was easier on the palate than that made of bitter buckwheat.

Villagers would grow buckwheat on the highest, most distant mountains. They chose to grow more bitter buckwheat, because of its higher yield, than sweet buckwheat. Buckwheat is an autumn crop. Bitter buckwheat flowers, as white as snow, bloom on high mountains. Fuchsia is the color of sweet buckwheat flowers.

Buckwheat flowers are beautiful. How come a crop of hard times can

---

1. The two short pieces are from the author's prose "Womanly Crops," *Literature of Nationality*, No. 1, 2012, pp. 101–104.

Translated by Dong Isbister

have such beautiful flowers, as simple and pretty as village girls? I wonder about that.

Nowadays, buckwheat has largely vanished as a staple crop. Occasionally, someone in a remote village grows one or two patches of buckwheat, but buckwheat flour has assumed a completely different identity as it is now a rarity. Buckwheat food is said to help improve diabetic conditions. Many people with diabetes now ask around for buckwheat flour. Sometimes the best hotel in the small town of Yangbi serves buckwheat cakes with honey dip. Customers battle each other to get at these cakes and sing the praises of this genuine organic food.

On an autumn day, the county writers' association took us to Shimenguan to *caifeng* (gathering story materials). As our vehicle was halfway up the mountain, I saw fuchsia flowers, but I had to look really hard before I was sure they were indeed buckwheat. A narrow stretch of fog gently hugged the mountain. The buckwheat flowers were blooming beautifully.

I hadn't seen buckwheat flowers like these for years.

Wheat

"Like wheat seedlings," this was how farmers around would describe a lovely girl. Its connotation is twofold. First, as the expression suggests, the girl is slender. Second, the girl is well-behaved and clever.

Farmers in my hometown don't grow a lot of wheat. After the autumn harvest, they mostly grow peas that have a shorter growing season. This tradition seems to be attributable to the dryness in the area. My Yi ancestors named our village *mixiba*, meaning a good place, but it is always dry. The arid fields are obviously unfit for growing wheat. The only patches of wheat fields in my village are in places with more moisture. Wheat grown in dry fields yields shorter seedlings. The ears are generally smaller and thinner. Farmers living in the valley also plant wheat. They are able to water their wheat fields many times during a season, but the wheat grown in my hometown does not have this luxury.

Because we produced less wheat, we didn't eat wheat food often. But there was one particular day each year, the Dragon Boat Festival, that we were obligated to eat wheat food. My family had a tradition of making *baozi* during this holiday. If wheat was available, Nainai, my grandma, would grind wheat flour in advance. At times if we had none, we would go to our neighbors and offer something to exchange for wheat. It was hardly proper *baozi*, nothing more than buns filled with a little brown sugar. And yet, I felt they were very tasty, since wheat food was usually such a rarity and so was sugar. In my hometown, wheat flour is always held in high regard, as *jingliang*, meaning refined flour.

Farmers in my hometown didn't grow much wheat, but raised many beautiful girls like "wheat seedlings." As a child, I learned from elders that many good-looking girls had grown up in the village. Actually, the village was locally known for the beauty of its girls. Generation after generation of beautiful girls had grown up here, like "wheat seedlings."

I remember a TV drama that I watched years ago. Two sisters left their village. The older sister is Xiao Qiao (little buckwheat) and the younger one is Xiao Mai (little wheat). Farmers are alike everywhere, because they love their children like their crops, and love their crops like their children.

Wheat seedlings, may you grow fast. Wheat seedlings, may you never stop growing.

About the Authors

Ayinuer Maowuliti (Kazakh) is the author of the poetry collection *Alima's Prairie*. Her prose "Apa" won a Bing Xin Prose Award. Her translation of *Poetry of Tangji-aleke* received an "Akesai" Kazakh Literature Translation Award. Her publications have appeared in *Poetry, October, Literature of Nationality, Green Breeze*, and other literary periodicals.

Bamo Qubumo (Yi) is a researcher at the Institute of Ethnic Literature of Chinese Academy of Social Sciences (CASS) and director of the Oral Traditions Research Center of CASS. She has published numerous books, articles and poems and is the co-author of *Mountain Patterns: The Survival of Nuosu Culture in China* (2000).

Burao Yilu (Va) is the author of *Pledge to the Sacred Tree* (2010). Her poem "Moon Mountain" (2011) was translated into English and published in *Asian Highlands Perspectives*. "Language of Bauhinia Flower" received a Silver Award for the World Chinese Poetry Contest. She was included in *The Famous Figures of the Contemporary Art's Circles in China* (1997) and *Encyclopedia of Chinese Ethnic Minority-Va* (2014).

Cen Xianqing (pen name Ping Chang) (Zhuang) (BA Chinese literature, Beijing University) is a native of Longzhou, Guangxi Province. Her works include *Fireflies* (essays), which won the Fourth Ethnic Literature Creative Writing Award, *Fissures* (novellas), which won the Third Zhuang Creative Writing Award, and "Eternal Spirits" (prose). She is the director and associate editor of the China Writers Association literary journal, *Literature of Nationality*.

Chen Danling (Tujia) has published works in Chinese literary periodicals, including *Literature of Nationality, Mountain Flowers, Frontiers, Meiwen, Sichuan Literature, Dianchi, Bianjiang Wenxue, Readers, and Xiangtu*. She has published *Expressions of Dewdrops* and *Notes on the Village*. She won a national award for Outstanding Tujia Literature.

Dekeli (Evenki) was born in Aoluguya, and her childhood nomadic experience of living with her grandmother and reindeer in the forest has inspired and informed her poetry and prose. She has published *Ewo, In Search of the Legendary Prairie, Kangnalikan the Little Reindeer of Aoluguya, Seven Hundred and Eighty Years of Loyalty, My Melancholy Northern Woods, The Hunter and Tea, A-er-ba-ji-kan, Mother's Forest*.

Han Jinghui (Mongolian) has received numerous awards, including the Jun Ma Award, a book award of Bing Xin Children's Literature, and a Bing Xin Book Award. She has published over thirty novels and short story collections, including *For Whom Do I Live?*, *The Girl from Saihansaer River*, *Erji and Poppies*, *Uncertain*, *The Bachelor's House*, and *Grandpa's Passive Resistance*.

Lei Zhifen (Xibo) was born in the Morin Dawa Daur Autonomous Banner of Inner Mongolia in China. Her works include *There Is Only a Leaf Here* (collection of short stories) and other fictional or nonfictional writings published in *Chinese Writers*, *Prairie*, *Jun Ma* and other literary magazines or periodicals. She is a recipient of the Hulunbuir Jun Ma Literary Award for *There Is Only a Leaf Here*.

Ma Jinlian (Hui) is the author of *Father's Snow*, *Daughter-in-law*, *Long River*, *Brine and Pickles of 1987*, *Embroidered Mandarin Ducks*, and *The Child Who Counts Stars*. She is also a recipient of numerous awards, including an Annual Literature of Nationality Award, a Liupanshan Literary Award, a Suofang Literary Award, Yudafu Fiction Award, the Best Works Award, the Maodun Literature Award for Emerging Authors, and a National Jun Ma Award for Ethnic Literature.

Maidina Seyiti (Uyghur) (MA Uyghur literature, School of Ethnic Studies and Sociology, Minzu University) was born in Ürümqi of Xinjiang Uyghur Autonomous Region. She writes in Chinese and her translated works have appeared in *Literature of Nationality* and other literary periodicals. She has been an editor at the Uyghur Ethnic Literature Publishing House since 2011.

Mao Mei (Hui) has published over twenty pieces of prose, including *My Home Is on the Northern Slope of Tianshan*, *In Search of the Philosophies of Hatred*, and *Seeking Warmth in Deep Culture*. She has received the award for "The Best Place Names" Writing Contest of *Guang Ming Daily* sponsored by the Ministry of Civil Affairs of the People's Republic of China, the Literary Award for Western Literature, and the Tianshan Wenyi Award.

Naye (Manchu) graduated from the Chinese Department of Nanjing University. Her collections of poems include *Poems of Naye*, *Selected Poems of Naye*, *The Wind Arises*, *Writing Before Sleep*, and *Personal Sketches*. She is a recipient of the People's Literature Award, Shiyue Literary Award, and Tianwen Poet Award. *The Selected Poems of Naye* received the Lu Xun Literature Award.

Nuryla Qiziqan (Kazakh) is a writer, poet, and folklorist from Xinjiang Uyghur Autonomous Region. In 2009, she published *Hunter's Stories* to commemorate her hunter father Qiziqan Ahman. Since then, she has been active in archiving pastoral and hunting knowledge, folktales, hunters and herders' experiences in Northern Xinjiang.

Patigül (Uyghur) has published in literary periodicals, including *People's Literature*, and *Literature of Nationality*. Her novel *Keka's Love* received a Best Fiction of Beijing Award. *One Hundred Years of Bloodline* (novel) was on the list of One Hundred Best Ethnic Books and won the Best Books of Beijing Award and the Best Fiction of Beijing Award. Her prose "The Tongue Stolen by Language" won the 2014 *People's Literature* Award.

Sana (Daur) is the author of the novel *Duobukuer River*. Her fiction has appeared in *Harvest*, *Dang Dai*, *Zhong Shan*, *Flower City*, *October*, *People's Literature* and been selected for publication in *Xiao Shuo Xuan Kan* and *Fiction Monthly*. Her work of collected fiction, *Stagger on Your Face*, received a Jun Ma Award for Best Ethnic Literature in China. She is vice president of the Writers Association of Inner Mongolia.

Su Hua (pen name Nadiya) (Daur) has published a collection of short stories, *Pastoral Songs* and a collection of prose pieces, *Doe Suwa*. Both collections have been added to the collection of National Library of China. She is listed in *Biographical Sketches of Contemporary Writers in Inner Mongolia, History of Daur Literature, Annals of Molidawa Autonomous Banner, Encyclopedia of the Daur, Titles and Abstracts of Studies of Daur Literature,* and *Writers from Hulunbuir.*

Ye Guangcen (Manchu) is a native of Beijing. She has published four novels, including *Behind the Gate of Heavenly Purity, Collecting Mulberries, Bear Alert,* and *Qing Mu Chuan*. She has also published *Luofu River with No Journals* (autobiography and recipient of a National Jun Ma Award for Ethnic Literature). Her novella *Following My Dreams to My Love* won a Lu Xun Literature Award.

Ye Mei (a.k.a. Fang Guanglan) (Tujia) has published many fiction and nonfiction collections, including *The Lantern Is Like Her Eyes, Dragon Boat River in Grief* (recipient of *Chinese Writers'* Outstanding Novella Award), *May Moths* (recipient of a *Hubei Literature Award* and a *National Jun Ma Award for Ethnic Literature*), Many of her works have been translated into English, French, Japanese, and Korean.

Yilan (pen name Zhang Hua) (Daur) has published five books, including the novel *Ya De Gen* included in *Selected Excellent Original Works* and on the list of One Hundred Ethnic Minority Books by National Ethnic Affairs Commission of the People's Republic of China (NEAC) and State Administration of Press, Publication, Radio, Film and Television of the People's Republic of China (SAPPRFT). She has received over thirty awards, including the Inner Mongolian Suolongge Literature Award.

Zhao Yan (Zhong Xiuhua) (She) has published works in numerous literary magazines including *San Wen, Mei Wen, Mang Zhong, Youth Literature, Bai Hua Zhou,* and *San Wen Xuan Kan*. She is the recipient of the annual award of Literature of Nationality, Jing Gang Shan Literature Award, and Hong Kong Youth Literary Award. She is the author of the prose collection *Maicai Ridge Under the Sky.*

Zuo Zhongmei (Yi) has published multiple prose collections, including *Missing Autumn, Penning Time on Paper, Encounter at the Corner,* and *Peaceful Land*. She is a recipient of the Dali Literature and Art Award, the Yunnan Provincial Foundation Award for Creative Works, and the "Lingshui Cup" Ethnic Literary Award. She is a member of the China Writers Association.

About the Translators

Alexandra Draggeim is a conference interpreter and translator based in Paris, France. After completing a year at the Inter-University Program (IUP) for Chinese language studies at Tsinghua University in Beijing, she went on to complete a master's degree in Chinese language and culture from the Ohio State University.

Heidi Emerson holds a bachelor's degree in Chinese civilization and culture and a master's degree in Chinese language and literature from the University of Colorado at Boulder. Her primary interests involve the evolution of modern language, particularly internet slang. She is a freelance translator based in Denver, Colorado.

Jesse Field is the Dean of Studies for Bard Early College at Houde Academy, Shenzhen. Born and raised in Texas, he first became interested in Chinese literature and culture while studying science and mathematics at Harvard University. His previous translations include the memoirs *We Three* and "On Qian Zhongshu and Fortress Besieged" by Yang Jiang, and "Writing Lives in China: The Case of Yang Jiang."

Weihong Gao is the ESL Director of the English as a Second Language Program in the Institute for International Studies at Murray State University. Her research interest is in second language vocabulary instruction and acquisition.

Stacy Jane Grover is a nonfiction writer and transgender educator whose work has appeared in numerous literary journals and websites including InsideHigherEd, Belt Publishing, and HeARTOnline Journal. Her work has been assigned as key readings at conferences across the U.S. and cited by multiple university policy websites.

Anne Henochowicz is a translator and digital journalist. She is a commissioning editor at the China Channel, an affiliate of the *Los Angeles Review of Books*, and the former translations editor at *China Digital Times*. She studied Inner Mongolian folk music at the University of Cambridge and the Ohio State University.

Dong Isbister is an associate professor of women's and gender studies at the University of Wisconsin–Platteville. Her research and teaching interests include collective memory, immigration, transnational feminisms, environmental humanities, women's literature, and translation and interpreting studies. She has published scholarly and creative works in English and Chinese.

Xiumei Pu is an assistant professor of environmental studies at Westminster College, where she teaches indigenous environmental thoughts, multiethnic environmental literature, ecowomanist and ecofeminist theories, and other related areas of inquiries. She is the author of "Turning Weapons into Flowers: Ecospiritual Poetics and Politics of Bön and Ecowomanism" and other publications about transcultural understanding of gender and the environment.

Stephen D. Rachman is an associate professor in the department of English and former director of the American Studies Program at Michigan State University. He is the editor of *The Hasheesh Eater* by Fitz-Hugh Ludlow (2006), co-author of the award-winning *Cholera, Chloroform, and the Science of Medicine: A Life of John Snow* (2003) and coeditor of *The American Face of Edgar Allan Poe* (1995). He has written on the Chinese artist Lam Qua and his relationship with the American Medical Missionary, Peter Parker, and on Pearl S. Buck as a transnational Sino-American figure.

Guldana Salimjan is the Ruth Wynn Woodward Junior Chair and an assistant professor at the Gender, Sexuality, and Women's Studies Department at Simon Fraser University. She received a Ph.D. at the Institute for Gender, Race, Sexuality, and Social Justice from the University of British Columbia. Her research focuses on the politics of memory, knowledge production, and women's history in China and Central Asia.

Ann Waltner's reading group has met on a weekly basis to read and translate classical Chinese since 1987. It is run by Ann Waltner who teaches in the Department of History at the University of Minnesota–Twin Cities. Members of the group who contributed to the translated anthology include: Rivi Handler-Spitz, who teaches Chinese and Chinese literature at Macalester College and is the author of *Symptoms of an Unruly Age: Li Zhi and Cultures of Early Modernity*; Ben van Overmeire, a faculty member at Duke University–Kunshan; Rachel Kronick, a translator in Taiwan; and Han Jiangxue, a graduate student at Yale University. Contributors also include several graduate students in history: Li Kan, Jiang Yuanxin, Gao Ruchen, Zhu Tianxiao and Eric R. Becklin, and one graduate student in musicology, Lars Christensen.

Guangrong Wan is a professor of linguistics at Hunan Normal University. Her research interests are syntax, comparative linguistics and linguistic typology. She has published monographs on Chinese syntax and a number of scholarly journal articles. She is working on "Mirativity in Chinese Language," a research project funded by the National Social Science Fund of China.

Wendy Mina Wang spent three years studying Chinese in Beijing, where she also worked as a translator and voice actress for the animated TV series *Colorful Crayons*. After receiving a MSc in management from Ivey Business School, she began her career in blockchain and cryptocurrency as an operations manager. She is also a freelance translator.

Seth Wiener is an assistant professor of second language acquisition and Chinese studies in the Department of Modern Languages at Carnegie Mellon University. His research program involves experimental investigations of the perception and production of speech. He teaches courses on psycholinguistics, experimental methods, and the Chinese language. He serves as an associate editor for the journal *Applied Psycholinguistics*.

Xiangyang Xiao is a professor of English at the School of Foreign Studies in Southern Medical University, People's Republic of China. She earned a BA in English from

Wuhan University, and an MA in English language literature from South China Normal University. Her research fields are English literature, translation, and education.

Daniel M. Youd is a professor of Chinese language and literature in the Department of Modern Languages and Literatures at Beloit College in Beloit, Wisconsin, where he has taught since 2002. His teaching and research interests include Ming and Qing dynasty vernacular fiction, translation studies, science fiction, and intellectual history.

Jennifer Young is a postdoctoral fellow at Stanford University. She earned a Ph.D. in family science at the University of Maryland, an MA in East Asian languages and literature from the Ohio State University, and an MS in couples and family therapy from the University of Maryland. She has done clinical work and research with Chinese American families in Baltimore, Maryland.

Zhou Xiaojing is a professor of English at the University of the Pacific, where she teaches literature and ethnic studies courses, including Asian American literature, environment and literature, multiethnic American literature, and ecocriticism. Her publications include "'Slow Violence' in Migrant Landscapes: 'Hollow Villages' and Tourist River Towns in China" (2017).

Index

www.ingramcontent.com/pod-product-compliance
Lightning Source LLC
Chambersburg PA
CBHW021423110726
47901CB00008B/2281